COOL PASSION
Challenging Higher Education

NASPA
Student Affairs Administrators
in Higher Education

COOL PASSION
Challenging Higher Education

ARTHUR W. CHICKERING
and Associates

FOREWORD BY *Alexander W. Astin* AND *Helen S. Astin*

NASPA
Student Affairs Administrators
in Higher Education

NASPA
Student Affairs Administrators
in Higher Education

Cool Passion: Challenging Higher Education

Published by
NASPA–Student Affairs Administrators in Higher Education
111 K Street, NE
10th Floor
Washington, DC 20002
www.naspa.org

Additional copies may be purchased by contacting the NASPA publications department at 202-265-7500 or visiting http://bookstore.naspa.org.

NASPA does not discriminate on the basis of race, color, national origin, religion, sex, age, gender identity, gender expression, affectional or sexual orientation, or disability in any of its policies, programs, and services.

Library of Congress Cataloging-in-Publication Data

Chickering, Arthur W., 1927-
  Cool passion : challenging higher education / Arthur W. Chickering. -- First edition.
    pages cm
  Includes bibliographical references.
  ISBN 978-0-931654-89-3
  1. Chickering, Arthur W., 1927- 2. Educators--United States--Biography. 3. Education, Higher--Philosophy. I. Title.
  LA2317.C52A3 2014
  371.10092--dc23
  [B]
                          2013050219

Printed and bound in the United States of America
FIRST EDITION

This book is dedicated to Jo Chickering, my loving wife, partner, and constant source of support for 62 years. Her deep compassion for all creatures and our earth, her courage and spiritual strength, not only sustain me but inspire all who enter her shining orbit.

Contents

Part Three: "Retiring" to Vermont

Acknowledgments

My career has been anchored in what I learned from Tim Pitkin, Forest Davis, George Beecher, and Robert Mattuck, from rich experiences being immersed in the Goddard College culture from 1959 to 1964, and from the subsequent Project on Student Development in Small Colleges. Since then, I have stood on the shoulders of fellow researchers whose work has been so well summarized, first by Ken Feldman and Ted Newcomb and subsequently by Ernie Pascarella and Pat Terenzini. I have been fortunate to collaborate with and learn from colleagues, several of whom have become good friends. Numerous fellow practitioners by word and deed drove home important lessons—some of them models and a few anti-models—at Empire State College, the Center for the Study of Higher Education at Memphis State University, and George Mason University. Colleagues who have been friends and collaborators are so widespread and numerous I cannot list all of them here.

But two colleagues, Sandy and Lena Astin, stand far above the rest. Sandy took me out of the woods of Vermont and onto the national scene when he invited me to come to the American Council on Education as a visiting scholar from 1969 to 1970. He and Lena warmly welcomed me and my wife, Jo, sharing their home and friends. Lena served on Jo's doctoral committee when she received her PhD in counseling and higher education from the Union Institute in 1973. Since those beginnings, we have shared many joint ventures; most were highly productive, some less so. They have been enduring friends for more than 40 years.

I am indebted to my coauthors in Part Two of this book. Without their wide-ranging, complex, historical perspectives this book would simply be a shallow memoir, and only of passing interest to some friends and fans.

Embarking on this combination of professional memoir and commentaries on changes in higher education was triggered by the autobiography I wrote for my Master of Fine Arts in Creative Writing degree from Goddard College. I want to thank Academic Vice President Kabba Colley and former President Mark Shulman for supporting tuition waivers for my first terms. I also want to thank Barbara Vacarr, the current president, for continuing that support. With persistent tough love—excellent criticism and solid support—from Nicola Morris, my advisor, and her colleagues Jeanne Mackin and Richard Panek—I learned about a new genre that I will continue to try to improve.

Finally, I want to thank the National Association of Student Personnel Administrators (NASPA) for its willingness to publish this somewhat unusual work.

Foreword

Arthur Chickering's *Cool Passion: Challenging Higher Education* will be enjoyed by students and professionals for years to come. Chick, as his friends and colleagues call him, touches the reader with his honesty and courage as he reveals himself so publicly, but he also educates us with astute insights about American higher education during the past five decades. His personal story illuminates his enduring commitment to helping students become lifelong learners, dedicated workers, and caring and engaged citizens.

In an era when we are treated to an abundance of memoirs by artists, writers, and scholars, it is a delight to see one of our own, a scholar of higher education, a consummate professional, a passionate teacher and researcher, take on the task of sharing with the reader an intimate and powerful story about himself, a story he tells with candor and authenticity. One of the critical messages of this book is that we can be authentic, whole, and vulnerable at the same time that we function as objective researchers and analysts. Chick models this rare ability with clarity and honesty.

The five areas of work that Chick has singled out for special commentary in this book—civic learning, assessment, pedagogy, student services, and student diversity—reflect both emerging issues in higher education as well as many of his major accomplishments. Chick focused attention on the rapidly expanding but neglected student population of adult learners through a longtime association with the Council for Adult and Experiential Learning and his pioneering work in helping to bring the State University of New York's Empire State College into being. He pursued his goal further by creating innovative educational programs to serve this population. Chick's work at Empire State College laid the groundwork for today's focus on civic learning and democratic engagement. His scholarly work, in particular his classic works *Education and Identity* (Chickering, 1969) and *The Modern American College* (Chickering, 1981), broadened and clarified conceptions of liberal learning, encouraged college faculty to view their work with students in terms of theories of developmental psychology, and provided the field of student services with a solid conceptual foundation.

Chick's lifelong dedication to enhancing understanding of student growth and his many contributions to instructional innovation highlight a tension that continues to plague the system of higher education: The relentless institutional and individual competition for greater prestige and resources is often in conflict with ongoing efforts to improve the quality of the student experience. Chick has consistently been a champion of the latter.

Chick's career as revealed in the candid autobiographical material in this book shows little evidence of the striving for status that characterizes the lives of many academics. Rather than searching for the next job that would provide him with a higher status position or land him in a more prestigious institution, his career decisions were guided by considerations of substance: It is as if Chick asked himself, "Will this job enable me to further our understanding of student growth and development and further my opportunities to engage in innovative educational improvement and reform efforts?"

Chick is a Renaissance man, an adventurer, and a forward thinker. He lives in rural Vermont where he is an avid athlete and tennis player, and he also enjoys nature, hiking, and chopping wood. When he needed to replace his knees because of years spent running around tennis courts, he chose to replace both at the same time, which is no easy task for a man well into his seventies. When some of his friends first suggested that higher education needed to pay more attention to issues relating to spirituality, Chick was skeptical of the "S-word." But he was willing to discuss and debate the issue. After much reflection, he championed the cause, becoming one of the most loyal and engaged members of the spirituality steering committee and eventually coauthoring a book on spirituality and higher education.

What may be Chick's most remarkable professional accomplishment is something that he gives only modest attention to in this volume: the establishment of Empire State College. Empire State is one of the country's most innovative and remarkable higher education institutions, and Chick can take much of the credit for the fact that it exists and has thrived since its founding.

Chick has been a dear friend and a wonderful colleague for more than 40 years. We have personally shared many of the experiences that Chick describes in this volume; in reading his own telling of the events, the power of his storytelling and the openness with which he writes about his life have touched us deeply. We hope that this book will help all those who read it, and in particular, graduate students and young professionals, to change the way they work and relate to each other in higher education, so that our institutions can become more authentic, more whole, and more responsive to the needs of students and society.

Alexander W. Astin and Helen S. Astin
University of California, Los Angeles
July 31, 2013

REFERENCES

Chickering, A. W. (1969). *Education and identity*. San Francisco, CA: Jossey-Bass.

Chickering, A. W. (1981). *The modern American college: Responding to the new realities of diverse students and a changing society*. San Francisco, CA: Jossey-Bass.

Preface

In the summer of 2012, I noticed a dandelion that had fought its way up through a crack in the asphalt at Shaw's supermarket in downtown Montpelier, Vermont, 7 miles out of town from our house on a dead end dirt road, up a little watershed. I stepped around the yellow blossom when I went in to shop. I had been doing this for the last couple of weeks. Why was I so careful about stepping around that dandelion? Perhaps because the dandelion's struggle was an echo of my own birth on April 27, 1927—a 14-hour struggle to push through and come into life. I was pulled out with forceps, so I did not emerge as pretty and symmetrical as that bloom. My skull was shaped like the "pointy-headed intellectual" that Nixon's Vice President Spiro Agnew decried, and that I later became as a "Distinguished Professor."

I watched the dandelion create a small life space in that challenging environment. Tough and persistent, through searing sun and heavy rains, it spread a circle of green leaves. During the next two weeks, grey-headed like me, it released seeds to passing breezes. Although that dandelion's lifespan was much briefer than mine, the challenges I experienced in my 86 years have been not unlike that dandelion's: the struggle to live, grow, and thrive among the conventions and constraints of schools, colleges, and universities, to blossom and, finally, grey-haired, to watch the seeds of my career spread and influence higher education.

Since my wife, Jo, had a stroke in 1999, our lives have become increasingly constrained. The domestic and international travels that used to fill our lives are difficult. She can no longer drive. I have become chief cook and bottle washer. Although I can still work part time, mostly from home, if I am away it puts a burden on our two daughters, who live nearby, so my professional travel and consultation are limited. Jo and I were looking for something that we could do together besides reading, playing Scrabble, watching television, and occasionally entertaining at home or going out for dinners with friends. We both enjoy writing—poetry for her, professional books and articles for me. We thought it might be fun and challenging to write about our 60-plus years of marriage, with its many ups and downs and four wonderful children, now in their 50s. In January 2009, I enrolled in Goddard College's Master of Fine Arts in Creative Writing program. It was an interesting challenge to tackle creative nonfiction that called for a kind of writing very different from my professional publications. And Jo wrote about our life together through poetry. We shared drafts and relived parts of our rich history. The autobiography I wrote focused almost entirely on my growing up and on marriage and family. I did not take time to share details about my career in higher education and to reflect on the changes that I have been part of since 1958, when I left work as a school psychologist to start a new department as director of teacher education at Monmouth College in Long Branch, New Jersey. I hope this book, with its sharing and associated reflections, may help to enrich conversations about current issues facing higher education.

Because the chapters that follow share personal experiences, values, and beliefs—as well as professional contributions and reflections—it seems only fair that I ask myself what less lofty purposes or motives may be at play. First, I guess, reflecting on my past life and on these issues that have occupied it keeps me engaged. It is an enjoyable use of discretionary time and gives me at least the illusion of doing something useful. Mind you, it is not like mowing the lawn, picking blueberries, or getting in our winter wood supply. When the lawn is nice and trim, or when my gallon jug is overflowing with blueberries, I know I have done something. After I have felled enough trees to heat our house for the winter, limbed them off, cut them up with my chainsaw, pulled five or six trailer loads into the garage with the old Ford tractor, and stacked three-and-a-half or four cords, the evidence of time well spent is unequivocal. And my aching back and shoulders tell me I have done more than sit around reading, talking, or typing. Teaching, research, writing, and administrative decisions may do some good in the world, but whether they make any lasting difference is much more uncertain.

Then there is the question of self-aggrandizement. When I shared the idea for this book with Jo, in her usual candid, penetrating way, she said, "Watch out for hubris." Dame Judi Dench, that wonderful actor, said that the older you get, the louder you should sing. Maybe my most fundamental motive is just to remind folks out there that I am still alive and kicking, to recall some of the potential contributions I have made, to sing my swan song, to take one last bite of the apple.

Arthur W. Chickering
East Montpelier, Vermont
Fall 2013

Introduction

Things fall apart; the center cannot hold;
Mere anarchy is loosed upon the world,
The blood-dimmed tide is loosed, and everywhere
The ceremony of innocence is drowned;
The best lack all conviction, while the worst
Are full of passionate intensity.
—W. B. Yeats, "The Second Coming" (1921)

I do not know what conditions prompted Yeats to write those words, but they certainly seem apt today. In *A Crucible Moment: College Learning and Democracy's Future,* the Association of American Colleges and Universities (AAC&U, 2012) issued a national call to action. The document argues for higher education's critical role in our pluralistic, globally interdependent country. As in earlier publications, AAC&U calls for fundamental outcomes substantially beyond professional and occupational preparation. These outcomes are critical not only for civic engagement but also for a successful career, effective parenting, and a meaningful life. Educationally powerful activities and experiences during the college years set a solid foundation, but a citizen's social contributions depend on lifelong learning that responds to changing circumstances and unanticipated challenges.

In 1981, in *The Modern American College: Responding to the New Realities of Diverse Students and a Changing Society,* I wrote:

Frenzied, unbridled passion, whether in love or work, seldom serves us well. Indeed, it often harms more than helps. To be enflamed, carried away, by an affection, ideology, or cause is easy, but such a state shrinks from reflective thought, public scrutiny, and tough-minded testing. Maintaining a steady fire that is critical as well as creative is more difficult, especially when it suffers frequent doses of icy logic and frigid resistance. Cool passion seeks fulfillment by joining the forces of heart and mind, commitment and critical analysis. (p. 783)

This is still the posture we need in order to keep strengthening our institutional effectiveness and addressing the daunting issues facing our struggling democracy. It has characterized my 55 years of challenging higher education to broaden its purposes, improve its teaching, undertake research for action, and create more powerful curricula, cocurricula, and educational practices that respond to adult learners. That work has given purpose and meaning to my life, and continues to do so.

In Part One of this book, I share the educational experiences that laid the foundation for my professional orientation and career. In many ways, those experiences also underlie some of the attitudes, values, and educational positions I have taken.

The chapters in Part Two are the guts of the book. They address five areas that absorbed most of my professional time and energy: the purposes of higher education, research, teaching, student affairs, and adult learners. My coauthors, who are more broadly experienced and up to date than I am, have greatly strengthened the discussion by putting my work in the larger contexts to which it contributed. They identify important changes that have occurred, note continuing challenges, and suggest agendas for further work.

Our purposes in higher education have broadened from merely cultivating the intellect and transferring knowledge to emphasizing critical thinking, professional training, civic engagement, authenticity and spiritual growth, with student development on the margins. Becoming more sophisticated about our global interdependence, coping with new technologies, and lifelong learning for lives of purpose and meaning need further work.

Research in higher education has moved beyond the scattered scholarly work pulled together by Nevitt Sanford (1962) in *The American College* to sustained efforts generating findings for disaggregated subgroups and subcultures that can be applied to particular institutional contexts. The assessment movement has helped move us toward evidence-based decision making. But moving from research to action and applying these findings to create systemic and localized change remains a challenge.

Teaching has advanced beyond lectures and texts to more active learning that is experiential and collaborative, that involves communities of learning, and that offers individualized education. However, we continue to be put to the test to promote learning that lasts and individual self-realization.

Student affairs officers and practitioners have progressed from a student services orientation to a more intentional educational role, strengthening student learning and increasingly collaborating directly with academic affairs professionals. Those collaborative relationships still need strengthening, and student development agendas must yet be pursued.

The influx of adult learners in higher education has stimulated the assessment of prior learning, new learner-centered programs, and innovative organizational structures. But entrenched interests and traditional governance arrangements make it difficult to become more nimble and creative in response to changing conditions.

Part Two closes with a chapter of personal reflections on the real progress described by the coauthors and also on the work that remains to be done in these areas. I argue for the continued relevance of developmental-stage theories and the need to keep a broad-gauged perspective on human development as the organizing purpose for teaching and learning in our colleges and universities.

Part Three brings readers up to date on my recent past and what life is like for me and my wife at the old homestead in Vermont, in case the reader is curious about where all this has left me. The end of the book includes my curriculum vitae, which provides an overview of my work and career, and brief biographical notes on the coauthors who contributed so generously and wisely to Part Two.

I have been committed to human development as a critical organizing purpose for higher education since before *Education and Identity* won the American Council on Education book award in 1969. This orientation has been the organizing framework for my research and writing, teaching and professional development workshops, and educational leadership. During those 40-plus years of my career, I experienced the significant changes in all these domains in higher education. Now, at age 86, I want to provide a personal perspective that can put flesh and blood on these changes and suggest where to go from here consistent with that longstanding commitment. Perhaps this perspective can enrich current conversations and deepen our debates.

I am hardly in a position to judge the balance between such highfalutin purposes and the baser self-interests I recognized in the Preface. I have enjoyed the process, and readers will let me know how it turns out.

REFERENCES

Association of American Colleges and Universities. (2012). *A crucible moment: College learning and democracy's future.* Washington, DC: Author.

Chickering, A. W. (1969). *Education and identity.* San Francisco, CA: Jossey-Bass.

Chickering, A. W. (1981). *The modern American college: Responding to the new realities of diverse students and a changing society.* San Francisco, CA: Jossey-Bass.

Sanford, N. (1962). *The American college: A psychological and social interpretation of higher learning.* New York, NY: Wiley.

Yeats, W. B. (1921). The second coming. In *Michael Robartes and the dancer* (pp. 19–20). Dublin, Ireland: The Cuala Press.

PART ONE

Roots

My father, Rowell Osborn Chickering, also nicknamed Chick, was fond of saying that Chickerings fought in the Lexington Alarm. In one of my file cabinets I have a multipage genealogy that he commissioned. My roots go deep into New England soil. There are Chickerings scattered all over Vermont and New Hampshire. We are distantly related to the Chickering piano branch of the family. The pianos were top of the line when they were made in Brattleboro, Vermont, during the 1800s. None of that wealth trickled down to Dad's parents. He worked during high school and was a traveling salesman for Uneeda Biscuits when he married my mother in 1926. I was born in 1927.

My mother, Thelma Halley Wright, was 21 years old when she married my father. She was born to George and Bertha Wright in Natick, Massachusetts, 20 miles west of Boston. I was told that George was descended from a Native American member of the Wampanoag tribe that was based on Cape Cod and Martha's Vineyard; this forebear was called "King Phillip" because of his tribal leadership. Grampa's hatchet-shaped face, high cheek bones, and ruddy complexion lent credence to the story. George and Bertha had several acres of land—with a substantial apple orchard, large vegetable garden, chickens, and a cow—that supplied much of their food. George was always in demand as a carpenter and house builder, as much for his total honesty and frugality as for his excellent workmanship. The Wright side of my family had relatives nearby in Massachusetts and also in Vermont and New Hampshire. Mom and I visited some of them in Rochester and Hancock, adjacent towns in Vermont, during the summers of 1937 and 1938.

Handsome, smart, and opportunistic, Dad became a modestly successful salesman and part owner of a heating oil business, selling Timken burners and supplying oil to run them. He became a staunch Freemason and president of the Natick Rotary Club. He also drank and gambled, introducing me to poker in my teens and booze when I came of age. Whatever entrepreneurial opportunism characterized my growing up and later life came from my father. My mother earned A's in high school, played on the girls' basketball team, and was very good-looking. Anxious to get away from her strict and domineering father, she did not hesitate to marry Dad when she got pregnant. We lived near my mother's parents. As the first and only grandson I spent a lot of time with George, helping out around my grandparents' place and learning how to handle a hammer, saw, and paintbrush, how to mow the lawn without leaving "vacations," and other basic life skills. From him, and from my mother, came my frugality, willingness to work hard, and respect for others, whatever their backgrounds. These characteristics served me well during the early years of my marriage and as I banged away trying to challenge unquestioned assumptions and conventional practices in colleges and universities.

Basic semi-Puritan, human values permeated our rural, small-town environment. They were reinforced by the Methodist church where my mother and grandmother were active, and where I sang in the choir. The local schools were White, with very few Jewish kids, and with teachers and administrators anchored in the New England heritage and its associated values. The following Part One chapters share the sprouts and saplings of my personal development that grew from these roots.

CHAPTER 1

Schooling

"Schooling" means "to discipline or habituate to something" or "the training of a horse to service" (*Merriam-Webster's Collegiate Dictionary*, 2005, p. 1,045). However, neither of these definitions of schooling applied to me during my years in the Natick, Massachusetts, schools or after my mother shipped me off to Mount Hermon for my junior and senior years. I wasn't about to let myself be disciplined, habituated, or trained.

About 7:30 a.m. on September 5, 1932, the Tuesday after Labor Day, Mom and I began the mile-long walk to first grade at the Bacon Street School. I wore clean khaki shorts, a green shirt, my Red Sox baseball cap, and my brand-new ankle-high red-and-white sneakers. They had a round disk on the outside with wings on a foot and "KEDS" in the middle. My lunch pail was just like Grampa's. When I opened it, I had a thermos of cold milk in the rounded top, held in place by a

5

metal clamp; in the ample bottom there was a peanut butter and jelly sandwich with my favorite oatmeal bread that Mom had made. It was crumbly, but the peanut butter kept it glued together pretty well. I had to be careful of the homemade apple jelly in the middle; it would ooze out the side when I took a bite. I also had a big Baldwin apple I helped pick the day before and two brownies with walnuts. Thirty-five cents jingled in my pocket; 10 cents from my weekly allowance and 25 I earned helping Grampa pick apples. I also had my favorite blue aggie flecked with white clouds. The 3-inch jackknife Grampa gave me for my fifth birthday was always in my right-hand pocket. It had a 3-inch blade and a short one. The long blade was so sharp I could shave the hair off my father's forearm just by sliding it along.

Other parents were arriving with their boys and girls and going into the school. One small boy about my size cried and dug in his heels as his mother dragged him along. Feeling courageous, I walked ahead of him through the big door and was confronted by a wide green sash tied over a round belly. Looking up I saw Mrs. Lawson's square face, gray hair, and forbidding smile. She was the principal and sixth-grade teacher.

Holding out her hand, she took mine in a firm grip.

"Good morning," she said. "What's your name?"

"Arthur Chickering," I replied.

Mrs. Lawson pointed me toward my classroom and said, "You are with Miss Dudley in Room One, right down there on the left."

Miss Dudley welcomed other kids and their parents. She was young, pretty, full of energy, and warm and smiley as she showed us to our desks. There were 23 kids, 10 boys and 13 girls. The sloping surface on my desk swung up on hinges along a 3-inch flat board. A hole in the upper right-hand corner held an inkwell; a yellow pencil and a pen with a metal tip were in a center groove. When I lifted the hinged top I found an 8.5-by-11-inch lined pad and a red rubber eraser.

Miss Dudley asked us to take out our pads and pick up our pens. She showed us how to dip our pens carefully into the inkwell; she wrote a cursive letter *A* on the blackboard and asked us to copy it with our pens. For some reason, I picked up my pen with my left hand. In order to make the *A* slant toward the right I looped my hand around above the letter. If you have ever seen a great blue heron bending over to stab a frog, that's what my writing hand looked like. The pen is his beak, my fingers are his head and neck, my hand is his body, and my arm is his legs. With the heel of my hand resting on the paper, it scraped across the wet ink. When I tried to hold my hand up off the paper, the whole process was a major test of my coordination. The sharp metal point dug into the paper and the ink splattered onto the page. When I looked at the classmate on my left, her right hand moved smoothly along, making multiple *A*'s with no problem. Later, when we wrote with our pencils, the heel of my hand became black from the soft lead.

We worked our way through the endless alphabet. The 20 or 30 minutes felt like an eternity. The heel of my hand was black and my fingers ached. But there was more in store. The Palmer Method of penmanship instruction called for exercises where you made half-inch lines up and down, next to each other, slanting to the right, across the page. Then you went down to the next line and made overlapping *O*'s across the page. My lines became full of blue smudges where my hand had dropped down onto the paper. What a mess! Miss Dudley walked around the room as we were working. She sympathized with my problem but offered no solution. She encouraged me to keep trying. I wondered whether the long years of school ahead would be filled with other challenges for which there would be little help. Was I always going to be somebody who was different, who couldn't do things the right way? Maybe my later career, pushing for better teaching and for recognizing individual differences, was in part motivated by her unresponsiveness to my difficulty.

Recess was at 10:00 a.m. for 20 minutes. We ran and screamed, took turns on the swing and slide, and played tag. At 11:45 a.m. we ate lunch at our desks. When we finished lunch, we could run and play until 12:30 p.m. I gulped down my milk, inhaled my sandwich and brownies, and saved my apple for later. Then, I ran outside and spotted a large apple tree to climb. I had lots of practice climbing trees in Grampa's orchard to help him pick. I easily climbed up the spreading branches of the schoolyard apple tree.

Miss Dudley appeared below me, at the base of the tree. "Arthur, come down out of there," she yelled. "We don't want you falling and hurting yourself!"

"Aw, I won't fall," I protested. "I climb apple trees all the time and never fall."

"Come down out of that tree right now," Miss Dudley demanded.

With consummate agility and grace, like those monkeys I saw in Nana's *National Geographic,* I swung down from branch to branch, and dropped lightly at her feet.

During afternoon recess, I sat against the chain-link fence that bordered Walnut Street and nibbled my apple. I took out my jackknife and pencil. Even though the pencil had made my hand black, there was one good thing about it: I could sharpen it to a nice point with my well- honed knife. There was a pencil sharpener on the wall by the blackboard, but I wanted to use my knife. I didn't dare do it in class—I didn't know what to do with the little wood chips and was afraid Miss Dudley would stop me and take my knife because she thought I might cut myself. I didn't think she would notice me over by the fence, so I went ahead. It felt really good doing something familiar and doing it well. Thinking about all that had happened this first day, I didn't feel as though I was off to a great start. Was school always going to be like this; teachers telling me to stop doing things that were fun? Would I just have to sit around and only do things that were safe and easy? Early on I was looking for risk and challenge. It's not surprising my childhood orientation became a cornerstone for my thinking about education, for recognizing that significant learning and personal growth occur best when you run into something you don't understand or don't know how to manage.

After school that first day, Mom was waiting to walk me home, I told her about the kids I played tag with during recess and about my penmanship difficulties. I asked her why I wrote with my left hand when I threw and batted rightie. I told her I liked Miss Dudley but decided it was probably best not to tell about climbing the apple tree.

My first serious challenge hit in late September when I started home on a sunny afternoon. A big maple tree, about four feet in diameter, stood on the left beside the road just after the intersection, next to a stone wall at the edge of Barstow's pasture. I had just passed it when Billy Barstow and Paul Mynaris jumped out, grabbed my hat, and pushed me down. Billy, who was about three-and-a-half feet tall, was built like a fireplug, with solid muscles from helping around his father's farm. Paul was skinny and a little taller than me, at about 3 feet 4 inches. He sat a couple of rows behind me and always had his hand up when Miss Dudley asked a question.

I got up. They tossed my cap back and forth as I ran from one to the other. When I tried to take it from Billy, he gave me a hard shove. I came back and swung my lunch bucket at him, but he stepped aside and tossed my hat back to Paul. After 10 minutes or so they tossed it on top of a nearby lilac bush, vaulted over the stone wall, and ran up to Billy's house. By this time, I was crying. I shook the bush, pulled down the branches, and recovered my cap. Two days later Paul jumped out from behind the tree. I ran down Bacon Street. I knew from games of tag that he could never catch me. But at the end of the pasture Billy jumped over the wall and cut me off. I grabbed my hat. They pushed me back and forth between them, calling me "chicken feathers" and "chicken shit," yelling "cock-a-doodle-doo." Crying again, I dodged away from Paul and ran toward home.

Over dinner that night I complained to Mom and Dad.

"I'm really sorry," Mom said. "There are bullies in this world."

"What are you going to do?" Dad asked.

"I don't know. Maybe I could go to the Felchville School. It's only a little farther away."

"No," Mom said. "There's no way you can change schools. Eat your dessert and let's see how things go."

After dessert I went up to my room, rearranged my lead toy soldiers on my bureau, brushed my teeth, undressed, and crawled into bed. I lay there and worked out a route home where I could go down Walnut Street a short way, back around behind Barstow's farm, through the Nelson's backyard, and over the wall to cross Bacon Street just above where Wilson's Lane went off. I dropped off to sleep feeling better. The next day I found my way along that route and they never saw me.

During supper I told my folks about my successful trip home. Mom said, "Good enough. Let's see how that works."

The next day at morning recess Billy pushed me down in front of Mary Bledsoe, a girl I liked, and some other kids. He said, "Hey, chicken shit, we didn't see you after school yesterday. What happened? Where'd you go?" I jumped up and threw myself into him. My head and shoulders hit his chest and knocked him over backward. On top of him, I pounded his face with my small fists. His nose bled. Miss Dudley pulled me off.

"Shame on you fighting like that. We're going to see Mrs. Lawson."

She marched me into Mrs. Lawson's office.

"Arthur knocked Billy Barstow down and gave him a bloody nose."

"Why did you do that?" asked Mrs. Lawson.

"He and Paul have been teasing me. He pushed me down and I got mad. I don't like being pushed around."

Mrs. Lawson replied, "Come to my office after school today. You'll sit here for half an hour to think about what you've done. I'll speak with Billy and Paul to see what their story is."

When I headed home at 3:00 p.m. that day, Billy and Paul were nowhere to be seen. During dinner I told Mom and Dad what had happened. Mom and Dad were both pleased with how I had handled the situation. I fell asleep ready to tackle the world.

On a Sunday morning in May 1936, soon after I had turned 9 years old, I woke up to screams and curses coming from Mom and Dad's bedroom. I crept down the hall and cracked open their door. They were kneeling on the bed facing each other. Dad had on his red and green pajama top and pants, Mom was in her short blue nightie with the white flowers and little eyelets. The bedspread was on the floor, and the sheet and blanket were tangled up. Mom was shaking Dad's head with both hands, pulling his hair and yelling at him. He was holding both her wrists, trying to stop her. His shoes were beside the bed, pants slung over the ladder-back chair. I noticed the picture on the bureau of them standing with their arms around each other on the beach at Dug Pond. The west window was open halfway and a balmy breeze ruffled the yellow chintz curtains, a striking contrast to the storm raging on the double bed.

When Mom saw me at the door, she let go of Dad's hair, turned, and said, "Go to your room and stay there."

I ran back to my room. In a little while I heard someone run down the stairs, slam the front door, and start the car. Then I heard its wheels spin, spraying gravel, and drive off. Mom was sobbing. I crept to the bedroom door and looked in. Sitting on the bed holding her head in her hands, she looked up and said, "Help yourself to some breakfast.

You can go out and play. I'll talk with you about all this after a while."

Totally bewildered, anxious, and sad, I went back to my room and dressed. After tiptoeing down to the kitchen, I sat at the table staring out at the apple tree and blue sky. A robin was pulling worms out in our backyard and the daffodils Mom planted last year were blooming. I didn't feel like eating, but got out some corn flakes and milk, filled my teddy bear bowl, and put on two extra teaspoons of sugar.

I didn't really want to go out and play. My mind was whirling. Climbing the apple tree, playing with the dump truck in my sandbox, or riding my bike did not feel right. The whole house was silent, as when we all stood around the graves at the Wayland cemetery. In the living room, I sat on the couch to read my *Outdoor Life* magazine. But I couldn't get into it. I finally went out back and slowly pushed myself back and forth on the swing that Dad had hung from the apple tree.

After what seemed like hours, Mom came out. I got off the swing and she gave me a long hug and said, "Your father is going to live somewhere else for awhile. He and I need to have some time apart. You two will have Sundays together, but the rest of the week it'll be just you and me."

I didn't know what to say and just stood there while she held me.

Taking my hand, she said, "Let's go over to Grampa's and Nana's. They'll be back from church by now."

So we walked over and went in.

"You're early for Sunday dinner. Where's Chick?" Nana said.

"He's gone," said my mother.

Nana replied, "Oh dear! I wondered if that would happen. Well, come in. You can help me get dinner on the table."

Mom asked me, "Art, why don't you go get Grampa from the orchard?"

A few minutes later, when Grampa and I came in, a rack of lamb, oven-roasted potatoes, beans, and boiled onions were on the table.

Mom told them the whole story. Dad had lost his job due to

drinking and driving. I guess that must have happened when he was on the road because I never saw signs of it or smelled anything when he came home. She also had found a bundle of love letters from her friend Susie, dating back to last fall, tucked up in the rafters in the cellar. Last Saturday Susie had cried and said she just couldn't resist Chick. He had come home late last night and that's what they fought about this morning. She had told him to get out.

"What are you going to do?" Nana asked.

"I'll have to get a job. We'll sell the house and that should give me something to live on until I find work. And Chick will have to help with child support."

"But he's just been fired and his driver's license is suspended. How can he help?"

"It's only a month suspension. He'll just have to renew his license and find another job. When he gets one maybe he can slack off on the liquor. And maybe my good old high school buddy Susie will help out in return for the good sex they've been having."

Grampa said, "You're well rid of that son of a bitch. I can help you move after we sell the house."

Even though I was only 9 years old, I realized that life was full of temptations. Staying married was not easy. I wondered how well I would manage when I grew up.

Mom's brother, Charles, and his wife, Maxine, lived in a duplex close to downtown. Mom learned that the top-floor apartment would be vacant. She could rent it and they could help look after me while she was working. The apartment had a small kitchen with a brick-colored linoleum floor. The living room, with soft red roses on the wallpaper, was big enough to hold our piano, couch, and an easy chair, and had a door that opened out onto a screened porch overlooking Winnemay Street. We each had our own small bedrooms. My familiar world, where

I had spent my first 9 years, was gone. So was my familiar family, with Grampa and Nana nearby, and with Dad there most evenings, breakfasts, and weekends.

Because work was scarce, Mom couldn't find a job in Natick or other nearby towns and ended up as a secretary with the John A. Roebling Company in Boston. Every morning she boarded a 7:15 a.m. train to South Station, only 5 blocks from her office. At 6:30 p.m. I ran down and got a hug as she stepped off the train. We walked home slowly while I told her about my day. We usually listened to the radio for the news while she was getting supper. She was pretty devastated when Amelia Earhart got lost out in the Pacific. She'd always followed Earhart's exploits and admired her courage. After we ate I listened to radio programs—*Little Orphan Annie; Mr. Keen, Tracer of Lost Persons;* and *The Lone Ranger.* Sometimes we sang at the piano or I did homework while she read.

Being there with Maxine and Charles and with the other kids exposed me to things going on in the rest of the world, more so than when my life revolved about Grampa and Nana. The kids told me about the Hindenburg bursting into flames in New Jersey. Most important, for the first time I realized there was a Depression. I heard about Roosevelt's New Deal and his trying to increase the size of the Supreme Court. We talked about heavyweight boxer Joe Louis, the "Brown Bomber," and how tough and unbeatable he was, and we sparred with each other imitating his stance and left jab.

Each Friday evening Mom put $21.50 in small bills and coins on the kitchen table. From the cupboard above the sink she took down a green metal box with a hinged top. Inside were several plain brown envelopes labeled *food, rent, clothing, transportation, medical, cleaning supplies,* and *entertainment.* Her fine hand had written dollars and cents down to the penny on each envelope. After handing me my week's allowance of a dime, she divided up the rest. As time went on, the numbers on the envelopes changed as her salary went from $21.50 to $25.00 to $27.50 and as unexpected expenses caused different allocations.

We never thought we were poor, but it was clear that every penny counted. We knew families who were worse off, and we also had neighbors who did not have to be so careful. Trying to manage, with a hungry, active, growing teenager, was tough for Mom. Hamburger was 12 cents a pound and bread 9 cents a loaf, so we often had well-seasoned meat loafs, cabbages and potatoes, and soups and grilled sandwiches. With lots of peanut butter and jelly sandwiches, I never felt especially hungry. Fortunately for both of us, I was a healthy kid. During the winter she made me take a tablespoonful of cod liver oil with a large glass of tomato juice before dinner each night, and that kept me free from colds. Despite my perpetual running around and tree climbing, I never broke a bone or had any sustained illnesses except for the usual childhood chicken pox, mumps, and measles.

I wondered how Dad and I would spend Sundays together. The first Sunday after we moved he drove up in the Ford about 9:30 a.m., just before Mom started walking to church. He never got up early on weekend mornings, so I was not anxious while I sat waiting on the back steps. He said he'd be there, and I knew he would. The top was down. I climbed in, leaned over, and gave him a hug.

"What are we going to do?" I asked.

"I thought we could go over to camp for the day," he replied. "There's no wind so we can take the canoe up the river and see if we can pot-shot some turtles."

"That sounds great," I said. I took the box of shorts for his .22-caliber bolt-action rifle off the dash.

His parents had a camp on Box Pond in Bellingham, Massachusetts, about half an hour away, at the head of the Charles River. Mom, Dad, and I had spent many weekends there with his folks and by ourselves. Pine trees shaded a roughly built two-story building with pine floors, a kitchen, a dining room, and a big fieldstone fireplace. Three bedrooms were upstairs, but the partitions only went up about eight feet, well short of the roof. At night Nana and Grampa Chickering snored so loudly it seemed like those partitions went in and out with each breath. When I was little I'd wake up scared, so Mom would come and lie beside me until I dropped off to sleep.

Dad and I didn't talk much on the way over. I didn't know what to say, and I guess he didn't either. We pulled in on the short, sandy road. When I jumped out, a beautiful scarlet tanager, bright red and black, sat right above us on a low pine branch. It seemed like a good sign for beginning our first day with this new life. He took the padlock off the back door. I got a pail of water from the pond to prime the hand pump at the kitchen sink, filled a large kettle with the cold water, and stuck in the hotdogs and a quart of milk Dad had brought.

Dad got a glass flask from the Ford, filled a tumbler about a third full with whiskey, and topped it off with the well water. We took two rockers from the living room out onto the porch and flopped into them.

"So how are things going?" he asked.

"Okay," I replied. "It's kind of hard with Mom working. But I have good fun playing with the other kids. I seem to be passing my fourth-grade subjects all right. Even though Mrs. Lawson and I don't get along all that well together, I've only had to stay after three times, twice for whispering and once for throwing a spitball at Billy Barstow."

"Well," he said, "if there is anything I can do to help, just give me a call. You know my number."

I did know his number but couldn't think of anything he could do, except somehow get back together with Mom.

"Let's eat," he said. "We can build a small fire in the outdoor fireplace."

I collected pine needles, wood chips, and small sticks from under the pine trees. Dad got some scrap paper and matches from the kitchen, laid the fire, and lit it up. I fed more sticks to it while he put on the hotdogs and buns. He poured me a glass of milk and another glass of whiskey for himself. I got two plates from the china cabinet and we munched our lunch sitting on the ground near the fire.

"Let's go see if we can find some turtles," Dad said.

"Sure," I replied.

In the past we had shot at tin cans and bottles in a sandpit the Natick road crews used. After some practice, I hardly ever missed. He went and got the .22 and the box of shells out of the car while I opened the double doors to the shed behind the house that held the 16-foot Old Town canoe. The two paddles were in the bottom. I carried the bow, Dad the stern and rifle, down to the pond. The warm sun felt good; I peeled off my T-shirt as we moved quietly through the still waters. It was an easy 20-minute paddle to the shallow end of the pond where the river came in. There were lots of painted turtles, floating with just their heads— about the size of the end of my thumb—sticking out of the water. We'd sit or stand in the canoe and shoot at their heads, passing the rifle back and forth and keeping score. They didn't duck when a bullet hit the water near them, and if one was hit, the others didn't move. They just kept on floating where they were. It never occurred to Dad or to me that we were killing living creatures. The issue never came up. It was sport. They were just challenging targets.

After the leisurely paddle back, Dad put his arm around my shoulder and gave me a hug.

"I guess we better get going," he said.

I buried my head in his chest, sobbing. He patted my head.

"I know how hard this must be for you. I'm sorry things have turned out this way. But we'll have more good times together," Dad assured me.

I couldn't think of anything to say, so we just stood there a minute or two, with the breeze rustling the pines. Dad locked up the camp. We climbed into the Ford and drove home. It was the first Sunday we'd spent just by ourselves and one of the best times we ever had.

At age 12, moving from the Bacon Street Elementary School to Coolidge Junior High School for grades seven through nine was no big deal. It was only about a mile walk through downtown Natick to school. Most of the kids I had known at Bacon Street and my neighborhood pals went there. Kids were divided into seven sections—A to G. A had the dummies, G the geniuses. I started in E. My grades were mostly C's with an occasional B, D, or F. I wasn't very good at doing homework. When school let out, I was ready to run and play. I was free until Mom got home from work at 6:30 p.m. She would get on me to study in the evenings, but after supper I was pretty tired and although I sat with books and exercises in front of me, I did not learn much.

My main problem was deportment. My wrestling buddy Rob Nason and I were in the same homeroom and had English, history, and social studies together. Rob and I tossed erasers and pencils back and forth when the teacher was facing the blackboard and threw spitballs at other kids. We made wisecracks about things teachers were saying, trying to outdo each other. Our English teacher, Mrs. Noyes, was small, gray-haired, mild mannered, and could not control us. Sometimes she was reduced to tears by things we did or said, and she sent us to the principal, who sent us to detention after school for half an hour. But that did not make much of an impression. Mom couldn't stay home from work to come in for a conference. Finally, after several rounds of detention and letters to my mother, whose scolding had little effect, the principal moved me up to Division F. That separated me from Rob and gave me a new English teacher, Mrs. Baxter. She was large and stern. Even though the kids in F were supposed to be smarter and the work more difficult, for the first time I started to enjoy English. Mrs. Baxter assigned O. Henry short stories, and we wrote about our daily lives at home, at church, and in our neighborhood playing with other kids. With her, and away from Rob, I behaved and got my first A in English. Sometimes I would even read and write in the afternoon when I got home from school. This early interest might have laid the foundation for my comparative literature major in college.

Mom and I got along pretty well, though there was one perpetual problem area: my bedroom. I could not be bothered to hang up my clothes and put them away, and my school books and papers were also scattered around. She'd say, "Hang up your clothes. It's just as easy as dropping them on the floor and kicking them under your desk."

I rebutted that it clearly took more time and effort to bend over, pick up the pants, carry them to the closet, and put them on a hanger than to just let them lie where I had stepped out of them. Even back then I had a flair for logical argument. So I was not persuaded. There was a small tree I climbed just outside my bedroom window. Coming home late one sunny October day, I came around the corner of our street and saw my bedroom window open. My dungarees, underpants, shirts, and socks were decorating the slender maple tree. My playmates, Teddy, Bobby, and Georgie, were sitting on the curb across the street grinning at me.

"Those are pretty dirty underpants you've got there," said Bobby.

His brother Teddy added, "I can smell those socks from here."

And Georgie, "How'd you get that shirttail so frazzled?"

"Aw, shut up," I answered as I went over and climbed the tree to toss and shake my clothes down onto the ground.

Mom did not say a word as I walked through the kitchen with my arms full. It took me only about three minutes to put the dirty under-pants and socks in the hamper, hang up my school pants and shirt, and put on my dungarees to go out and play before supper. My room became a good bit tidier after that.

On December 7, 1941, Dad and I went to the camp to drain the water and close up for the winter. Driving home about 5:30 that evening, a special report on the Japanese bombing of Pearl Harbor interrupted the program.

"Wow! What's gonna happen?" I asked.

"We'll have to go to war with them. I'll have to find a way to do my part."

Mom was waiting when I ran in.

"What about this bombing?" I asked. "Will Dad have to do something or go somewhere?"

"I don't know. We'll just have to see what happens."

That spring Dad got a 2-year job with the Merritt-Chapman and Scott Corporation, painting Quonset huts at a U.S. Air Force base in Ireland. He was not having much luck selling coke contracts for local coal burning furnaces, and this job paid good wages plus his room and board. He would be supporting the war effort and able to save most of his pay. It would be easier for him to help out Mom with my expenses. There was no real danger of getting shot, bombed, or hurt. He said he would write to me once a week and I could write and let him know how things were going. On October 1, Mom and I drove him to the boat in Boston, and he left his car with her.

In 1941, we all moved to Natick High for tenth grade, except for most of the kids in Divisions A and B, who dropped out. If some of the current alternatives for students with varied handicaps and abilities had been available then, I'm sure many of them would have been able to continue. One of my most memorable experiences happened in a social studies class. I still had trouble keeping quiet and behaving. Rob was in this class and we got back into our junior high antics, tossing things back and forth, making wisecracks. Mr. Larsen, also the football coach, was casual and had a good sense of humor. He caught me tossing a balled-up piece of paper to Rob with a tic-tac-toe game. He took the paper and smoothed it out.

"Chickering, come up here," he said with a smile.

"Yes, sir," I said as I walked up to his desk.

He drew a tic-tac-toe design on the blackboard and said, "I'll play you. If you lose, it's half an hour after school. If you win, you get off. Okay?"

I had played a lot of tic-tac-toe, and I knew that if you started in the middle you could never lose. You wouldn't always win, but you could always at least tie. So I took a piece of chalk and put my X in the middle square. Mr. Larsen made the fatal mistake of putting his O in a side space and he was a goner. I put an X in the corner below my other X, and I had two ways to make a row. Rob and a couple of other kids clapped. Mr. Larsen smiled, shook my hand, and said, "Well done. If you applied some of those smarts to social studies you'd get an A. Have an enjoyable afternoon."

As my deportment grades over the years indicated, I was not very good about obeying rules or putting up with people in charge of me. I usually was on the lookout for a way to bend a rule or get around it. Winning that tic-tac-toe game in front of all my classmates was a public achievement I had never experienced before. It reinforced a characteristic that had both positive and negative consequences later on when the stakes increased.

The other high point of my high school years was being on the baseball team—sort of. It was spring of 1942, and though I had turned 15, I was still only about 5 feet tall. Quick and close to the ground, I could get to and catch a lot of hard-hit balls. But I couldn't throw very hard and sometimes from deep third or short I could barely reach first base. There were bigger guys, juniors and seniors, who had much better arms and could also hit the ball farther. Some of them had been on the team the year before.

After the third practice, Coach Victor had to cut the kids not good enough to make the team. He took me aside while others went into the gym to get uniforms and said, "I'm sorry, Chick, but I just don't think I can play you this year. You're a good little fielder. Maybe next year your arm will be stronger." I accepted his decision but asked if I could still come to practice.

For the next 2 weeks I joined the practice, mainly fielding grounders or catching balls thrown in from the outfield and giving them to Coach as he hit long flies to make the outfielders run. Once in a while he would let me take some batting practice. I could get my bat on the ball pretty well but seldom hit it out of the infield. I was the only kid who'd been cut who came back. On Friday after the second week, at the end of practice Coach said, "Next Monday get yourself a uniform before you come out."

"Wow! Really?" I said.

"Yeah, you're a nice addition to the team," Coach replied.

I floated home and spent the weekend on a cloud. Mom congratulated me. None of the guys in the neighborhood believed me. "Well, wait and see," I said.

That whole season I went to practice, sat on the bench, and traveled with the team. I never once started or played in a game. We had a great team, and after winning the regional championship went to the Red Sox's Fenway Park for the state finals. Coach let me go out and warm up on the field, on the very ground where Bobby Doerr and Johnny Pesky stopped line drives and dove for ground balls. In the eighth inning, our fast center fielder, "Scooter" McDonough, led off with a ground-ball double between first and second, into deep right field. Charlie Olson, our catcher, was thrown out at first on a perfect bunt that moved Scooter to third. One out. Our lead-off hitter, Larry Potter, a quick shortstop, came to the plate. The infield for the opposing team was in on the grass, playing to get Scooter at home on a ground ball. Larry put a perfect bunt up the third-base line that the catcher had to field. But Scooter took off with the pitch and slid by the catcher to score. Larry was thrown out at first but we were ahead. We all jumped up off the bench and cheered. Coach ran and gave Scooter a hug. He had called that squeeze play and they'd done it perfectly. We held them scoreless in the top of the ninth and were state champions. I'll never forget running out on the field with Coach and the other guys. I'm still thankful to Coach Victor for letting me be a part of that team. That was my first experience in learning how important just showing up can be. It has served me well since then.

I was not long for Natick High. I got in trouble with the teachers and just barely passed. I was getting more difficult for Mom to handle. She decided I would be better off in a private school than at home with no supervision. Mount Hermon School in northern Massachusetts, then for boys only, had scholarship money for needy kids. She was able to get my costs reduced so, with help from Dad's overseas pay, I could go. Arriving the first week in September, Mom and I signed a housing form that described rules about noise, 10:30 p.m. lights out, linen changes, cleaning, and an honor code. Rooms were never locked.

I was in Room 214 in Overton Hall. There was a single bed made up with sheets, a pillow, and a grey wool blanket. A wooden, four-drawer bureau stood between it and a closet with a bar, wire hangers, and a shelf above. The desk had three drawers and a goosenecked lamp. I had two suitcases and an apple box full of clothes, shoes, some basic school supplies, a wind-up alarm clock, toothbrush, toothpaste, the Remington electric razor Dad gave me before he left for Ireland, and my trusty Rawlings baseball glove. My school supplies left the desk mostly empty so I put my ball glove in the bottom drawer. The alarm clock and my razor went on top of the bureau with my toothbrush and toothpaste.

After I had settled into my new home, Mom and I took a walk

on a dirt path that went up a steep hill to the chapel. The pews, posts, beams, and arches were all made of dark, well-polished wood. Plain glass windows tapered at the top let in light along the sides. Grey carpets led down the aisles.

"Kind of gloomy," I said.

"Yes, but you will get used to it with morning chapel two times a week," she replied.

The path led around the right side of the chapel to the dining hall, which had double doors on either end. Large windows along the side and at each end let in plenty of light. Round wooden tables had black ladder-back chairs for eight people. The kitchen was behind swinging double doors.

We walked down the hill across the grass and playing fields to the gym. Inside was a basketball court, climbing ropes and ladders along the east wall, and weights on pulleys for working out. On the second level a green canvas-covered track, sloping gently inward on the corners, ran around the whole open space. Lockers and showers filled the south end.

"I'm going to enjoy this," I said.

We walked silently back along the road to the Ford, parked by Overton Hall. I was full of mixed feelings and had no idea what to say. Maybe Mom felt the same.

She gave me a long hug. Her eyes glistened as she looked straight at me.

"I'll miss you. Try to write and let me know how things are going. Be a good boy. Remember, I love you."

"I know you do. I'll try to do better than I have before."

She turned away, got in the car, and drove off, waving out the driver's side. I surreptitiously wiped tears from my eyes. In my room, I stretched out on the bed, hands behind my head. Now began a chance to turn over a new leaf, to behave and not get in trouble, to study hard and get good grades, to live up to Mom's high standards. I was determined not to disappoint her again, but that was not to be.

On Monday afternoon, a week after Mom left, I finished putting the lunch dishes through the machine, helped by two other guys, and went back to my room. My bureau drawers and all my clothes were in a pile on the floor. Spread over them were the sheets, blanket, and pillowcase, with the pillow balanced on top. My suit, sports jacket, and pants were off the hangers and under the bed; books and papers covered the floor beside the desk.

I was furious. Who was the son of a bitch that did this? I wrestled with that question all afternoon while participating in tryouts for the football team. Coach Forslund ran us ragged, up and down the field, blocking and tackling, chasing passes. Afterward, we all jogged to the gym. I tossed my helmet in my locker, stripped off my pants, hip and shoulder pads, and showered. Everyone was joking around, nobody paying any special attention to me. Tossing my sport jacket over my shoulder, I walked to the dining hall. As I strolled in, Dick Thurston said, "Welcome to Mount Hermon," he smirked and walked off to his table. His room was on the third floor; the seniors roomed on the top floor, where it was most quiet. I had occasionally run into him coming or going on the stairs. He had been here all 4 years and often had some crack to make about my clothes, or cowlick, or something else. I was sure he'd messed up my room.

I learned what I could about Thurston's schedule. He did not seem to be involved in any athletic activities during the afternoons. We all had classes in the mornings. Evenings before lights-out at 10:30 we all studied, went to the library, played cards, or just horsed around. I could not see any time when he was regularly away from his room. I figured lunch was the only possibility. Friday morning, after chemistry class at 11:30, I went directly back to my room. From my window, I watched Dick walk up the path to the dining hall. I ran up to his room.

Our rooms had large double-hung windows. I pushed his bottom window all the way up and threw sheets, blanket, and pillows out of it. The clothes in his closet went out on their hangers. The contents of his desk drawers littered the floor. Finally, I turned to the single-bed mattress. Folded in half lengthways, it slid through the window. Watching it float to the ground and land on all his stuff made my day. I thought about tossing the bureau drawers out, but I was afraid that if they broke I might get in even more trouble. I certainly didn't have the money to pay for them. I slammed his door shut and bounded down the stairs two at a time. Then I ran to lunch and slid into my seat in time for apple pie and a glass of milk.

I joined my dishwashing team. We were speeding along, hard at work, when, after about 20 minutes, Dick came steaming up to me. "You bastard," he said. "Wait 'til I get you."

"You know where to find me," I replied, as he stormed out. My two teammates stood there.

"What the hell was that about?" Harry, another senior, asked. I told them the story.

"Don't worry," he said. "I've known Thurston for 4 years. He makes a lot of noise, but he won't do anything." Ralph, my other teammate slapped me on the back. "Good for you. Nobody else will hassle you either."

When I walked back to Overton after football practice that day, there was no sign of Thurston's clothes or mattress on the ground. For the next couple of weeks, I watched my back, but nothing ever happened, except for icy glares when we chanced to pass on the stairs. No bumps, pushes, or other challenges. And there was never a word from a faculty member or administrator. Like taking on Billy Barstow in the first grade, this experience reinforced a readiness to fight back when someone tried to push me around, whether or not they were bigger or more senior than I.

We were back from the Christmas break. It was about 4:00 p.m. in early January and getting dark. The overhead lights were on in the gym and 22 of us were trying out for basketball. During the fall, when I had a few spare minutes, I enjoyed going to the gym and fooling around, either by myself or with a few other guys, just shooting or playing half-court pickup games. I never had access to a gym before and it was a real treat. I was only 5 feet 2 inches tall and not much help on defense under the basket or rebounding. Almost everyone shot over me or reached up and took the ball off the backboard above my head. But I was quick and could dribble, pass, and shoot pretty well.

Coach Forslund was a real taskmaster, running us through various drills. We were practicing simple layups. In my nonconformist way, I started passing behind my back and trying to go under the basket for a reverse layup instead of simply putting the ball up the regular way. After I did this two or three times, Coach yelled, "Okay, Chickering. That's enough fooling around. Go up and run around the track until I tell you to stop."

I went up to the track and started running. I was not sprinting, just rolling along comfortably, so I could keep going as long as I needed to. The guys finished drills and I enjoyed watching them scrimmage against each other. Coach stopped frequently to give them tips about defense and offense, court position, and passing patterns. Keeping them going fast, he rotated players so each guy got a chance to show what he could do. I just kept on jogging, learning what I could from his comments and watching the play.

At 5:00 p.m. Coach said, "Okay guys, knock it off. That was a good workout. We'll see you tomorrow at 2:00 p.m. The last man to leave turn out the lights." He went to his small office. Coming out in a down jacket, he left through the side door.

I kept jogging. About 20 minutes later, Billy Morris, who was always slow in the shower, came onto the gym floor. He looked up at me and said, "What do you want me to do about the lights?"

"Turn 'em out, like Coach said," I replied. So he did and left.

I sat down beside the track. Dinner would be served in about five minutes and I wouldn't be there. Someone might notice, and I could be in trouble. But I decided to stay at the track as I had been told to do. I thought about Winnie, my friend at the nearby Northfield School for Girls, and speculated about what Mom might be doing at home and what Dad was doing over in Ireland. I tried to remember the periodic table for chemistry and who the past U.S. presidents were. I wondered what would happen when they discovered I was still at the track and not at dinner. I knew I was out of line, staying there in the gym when I should be up at dinner. But I was not anxious. After all, I was just doing what Coach told me to do.

I kept an eye out the window. After what seemed like a long time, I saw Coach striding down the path. He had that kind of walk he used when he really meant business: long steps, standing straight, head jutting forward a little. I had been missed at dinner. When they checked, I was not in my room. They got in touch with Coach and asked if he knew where I might be.

I got up and started running at a good clip. Coach burst through the side door. "Chickering! What do you think you are doing?"

"Running sir, just like you told me to," I answered.

"You come down out of there," he ordered. "Don't bother to shower. Put on your clothes and go up to the kitchen. They'll give you some food. Show up for practice tomorrow, and if you try any more of that wiseass stuff, you'll never play on any Mount Hermon team."

I trotted down to my locker, dressed, and left as he stood by the door. Neither of us spoke. I jogged to the dining hall and went into the kitchen. No one was there. A plate of roast beef, mashed potatoes, green beans, and a glass of milk were on the counter. I ate, washed and put away my dishes, and went to my room. It felt good to have scored a small point against that domineering coach. The next afternoon when I went to my locker, the other kids wanted to know what happened with Coach. I told them and we had a good laugh. After we went out onto the court, I was meticulous about following Coach's instructions, not wanting to trigger his wrath again. I was not good enough or big enough to be a starter, but I did warm the bench and get to play occasionally. Sometimes I would get to practice early, in time to change and be running around the track when Coach and the rest of the basketball team came in

Singing, along with sports, playing cards, and eating, was one of my favorite activities. At home I sang around the piano with Mom and other relatives, and in the church choir. I had a good sense of pitch and could carry any tune. Mount Hermon had a boy's glee club and an a cappella octet. Anybody who wanted to could sing in the glee club, but an audition was required to join the octet. Mr. Turnbull, a young, athletic, music master during 1942–1943, sat at the piano. First, he played single notes and asked me to sing them. Then he played scales in different keys for me to repeat. Next, he played phrases from four or five classical and popular songs. I had to get the pitch correct and capture the phrasing and tones as well. I nailed these musical tests. Finally, he checked my range, from low to high. I was a tenor with a pretty good range. Turnbull was a wonderful conductor, quiet and constrained. He could communicate the expressions he was after with just his fist, fingers, and facial expressions.

Every a cappella rehearsal with the other seven students was a great experience. Turnbull helped us create a single, harmonious, unified sound. If one of us was too loud, he pointed a finger and dropped his hand slightly. If he wanted more volume, he would point, clench his fist, and raise it slowly. He helped us work together better than any coach, of any kind, I have ever experienced. Unfortunately, he left at the end of that year. Mr. Homer replaced him, and was just as good a musician, but he didn't inspire us. I still sang and enjoyed it but not as much as the year before.

Academically, my lack of study during 1942–1943 got me grades similar to those at Natick High: English, 70; Algebra II, 63; Spanish I, 65; American History, 68; and Bible, 70. These grades averaged 66, with a D-minus for Conduct. Mom was not pleased with these results, but she was willing to have me go back as long as I earned some money that summer.

The previous fall she left her job with Roebling and took a position as an executive secretary with American Bosch in Springfield, Massachusetts. She found a summer job for me in the shipping department at Bosch. They made all kinds of pumps. As they came off the assembly line, my job was to pack one or more into wooden boxes about three feet wide, two feet deep, and four feet long. Once I nailed down the top, I filled out and tacked on the appropriate shipping label and rolled the heavy box to the outside dock with a dolly. The factory was humming, with three shifts around the clock. I got up each morning at 6:00 to join three other guys in a carpool in time for our 8:00 a.m. to 4:00 p.m. shift. I liked the fast-paced, physical work, keeping up with the pumps coming off the line. I also enjoyed the good-natured kidding among the workers. I'd never had any real contact with blue-collar workers like these folks, who said what they thought with no beating around the bush. I didn't often agree with their thinking about Roosevelt and the New Deal, or their attitudes about Blacks, Jews, or other "foreigners," but I tried to understand where they were coming from. After awhile I seemed to fit in, joshing the girls with the best of them, and I never lost my respect for those hardworking men and women.

When I got back into Mount Hermon's academic environment and culture, I was startled at the differences from my summer job at Bosch. In contrast to Bosch, at Mount Hermon every opinion included something like "I may be wrong, but . . . ," or "on the other hand . . . ," or "so and so's study seems to support the view that . . . ." It was hard to nail other kids or the teachers down when I asked, "But what do *you* think?" or "Where do *you* stand?" And at Bosch, I could see clear results from hard work, and it felt good to pick up my paycheck every Friday. At Hermon, I couldn't see how anything I did made much difference or how what I was studying would be useful after I graduated. Sports, cards, singing, and eating continued to be my favorite activities. Studying ran a poor fifth. So, my grades were about the same as the year before, an average of 67, but my Conduct was a full grade better, a C-minus. I graduated 93rd in a class of 102. I have always wondered who those other nine guys were and how they managed do more poorly than I did. Mom attended graduation. When I walked out of the chapel after the ceremony, she heaved a big sigh and said, "Well, you finally made it." You could have given 1000:1 odds against this character ever becoming a Distinguished Professor.

During the Christmas holidays of my senior year, Mom and I went skiing at Pico Peak outside Rutland, Vermont. Pico was the first ski area in the country to have a T-bar lift, a great improvement over the rope tows that pulled my arms out. The Roebling Company, where Mom had worked in Boston, supplied all the wire rope for the T-bars and cable. Her former boss was still a good friend and got passes for our lift tickets. We stayed at the Berkeley Hotel in Rutland. While we were having dinner our first night, a well-dressed, square-shouldered man with well-trimmed hair on his upper lip came over and asked if he could join us. He had on a sport jacket over a white shirt, unbuttoned at the top, with a green silk cloth tied around his neck. His dark pants, with a sharp crease, dropped down to shiny black shoes.

Mom, apparently used to having men come up like that, pulled out a chair and invited him to sit down. "Captain Jack" Sibley was also there for a few days of skiing. We chatted about the snow conditions and the forecast for more snow and good powder. Mom told him about her past job with Roebling and her current one with American Bosch. I gave him an edited version of my Mount Hermon experiences. He had driven up from Middlefield, Connecticut, where he owned Happy Acres, a summer resort, and the Dainty Maid Corporation, which sold women's feminine hygiene products. We finished our meal and as we got up, he offered us a ride out to Pico the next morning.

Our skis, poles, and knapsack fit easily into his wood-paneled station wagon with "Happy Acres" on the doors. Jack was not a good a skier, but he seemed to like being with us. After a good day together on the slopes, he joined us for dinner and signed the check. After dessert, he and Mom wanted to talk over coffee and a drink, so I went up to our room. Mom came up an hour or so later and commented on what a nice man he seemed to be. That became our routine for the next 3 days, except on the third evening the clock beside our beds read 12:30 a.m. when she came in.

In January, Jack drove up to Springfield and asked Mom to be his executive assistant. She and I moved to Middlefield in April, and I went there after graduation. The appointment included room and board at a manor house, plus a salary, so it was a good deal for Mom.

I had a small bedroom upstairs in the manor house. Rosalie, a Dainty Maid secretary, was an attractive former ballet dancer whose bedroom turned out to be next to Jack's. Milton, a tall, lanky British man, kept the house and rooms tidy. Both of them had become good friends with Mom and welcomed me warmly. The place was full of guests playing tennis, swimming in the pool, rowing and sailing on the lake, reading, and lying around in the sun. Jack gave me a summer job as a waiter.

I had no special plans for college or anything else, and with my lousy Mt. Hermon record, it was doubtful any place would accept me. Mom heard about an Army specialized-training reserve program that was open to 17 year olds. They sent kids to college for a year and then into the Army. Mom and I thought this program was a good way to start my military service and try college at the same time. Maybe I could get decent grades that would help me when I finished with the Army. On June 15, 1944, in one of his Fireside Chats, Roosevelt announced that Rome had fallen. Soon after, we heard on the radio that Mount Vesuvius had erupted, maybe celebrating Mussolini's downfall. Mom was a Roosevelt fan and was certain that he and Truman would beat Dewey and Bricker in November. Even though the war was going well, and Roosevelt was likely to remain in office, the draft would continue. My 18th birthday would be the following April, and they surely would come after me. So on July 1, 1944, I enlisted at the recruiting station in Middletown, Connecticut. The second lieutenant told me to come back for a physical exam the next day.

When I arrived a sergeant was sitting at a small table. He told me to get in the line for my physical exam. I stood behind a huge guy, about 6 feet 2 inches, broad shouldered, with large arms and a belly lopping over his belt. "I'm Max. Just been drafted," he said, and shook my small hand with his large fist.

The first step for the physical was to have blood drawn. I had never experienced this or seen it done, so I was both curious and sweating. The corporal taking the samples beckoned to Max. He walked over and I moved up, just about three feet away. The small metal folding chair creaked in protest when Max sat down. The corporal hitched his chair closer, rolled up Max's sleeve, and wrapped a rubberband tight around Max's big, fat upper arm. Taking Max's left hand, he pulled his arm out straight and swabbed a spot inside the left elbow with something that smelled like the rubbing alcohol Mom used on our legs after a hard day of skiing. I was close enough to see a small blue bulge in the fold of Max's elbow.

The corporal lifted a needle and pressed it into that blue bulge. Max fainted dead away and fell off the chair with a thud. The corporal sighed, rolled his eyes, got up, leaned over, and stuck an adhesive bandage over the small hole that was oozing blood. This was clearly not the first time he'd dealt with something like this. He poured some of the alcohol on a gauze pad and passed it back and forth under Max's nose. Max woke right up. The corporal, with some effort, helped him get on his feet, walked him to the doctor at the next station, and told him to come back after he had completed the rest of the physical.

The corporal turned to me and said, "Next."

I paused.

"Come on," he said.

I went to the chair and sat down gingerly. "What the hell is this?" I thought.

I pulled up my sleeve. The corporal wrapped my arm, swabbed the inside of my elbow, and stuck in the needle. It was not bad at all. The times I hit my thumb with a hammer working with my grandfather were much worse! I was fascinated to see my blood flowing into that small capsule. He pulled out the needle and gave me a small gauze pad to put over the tiny injection hole, tore off a piece of tape, and put it over the gauze pad. "Over there," he said, pointing to the doctor at the next station. Max was gone and I never saw him again. I breezed through the rest of the physical. The following week a letter arrived telling me to go to the University of New Hampshire on the Tuesday after Labor Day weekend. I would be there until May 1945, when I would be sent to basic training.

REFERENCE

Merriam-Webster's collegiate dictionary (11th ed.). (2005). Springfield, MA: Merriam-Webster.

CHAPTER 2

The University of New Hampshire and Wesleyan

In September 1944 I was living in Hetzel Hall at the University of New Hampshire (UNH) with 24 other 17 and 18 year olds. We took five courses that met every day, ate in the campus cafeteria, did homework, and chased after the coeds, who outnumbered the men about 4 to 1. We had to be in by 10:30 at night, which limited my time with the girls. I was on the third floor with my roommate, Charlie, from New Haven, Connecticut, and we were lucky enough to have a tall tree outside our window. My childhood tree-climbing practice came in handy. With the top half of the window all the way down, I straddled the panes, leaned out, put one foot on the sill and the other on a strong branch close to the trunk, and stepped over. Three more branches brought me down to 12 feet above the ground, where I would swing down and drop to the ground. I soon found a poker game. And then found Jeannie, from Littleton, New Hampshire. With wavy black hair and high cheekbones, she looked like Ava Gardner, who held off Humphrey Bogart's advances in *The Barefoot Contessa*. We danced and she was not reluctant to share her body. My late nights with her and poker meant that I dozed off frequently during early morning classes and spent little time studying.

Devon McNamara, a First Lieutenant, was in charge of our unit. Young, red faced, and Irish, his mission in life was to whip us young recruits into line. His main leverage came from numerous rules about how we should dress, where we should be and when, and how we should salute and speak to him and to the colonel, to whom he reported. Ridicule, running laps around the dirt track, push-ups, and jumping jacks were his main tools. This was "schooling" with a vengeance. It strengthened my inclination to challenge authority and my resistance to arbitrary exercises of power that became part of the rest of my life.

My prior schooling had not succeeded very well in habituating me to rules. Neither my Bacon Elementary School years sitting in Mrs. Lawson's office after school, nor having my homeroom changed in junior high had had much impact on my independent, rebellious streak. I persisted in getting a D-minus and a C-minus for deportment at Mount Hermon. So this guy was not going to break me, to convert me into some obedient horse, plodding along in step with all the others. I cut corners and pushed the limits—sloppy dress, reporting late for morning formations. When he caught me, I did not mind the extra exercise. McNamara and I did not have a jolly relationship.

Classes stopped for the Thanksgiving weekend. Most of the girls went home, including my sweetheart, but the recruits could not leave. Things were pretty dull. Charlie liked to drink beer, so on Saturday morning he walked into Durham and picked up 4-quart bottles of

Budweiser. We drank and played gin rummy that afternoon and evening. He was a Sunday *New York Times* devotee and had it delivered to our residence hall. We stayed up fairly late Sunday night, drinking, reading, and playing cards. Monday morning our room was a mess, with empty bottles and the *Times* scattered around. Tired and hung over, we decided to chance leaving it that way until we got back from classes.

Thunder rolled, lightening flashed, and rain drenched us as we ran back after our last morning class. When we got to our room, the door was locked. Locking the door was against the rules, and none of us had keys. So we knew McNamara had caught us.

"Oh, shit," Charlie said. "What are we going to do?"

I was scared but had an idea. "I'll climb the tree and get into our room. Then I can let you in and we'll clean up. You can leave. I'll lock the door from inside and go back down the tree."

"Okay," Charlie said, "but you better hurry 'cause he may show up any time."

I ran down the stairs and out the side door. The tree was wet and slippery, but I made it into our room, let Charlie in, and relocked the door. We feverishly started scooping up the newsprint and stuffing the bottles into our bureau drawers. A key turned to unlock the door to our room, and I heard McNamara outside. "Colonel, I've told you about this Chickering guy. He's always pushing the envelope and has lousy grades. Wait 'til you see this room."

Charlie ducked into our closet and I plastered myself against the wall behind the door. My heart was pounding so loud I was sure McNamara could hear it out in the hall. I thought he was really going to nail me this time. I'd be lucky to get out of this in one piece.

The door opened. After a brief pause, his red face and sharp blue eyes peered at me around the door. He pulled me out by my right arm and grabbed both my shoulders. The Colonel was a ramrod behind him.

"How the hell did you get in here?" McNamara asked.

"Sir, I climbed up the tree and came in through the window so we could clean up—sir," I replied.

He let go of me, walked over to the window and looked down the three stories to the brick and cement patio. "My God! You might have been killed," he said.

"Yes, sir. I mean, no, sir. I'm a good tree climber. It's not really that dangerous."

Charlie stepped quietly out of the closet and saluted McNamara and the Colonel.

McNamara gave us our orders. "You guys make this room spotless. Chickering, I'll get to you as soon as the colonel and I figure out what to do."

Wednesday after lunch McNamara summoned me to his office. "You're out of this program. The semester is over in a week and a half. You can stay until the end or go home tomorrow. If you stay, you will be confined to your room after 8:00 every night, and I'll have someone watching your damn tree. Let me know what you want to do by supper time. Dismissed!"

I saluted and stepped into the hall. I had screwed up again, just after barely making it through Mt. Hermon. My stomach churned as worries raced through my head. *Mom is going to be livid. Will any college ever admit me? What the hell should I do?*

The afternoon was a blur. During dinner I told Charlie and a couple of other friends what happened. I skipped my classes and went for a long walk around the campus looking for Jeannie and trying to figure out my options. By the time I got back to Hetzel Hall, I had my decision. I told McNamara, "I'd like to leave Saturday morning. I need to pack up and check the bus schedules and I'd like to give my mother some warning."

"Okay. You're out of here after breakfast on Saturday," he said.

At the end of the day on Friday I told Jeannie what had happened. By then all the other recruits knew about the situation. Most of them wished me luck, but there was no way they could throw a going-away party.

I couldn't put it off any longer. I called Mom from the phone booth next to the dorm. "Hello, dear," she said. "This is a nice surprise."

"I'm coming home tomorrow."

"Why are you leaving early? Isn't there another week in the semester?"

"Yes, but I got into trouble with the lieutenant. It's too complicated to discuss long distance. I'll tell you all when I get there. I'll be at the Hartford bus terminal at 6:45 tomorrow evening."

"It better be a good story! Another failure for you. I'll be there." The line went dead.

The bus ride seemed to go on forever. I couldn't read or concentrate on anything other than what might happen when I got to Hartford. When I arrived at the station Mom was standing there bundled up in a jacket and scarf wearing wool pants and high-top boots. It had snowed and the pavement was slushy when I stepped down, duffel bag over my right shoulder. Mom had brought the nice wood-paneled Ford station wagon with "Happy Acres" on the doors. I tossed my bag into the back, and we both got into the car. Turning on the heater, she asked me what had happened. During the 45-minute drive to Middlefield, I told her about climbing the tree into our messy room, getting caught by McNamara and the Colonel, and getting kicked out. I didn't think she needed to know about the beer drinking or about my using the tree to skip out after curfew to dance and neck with Jeannie.

She listened with the stony silence I knew from my past escapades. When I finished she said, "Well, that's a nice opportunity down the drain. You'll be drafted in May or June. I suppose you can live with me at Happy Acres until then. Maybe Jack can find some work for you."

"I'd appreciate that. I think there's a college in Middletown—Wesleyan. Maybe they'd let me in for the spring semester."

"Perhaps," she replied, "but your high school record makes it seem unlikely."

When we pulled up to the main house, Jack came out and shook my hand. I told him I appreciated the chance to be there, and hoped I could help out in some way. He said we could talk about that after Christmas. Mom showed me to an upstairs room and took me to the kitchen for some roast beef, mashed potatoes, and beans left over from their supper.

After she got over the shock of my getting kicked out of the university, we discussed what I should do between that December and June or July, when I would be drafted. Wesleyan University was in Middletown, Connecticut, only 13 miles away. If I could get in, it would be a chance for a semester of college before the Army.

I made an appointment with Ralph Bischoff, the admissions officer, for Monday, December 3. Light snow fell as I drove to the campus. I didn't know what to expect and didn't have a clear plan. I knew my Mount Hermon record would be a problem, and I would not tell him about getting kicked out of the University of New Hampshire unless he asked me what I'd done during the fall.

I found a visitor parking space behind the administration building. Students trudged through the snow, heading for afternoon classes or back to their fraternities. Double doors at the top of four granite steps let me in. A sign on a dark wood door at the end of the hall on the first floor read, "Admissions." I opened the door, introduced myself, and the secretary told me to go right in, pointing to a door at the right of her desk.

Bischoff was leaning back in a maroon leather swivel chair, puffing on a briar pipe. His unbuttoned tweed jacket was over a white shirt.

A loosened red and black tie had the Wesleyan cardinal on it. A small picture turned half toward him showed a beaming woman and two grinning school-age boys. To the right, overlooking the snow-covered lawn, was a large window. In front of it was a round table on top of which sat copies of *Newsweek* and the *Saturday Review of Literature*. Two maroon leather armchairs, matching the one he sat in, faced each other on either side of the table.

"Hello, Arthur," he said as he waved toward the table. "Have a seat."

I took off my down jacket and hung it over the back of the armchair.

"What can I do for you?" he asked.

Rubbing my sweaty palms together, I leaned forward. "Well, sir, I'm living with my mother at Happy Acres in Middlefield. I'll turn 18 next April 27, so I will be drafted in June or July. I would like to get in a semester of college before I go."

"Where did you go to high school?" he asked.

"I graduated from Mount Hermon last May."

"Mount Hermon is a good school. We've had some graduates from there and they have always done well here. We have room for the spring semester, so just send me your transcript and test scores and we'll see what we can do." He took a puff on his pipe as I squirmed in my seat.

"Oh, you don't want to see those. If you do, you'll never let me in here," I said.

"Well, Arthur, we never let anyone in without seeing their past school records. After I get them, I'll give you a call. Leave your number with Betty." He stood up and went back to his desk, puffing as he went.

"Okay. I'll do that."

After giving my number to Betty, I drove slowly back to Happy Acres, wondering what I would do with myself during the rest of the winter and spring until the local draft board called me up. It seemed unlikely he would let me in once he saw my poor grades and test scores.

Mom agreed that probably I would not get in, but thought it was worth having my transcript sent, which I did.

On December 13, Mr. Bischoff called and asked me to come to his office the next day. During the drive, I anticipated his negative decision. Then a backup response hit me, and I entered his office feeling better than I had for the last week. At least I could take some initiative.

He got up and came to the table where we sat before. Same jacket, same tie, puffing on the same pipe.

"Arthur, I looked at your records and I'm afraid you are right," he said. "We have never let in anyone with the kind of grades or class ranking that you have. Even though the war is on and our enrollments are down, we have to maintain our standards."

"Yeah, I guess I can understand that."

"But one thing interests me," he continued. "Your grades are all over the place, your rank in class is close to the bottom, and your Scholastic Achievement Test scores are really low, but your Aptitude Test score is high. How do you explain that?"

A big puff blew smoke in the air above his head. I moved to the edge of my seat and leaned toward him.

"I've never really studied. I've always been more interested in sports, the outdoors, and other things. But now I realize this is my last chance to make some kind of record in college before I'm drafted. I'm at Happy Acres right now, and the resort is closed. There are no other kids around, no girls or other distractions. I am ready to study. I know I can do the work."

"That's helpful, but I still cannot see how we can let you in with that past record. Our best prediction of future performance is past performance."

"I tell you what. I'm going to be commuting. I won't take up any dormitory space. I will pay you my full tuition up front. You set any grade point average you want me to get, according to any testing schedule. If I don't make it, you can kick me out and keep the money."

He took two long puffs. I sat back, crossing my fingers in my lap.

"Well! That's quite a proposition," he said. "Let me think about it. I'll give you a call in a couple of days."

"Thanks, Mr. Bischoff, I hope you'll give me a chance."

We stood up, shook hands, and I walked out. He had not immediately said no. Maybe he'd give me a shot. After all, it was a no-lose situation for him. When I got back to Happy Acres, I told Mom what I had proposed. If he let me in, I would not ask her for any money because I had enough saved up from my summer job to pay the tuition.

"I know you can do good work if you just buckle down. I hope you are ready to do that," she said.

"I believe I am."

"I hope they give you a chance and I'm ready to be helpful in any way I can."

The next Thursday, before Christmas weekend, Mr. Bischoff called and asked me to come in the following day. My heart was racing and my palms were sweating again as I drove to the university. There was no sign of life on campus. Fresh snow made everything still. The administration building felt deserted when I walked through the double doors to his office. There was no secretary, but the door to his inner office was open.

"Come on in, Arthur," he said, staying seated behind his desk. He waved toward the table. "Have a seat."

Uh, oh, I thought. This doesn't look good. I sat down, not bothering to take off my jacket.

"How are you doing?" he asked.

"I'm okay. Nervous, I guess. What do you think?"

"Here's the deal. I'll let you in, but if you don't have at least a B average on your mid-term exams, you're out of here. How does that strike you?"

I jumped up.

"Thank you so much! I'm so grateful. You won't regret betting on me. What do I do next?" I asked.

"We'll be shutting down for the holidays, but after the first of the year, come on in and register. The Registrar's Office is at the other end of the hall—and don't forget to bring a check or cash. Get a catalog from the stack by Betty's desk and think about the courses you want to take. There's not a lot of flexibility for your first semester, but there are a couple of choices. Feel free to drop in and say hello if you want."

He got up, leaned over his desk and stuck out his hand. I took it in both of mine.

"Good luck," he said.

"Thank you. Thank you so much."

On my way out, I picked up a catalog from the stack and sped home, skidding a bit on the new snow, singing, "I Wish You a Merry Christmas."

I burst into Mom's office. "I got in!"

She gave me a big hug. "Great! Now the work starts. Let's look at that catalog after dinner."

The required courses were English Composition, History of Western Civilization, and Humanities. I could choose one more from a list of natural and social science courses and a foreign language. I wanted to continue Spanish because I had enjoyed it at Mount Hermon. Geology sounded good since I could go hiking to learn about how mountains, lakes, rivers, and the Earth were formed. Psychology might help me learn how to make out with girls, though I didn't share those reasons with Mom. We decided that after the Christmas holidays we could look at the textbooks and make my choices then.

After Christmas we drove to Rutland with Captain Jack to spend a long New Year's weekend skiing at Pico. When we returned to Happy

Acres, I went to the Wesleyan bookstore and looked at the geology and psychology texts. As long as I was going to be in the Army, psychology might be a more useful course than geology. I registered, gave them a check that about blew my small savings account, bought the texts, and started studying.

The history and humanities books were really interesting, much to my surprise. The psychology text was a huge disappointment. It was mostly about learning—experiments with dogs by Pavlov and rats in mazes. There was a section on perception that had detailed information about how we smell, taste, touch, hear, and see. Another section was on motivation, why we think what we think and do what we do. Most of this stuff did not give me much information about why I walked Dorothy Munroe home after choir practice, or wanted to make out with my girlfriend, or why I fought Billy in elementary school, or why I had battles with Mom, or had to take on McNamara. The personality theory was fairly interesting, but abstract. Freud's ideas about the id, ego, and superego gave me a general way to think about me and Mom and my problems dealing with who I was and what kind of person I wanted to be. The Oedipus complex made me wonder about my relationship with Dad and my problems with McNamara and other guys like him. But all in all, I didn't see how it would help me much with my upcoming Army experiences.

After classes started, Mom drove me to Wesleyan at 7:30 a.m. so she could be back at work by 8:00. I usually went to the gym and shot baskets or worked out with the weights. Sometimes I just ran around outside on the cinder track. When the weather got warmer, I borrowed one of their tennis racquets and hit against a backboard. Once in a while some other guy came out and hit with me and we would play. I regularly lost but was learning to play.

I liked that way to start the day and I liked having the access to those facilities, just as I had at Mount Hermon. I had one or two morning and afternoon classes and read in the library when I had some spare minutes. In the late afternoon I took the bus to Middlefield and walked the mile and a half home for dinner. In the evenings, I most always studied. Once in a while Mom and I would go to a movie in Middletown with Rosalie and Milton, who had become good friends with Mom and me.

One afternoon after I came home, Milton was serving tea with a black eye and bruised face. He had gone to a bar in Middletown and was ordering a drink when a burly young guy confronted him, asking if he was gay. When Milton equivocated, the guy grabbed him by the shirt front, pulled him off the stool, slugged him a couple of times, and said fruits of his kind were not welcome at that bar. This was my first encounter with homosexuality and anti-gay bullying. I felt more kindly to Milton after that.

At the time Wesleyan had only about 750 students. I participated in many activities because there were more things to do than there were students to do them. Sports, singing, and dramatic groups were always looking for participants. Classes were small and, for better or worse, the professors really got to know the students.

When midterm exams rolled around, I was better prepared than ever before. I had worked hard and felt I'd learned a lot, except for psychology. The exams took place over the period of a week. Each day Mom would ask how it went, and I would say that I did okay. When the grades arrived a week later, I had a B-plus average: A in Humanities, A-minus in History and Spanish, B-plus in English Composition, and a C in Psychology.

The day after I got my grades I walked into Bischoff's office. "Congratulations," he said. "I thought you had it in you."

"Thank you so much for giving me the chance. I don't know where I might have ended up if you had not bet on me," I said.

"We really were not taking a big risk. After all, you gave us your tuition. You were the one making the bet. We look forward to seeing you back here after you get out of the Army."

In mid-June I finished the semester with a B average. At Happy Acres, Mom was thrilled that for once I had done well in school. I had stayed out of trouble and gotten good grades. Jack and the others congratulated me. I put the books away and helped out around the place until I was called to serve my country on July 1, 1944.

When I returned to Wesleyan after a year and a half in the Army, the hard studying that had gotten me through the semester before I was drafted evaporated. Then I was highly motivated by the desire to ensure myself a place in college when I got out of the Army, and there was nothing much else to do at Happy Acres. But at Wesleyan, just as at the University of New Hampshire, poker, parties, and pretty girls were my top priorities, along with gin rummy, bridge, baseball, skiing, squash, and wrestling.

I joined the Sigma Nu fraternity. The suite I shared with Rob Nagle had a double bunk, two bureaus, and a closet in one small room. An adjoining room held a couch, two overstuffed chairs, and a small bar. As the semester wore on, we both became acquainted with some local girls who enjoyed dating college guys. Most Friday and Saturday evenings Rob and I joined other guys, playing records, dancing, drinking beer or blended whiskey and ginger ale. Those evenings often included songs and drinking games that loosened us all up. When the timing seemed right, Rob or I would invite our date up to our suite, replenish our drinks, put on some of our own 78s, dim the lights, and make out on the couch. The girls varied in what they permitted, but rarely actual intercourse.

Ever since my dad taught me to play poker when I was a kid, I'd enjoyed the game and was good at it. I had saved about $2,500 in winnings while I was in the Army, and Wesleyan kids just out of high school were easy pickings. You could get up a poker game almost any hour of the day, except perhaps between 9:00 a.m. and 12 p.m., when classes were in full swing. I walked around campus with a deck of cards in my hands, ready for a game anywhere, any time, for any amount. So with my G.I. Bill support, Army savings, and a steady stream of poor players, I had plenty of cash. I stashed $400 with Bill Bassett, our fraternity treasurer, in case I had a run of bad cards, but I never had to dip into it. That became an anchor for my identity during my first semesters back.

Not surprisingly, with studying still low on my list of priorities, I got lousy grades and was on probation for 3 semesters. The only courses I worked at were in American, English, and European Literature. I enjoyed both the classics and modern writers. During spring semester of my sophomore year, I had to declare a major. English, French, or Spanish were the only possibilities that appealed to me, but all of them were organized historically, starting with *Beowulf*, or *Chanson de Roland*, or *Don Quixote*, and working up to the present. I liked modern literature best, and the ways novels and plays interacted with social conditions, politics, and economics. With the deadline fast approaching, I made an appointment with Dean Mayfield. We were acquainted because he had called me in twice to discuss my probationary status, and also because he had to deal with complaints from a couple of parents about the money their kids were losing. I was not feeling optimistic as I walked into his office.

"Have a seat, Arthur. What's on your mind?"

I sat on the edge of the armchair in front of his desk and leaned forward. "Well, Dr. Mayfield, I've got to decide on a major and I'm stuck. I like literature, especially modern literature, but if I major in English, Spanish, or French I have to begin with the earliest writing and work up to the present. Isn't there some way you can slice this stuff horizontally? I really like how modern literature relates to what's going on in these various countries. But those majors don't really do that."

"It's nice to hear about your interest, Arthur. Comparative literature cuts across different nationalities and languages. We don't have that major here, but if Fred Mann for French, Juan Roura for Spanish, Nobby Brown for classics, and Fred Millet for humanities will put together a combination of courses and prepare your comprehensive exam, you can have that kind of major."

I walked out of his office at 10:30 a.m. and by 5:00 that afternoon I had met with all four professors. They all were glad to lay out a collection of courses and do my comprehensive exam. They seemed startled to find that I was interested in learning something and happy to give me a chance. The next morning I put "Comparative Literature" on the form for my major and left it with Dean Mayfield's secretary.

"Please give him a big thank you for me," I said.

The dean's flexibility and willingness to take my particular interest seriously, and the hearty responses of the faculty members, turned my Wesleyan life around. For the first time, I had a purpose for studying. I had enjoyed reading the *Saturday Review of Literature* and would look at Norman Cousins' editorials to try to figure out what made his writing so interesting. I wanted to make a living reading novels and plays and writing about them. The next semester I was off probation, and by my graduation in 1950 I had a B-plus average, good enough to get me into Harvard's Master of Arts in Teaching English program.

Sigma Nu also gave me my first experience of social activism. The fraternity was started in the South and did not admit Blacks or other minorities. We veterans were not willing to put up with that policy. We contacted the national office asking for permission to admit members regardless of race, ethnicity, or national origin. They sent an executive in his 60s to meet with us and explain why, given their long history, they could not make an exception for us. We said that if so, we would withdraw from the national and simply become a local Sigma Nu. They persisted in their decision, and with Wesleyan's backing we took out a mortgage from a local bank and bought the house. Our monthly payments were somewhat more than our dues to the national organization, but we all found great satisfaction in taking that action. This was in 1948 and 1949, years before *Brown v. Board of Education.* This powerful experience fit with my general anti-authoritarianism and readiness to tackle the establishment. It laid the foundation for my future membership in the National Association for the Advancement of Colored People and for my contributions to the activism of the 1960s.

Two brief conversational exchanges also had a major impact on how I thought about myself. During my first 3 semesters, my identity was anchored in gambling at poker, gin, bridge, and baccarat. To reinforce my distinctiveness, I also adopted the practice of going up to the second floor of the fraternity house, pausing a second or so between each step. That way everyone would know that Chickering was coming.

One afternoon I met Dick Holloway, a well-liked senior, coming down the stairs. He stopped, took my arm, and said, "Chick, why don't you just relax. We all like you and think you're a nice guy. You don't have to always put on a special show."

I looked down, mumbled "Thanks," and continued up the stairs. No one had ever said anything like that to me before. I don't remember coming to any grand conclusion, but I did start walking upstairs normally and after a while I kept my cards in my pocket. My shaky self-esteem had been given a small boost.

Another boost came from Juan Roura, my Spanish professor. I was finishing a second semester with him. He and his lovely Spanish wife had fled Franco's regime to come to Wesleyan. Once or twice a semester they invited his classes to their small apartment for sherry and tapas and to discuss plays we were reading. On one of those afternoons, I forgot to take my book of plays with me when I left. When I went back to get it, Dr. Roura said, "I looked at your book. You have underlined all the most important passages. Good for you." I thanked him and left feeling encouraged.

Three weeks later, I went back to see him. My Dad, whom I had seen during Christmas vacations and with whom I had taken a camping trip during the summer, was active in the Natick Rotary Club and had nominated me for a summer scholarship to study in France. I needed recommendations from two of my professors. I asked Dr. Roura if he would write one for me. He said, "I would be happy to. I think you would be a good representative for your country in Europe." I felt thrown off balance once again; with all my failures, gambling, drinking, partying, and chasing girls, I certainly never thought of myself as a good representative for anything. Perhaps I had something to offer after all, despite my mother's conscientious reminders about all my shortcomings.

My final Wesleyan challenge happened after I graduated. Although I was not much of a wrestler, I was on the wrestling team during spring semester of my senior year. At 155 pounds, I was quick and flexible but not as strong as most of the guys at other colleges. I won a couple of matches through escapes and take-downs, but I never pinned anyone. In April, we went to Boston to wrestle against Tufts University. I went to the mat against a small Samson and only just managed not to get pinned. The Doherty brothers, Tom and Terry, a sophomore and a junior, were also on the team. After the match and dinner we went back to the Copley Plaza, where we were staying before heading back to Wesleyan the next morning. As always, I had my Bicycle poker cards. I got a bunch of change and single-dollar bills at the front desk and six of us settled into an evening of five- and seven-card stud and five-card draw. I ended up winning $107. The Dohertys came out owing me $76; $52 from Tom and $24 from Terry. They promised to pay me when we got back. Graduation was fast approaching. They kept putting me off. I was preoccupied with preparing for my comprehensive exam, applying to the Harvard Graduate School of Education for the Master of Arts in Teaching English program, and making arrangements to go to the

University of Dijon for an intensive summer French language course. I also was busy packing up and getting ready for graduation. Whenever I ran into the Dohertys, they gave me excuses and promises. I ended up graduating without getting paid.

During Columbus Day weekend the following fall, I decided to go to Wesleyan for House Party Weekend. I wanted to collect from the Dohertys, and it would be nice to see Paula, a local girl I had dated. I arrived at Sigma Nu in time for drinks and dinner. Paula joined me and we had an evening dancing to records and drinking White Cargoes— vanilla ice cream blended with ample gin. After a while, we retired to an upstairs bedroom and slipped easily back into the lovemaking we had enjoyed the past spring. When I took her home at 1:30 a.m., we arranged for me to pick her up the next afternoon at 3:00, when partying would be getting underway at Sigma Nu and other fraternities across the campus.

I slept late, had a leisurely breakfast, and worked out at the gym. Paula was her usual lovely and lively self when I picked her up in the Olds that George and Mom let me borrow. We parked behind the fraternity and stopped in for a quick drink and dance.

"I've got some business to wrap up with the Doherty brothers at Eclectic. They owe me some money and I'm going to collect it. Do you want to come, or would you like to hang out here? I won't be gone long," I said.

"I'd be glad to join you. Sounds like it might be interesting," Paula said.

Eclectic was just 150 yards down the road. Their party was going strong when we got there. I found Ted Elbert, the fraternity president. I asked if the Dohertys were upstairs.

"Yeah, as far as I know they're up in their room. The same one they had last year."

"Good. Would you hold my watch?"

"I guess so. Why?" said Ted.

"I don't want to take a chance on breaking it. I'll be back soon."

I treasured my Longines Wittnauer wristwatch, a high-class timepiece I got as security during basic training when a guy to whom I'd loaned $50 never repaid me.

I went up the stairs and knocked. They both yelled, "Come in!" When I opened their door a smell like a well-used locker room hit me. They were stretched out on their beds with plastic Old Fashioned cocktail glasses half full of punch resting on their chests. The room was a mess. The desk was strewn with notebooks and papers, the bureau top was littered with toothbrushes, toothpaste, razors, pens, pencils, and small change. I could see a pile of dirty clothes through the half-open closet door, where two ties hung on the doorknob. I was glad to see that there were no women with them, and I understood why.

"Hello boys. How're you doing?" I asked.

Terry, on the farthest bed, put his glass on the table between them, swung his legs over the side, and sat up.

"We're doing fine. How's Harvard?" he replied.

"Harvard's fine. It's nice to be back for the weekend. I'm here for the $76 you guys owe me."

"Give us a break. We don't have that much cash on us," Terry answered.

"Well, I guess that's okay," I said.

I walked over to their clothes closet, kicking aside a jock strap as I went, and took a Harris Tweed sport jacket off a hanger. I slipped it on over my sport shirt.

"This is a good fit," I said. "And here's a nice gabardine suit. I may have to get the pants let out a bit, but it will do nicely. Do you want to get me the cash or shall I just go home with these?"

"You really mean that, don't you?" Terry said.

"I sure do," I said, heading for the door.

"Wait a minute. Maybe we can borrow it. Let's go downstairs. Our fraternity treasurer has cash that gets loaned out in emergencies."

"Okay. Let's go. Ted's downstairs and he can do it if your treasurer isn't here."

I tossed the clothes onto the nearest bed and followed them downstairs. Ted was dishing out the rum punch. Paula was sitting nearby. I thanked Ted for holding my watch and said, "These boys need your help. I'll just wait here. Hey, Paula, want to dance?"

By the time Artie Shaw's "Stardust" was done, the Dohertys were back with the cash, Ted behind them. He gave me back my watch.

"Thanks, boys. No hard feelings," I said.

"You sure take poker debts seriously," said Terry.

"I always have and I wasn't about to make an exception for you guys. Have a good weekend and a good year. I hope the wrestling season is better this year than last."

Paula and I strolled back to Sigma Nu. "Would you really have taken their clothes?"

"Yeah, they were a good fit and I can't afford stuff like that."

"What if they had tried to stop you?"

"That was unlikely. They came here straight from prep school, a couple of rich kids from Westchester County. They haven't been around much. Terry is the oldest and biggest, and was on the bed farthest from the door. Tom would look to him. If one of them grabbed for the clothes, I would have dropped them and hit him. Who knows what might have happened after that."

I kissed Paula goodbye after we had breakfast together Sunday morning and we've never seen each other since. When Mom and George asked how the weekend had gone I told them I had a great time partying and visiting old friends.

CHAPTER 3

Marriage, Harvard, and Columbia

I graduated from Wesleyan University in 1950 with a BA in Modern Comparative Literature. I enjoyed reading contemporary novels, poems, and plays, thinking about the societal contexts in which they were set, and writing about them. Each week, I eagerly ripped open my copy of the *Saturday Review of Literature* and read Norman Cousins's editorials not only for their wit and penetrating observations, but also to look at his sentence structures, paragraphing, metaphors, and analogies. I wanted to learn how his writing kept me riveted. John Ciardi was the *Saturday Review's* literary critic. I devoured his pieces. Reading contemporary literature and writing about it seemed like an interesting way to earn a living.

But I had to support myself after graduation. I could not just go to a writing program or graduate work in literature. School teaching seemed like the logical next step. Supplementing my G.I. Bill by working, and winning a fair amount of money at poker, gin, and baccarat had generated enough savings to pay the tuition for the Master of Arts in Teaching English program at the Harvard Graduate School of Education (HGSE). My mother had married George, and they lived in Cambridge. I figured I could live with them and teach high school for a year or two while I honed my critical skills and then, in my fantasy world, become a back up for Ciardi at the *Saturday Review*. So I entered HGSE in the fall of 1950.

Except for Robert Eulich's philosophy of education course, where I first encountered John Dewey, and Robert Sears's mildly amusing educational psychology course, the rest of HGSE's courses were a dead loss for me. Even the famous I.A. Richards class put me to sleep. Maybe others found these courses interesting and useful, but I did not. In contrast, the literature courses on the Harvard campus were fascinating. And I really enjoyed doing my MA thesis comparing Henry James and Marcel Proust. Those experiences led me to apply to the University of Wisconsin's PhD program in comparative literature. If I could not back up John Ciardi, maybe I could become a college professor. Or maybe I could do both.

The required "practice teaching" experience that spring turned me away from secondary school teaching and raised questions about my comparative literature career. I discovered that I was intrigued by how the high school students were using discussions of *Silas Marner* and *The Mill on the Floss* to process personal issues concerning relationships with their parents, with authorities, and with one another. I found myself more interested in trying to help them explore those issues, with all my 24-year-old wisdom, than in working on literary understanding and criticism.

Far and away the most important thing that happened to me that winter and spring was meeting Joanne Nelson. George had met her in July while Mom and I were in Europe. I had taken an intensive summer course in French at the University of Dijon, and Mom was a Cambridge League of Women Voters delegate to a convention in Brussels. George, Mom, and I were having lunch on the Saturday of Labor Day weekend, 1950, when he said, "I've found just the girl for you. Jo Nelson. She's beautiful, smart, lively, and volunteers for the World Federalists." George and I had interesting conversations when I came home for vacations while I was at Wesleyan. His penetrating questions and observations took my thinking to new depths. I admired his rock-solid values, stoic responses to pain and difficulties, active engagement with social concerns, and dry wit. He had become a strong and supportive partner for Mom after Dad's deceit and subsequent short-term relationships. So I took his suggestion seriously. Two weeks later my mother invited Jo, her father, Larry, and Barbara, her stepmother, for a Sunday afternoon tea where we sipped Madeira and ate sugar cookies and cashews. We discussed local, state, and world politics. Jo was much better informed than I and not shy about sharing her views. We discovered we both were enrolled in the HGSE program and were in Robert Eulich's Philosophy of Education course.

Just as George said, Jo was beautiful and lively. On warm evenings, after ice-cream cones at the Howard Johnson's on Memorial Drive, we interrupted walks along the Charles River for hugs and kisses. We shared some movies and "Breakfasts with Bertocci," a Boston University philosopher who discussed religious and spiritual issues with graduate students on Sunday mornings at the Cambridge Methodist Church. Jo visited our place in Hancock, New Hampshire, over New Year's weekend. We skied in the fields and woods behind the house. In front of the large, open-hearth fireplace, we listened to George recite poetry he had memorized in the trenches during World War I, and we read some of our own favorites. We danced until 5:00 a.m. at the Fireman's Ball in Peterborough on New Year's Eve. By then I was well hooked.

On Tuesday afternoon, April 10, 1951, Jo sat opposite me at a small, round table at "our" Howard Johnson's. Her tan was the color of coffee with cream; her black wavy hair fell to her shoulders; and she wore a white, scoop-neck peasant blouse. For the past 6 months, we had been meeting here a couple of times a week. Jo took the bus from Watertown, where she taught at the Perkins School for the Blind. I walked from my mother and stepfather's apartment on Forest Avenue.

Marianne, our waitress, came over.

"Hi there. The usual?" Marianne asked.

"No. Not today. Let's have two hot fudge Sundaes," I answered.

"Wow. We're splurging," Jo said.

"Yeah. This is a special day," I replied, rubbing my sweaty palms.

I reached across the table and took Jo's left hand.

"Will you marry me?" I asked, looking down at our clasped hands.

There was a long pause. I held my breath. A truck rumbled by on Memorial Drive. Looking up, I saw those deep blue eyes meeting mine.

"Yes, I will," she answered. "When?"

Trumpet fanfares sounded, birds sang, flowers nodded their heads. I grinned, leaned across the table, took her face in my hands, and we kissed.

"Whew! How about late August after my summer school classes are over?"

She swiveled to the side, crossed her lovely legs, and tossed that long black hair. "Sounds good. I guess I can wait that long."

We agreed we wanted a simple wedding, maybe in the Cambridge Methodist Church where we had been sharing those breakfasts with Bertocci.

The week went slowly until Jo and I met for ice-cream cones again. Jo looked me in the eye and said, "I've got a job with the New Jersey State Commission for the Blind. I'm going to begin work at Camp Marcella in northern New Jersey on May 15, and I never want to see you after today." Her chair fell over as she jumped up. With excellent timing, she ran out of the door and stepped up into the arriving bus.

I was stunned. What could have happened? Why no explanation? We had always shared our feelings and talked through difficult times before. Bolting out like that was not like the Jo I knew and loved.

I managed to get through the semester finals, even though I could not concentrate on studying. My mind was spinning, wondering why she left, where she was, what she was doing. I had been accepted for a PhD program in comparative literature at the University of Wisconsin, but I had to complete two Latin courses before I could be formally admitted. Plunging into summer school, I enrolled in two morning courses, worked in the Harvard University machine shop from 1:00 p.m. to 5:00 p.m., and also on the maternity ward reception desk at the Cambridge City Hospital from 11:00 p.m. to 7:00 a.m. After supper I slept from 7:30 p.m. to 10:30 p.m. and then went to the hospital. Usually, only three or four pregnant women showed up and it did not take long for them to fill out the forms and go to their rooms, so I could doze on a couch in the waiting room and work on my Latin.

This around-the-clock routine helped distract me from agonizing over Jo's summary departure. I felt empty, as though I were wandering in a desert without food or drink. I just could not let her go. I had to see her. I had to find out why she had broken off so suddenly.

Mom was skeptical when I asked to borrow the Olds so I could go to Camp Marcella in northern New Jersey to see Jo. But she knew how unhappy I had been and didn't like the hectic schedule I had created. Maybe a trip down to New Jersey would resolve things so I could get back to a more normal life. I quit my hospital job and got a couple of night's sleep before heading south on Friday morning. At 6:15 p.m., I pulled up in front of a spacious dining room full of children and staff. I stood in the double-door entrance. Talk gradually died down as word went around about this immobile young stranger in a white T-shirt, tan slacks, and tattered sneakers. For a moment I felt like a western gunslinger busting into a saloon. Then Jo stood up from among the children, one hand over her mouth. She came toward me slowly, as beautiful as ever, in a flowered blouse, cut-offs, and sandals. She took my hand, led me outside, and let go. She did not speak as we went down a gravel path toward a swimming area, and neither did I.

She stopped abruptly and turned to face me head on. "What on earth are you doing here?"

I shrugged and looked down.

"I had to see you. I couldn't stay away any longer. I have to go back Sunday afternoon, so I won't be here long."

She took my hand and turned back up the path.

"Come and get some food. Then we can talk. I'm free this evening."

We walked back to her table in the dining room. I took a tray from the end of the serving line and filled a plate with meat loaf, boiled potatoes, green beans, a piece of apple pie, and a glass of milk. We went to a bench near the swimming area. I dug into my food. Neither of us spoke. The six or seven minutes it took for me to finish my plate seemed to go on forever.

She let me take her hand.

"Why did you just up and leave? I thought you really cared for me."

"I did. I loved you and said I would marry you. But when Shari told me you'd been making out with Lynn, one of my best friends and married no less, I was so hurt and mad I couldn't talk. I just had to get away."

"That's crazy! I never made out with Lynn. You know I went out to Sherborn a couple of times and helped her and Tommy put the roof on their house. In fact, after we had supper one night she drove me back to Cambridge, turned off the car in front of the apartment, grabbed my left thigh, and turned toward me. I thanked her for the ride and told her I had to go. I got out of the car and left. That was the last time I went to help them out. Where Shari got the idea that something more was going on is beyond me."

"Well, I don't know. I guess I'll have to take your word for it, for now at least."

"Where do we go from here?" I asked.

"There are a couple of cots in the infirmary here at the camp. You can sleep there. Tomorrow you can do stuff with the kids. We can have dinner tomorrow evening at the Hideaway Inn down the road."

By the end of that leisurely dinner, she had agreed that we could see each other again. The next day her boss offered me a job painting the camp buildings in September. I canceled my application for the University of Wisconsin and applied for the school psychology doctoral program at Columbia University Teachers College to pursue that new interest. I moved into Camp Marcella after Labor Day. Jo had begun work in Newark at the office of the New Jersey Commission for the Blind, and we saw each other on weekends. At the end of September, Jo agreed again to marry me. In October I went back to Cambridge and Jo started working in South Jersey, placing blind children in elementary schools—the first mainstreaming program in the country. We got married on November 22, 1951, Thanksgiving Day, in the Cambridge Memorial Church and honeymooned that weekend at Mom and George's house in Hancock, where we had first really connected. We drove down to South Jersey on Sunday and found living space in Mt. Laurel with a Quaker couple and their four children. They rented a large room to us, with a small kitchen and a bath. During December, I volunteered at a school just a few miles away, the Moorestown Friends School, suggested by our landlords, and sold *World Book Encyclopedias* during weekday evenings.

In January I began classes in the school psychology program at Columbia Teachers College. I took Mental Hygiene, and Individual Psychological Testing of Children. Jo enrolled in the University of Pennsylvania's master's degree program in special education and took two evening courses paid for by the Commission for the Blind. After a quick supper on Tuesdays and Thursdays, Jo went back and forth to Philadelphia, which was a half-hour drive each way. After lunch on Fridays, I raced up the New Jersey Turnpike to New York City for my Friday evening course at Columbia. When class finished at 9:00 p.m., I studied in the library until it closed at 11:00 p.m. My resting place was next to Grant's Tomb, where overnight parking was allowed. I tipped back the passenger seat on our little Morris Minor convertible as far as it would go, about 45 degrees, pulled my sleeping bag up around my ears, and slept fitfully to the traffic noise below me on Riverside Drive. Once in a while a police officer's flashlight would startle me awake. I rolled out creakily between 6:00 and 7:00 a.m., got a cheap breakfast in the Teachers College cafeteria, and read until my 9:00 a.m. class. I was off with the bell at noon and, depending on the traffic, hugging Jo by 3:00 p.m. We continued this commuting life for the rest of the semester. Despite how busy we were, we both enjoyed starting to create a new life together.

The following summer of 1952 we took a honeymoon camping trip through the Southwest and the West Coast of the United States, the Canadian Rockies, and Glacier and Yellowstone Parks. Jo's boss had thoughtfully transferred her to northern Jersey so we would be close to Columbia. I got a job at the Wardlaw School in Plainfield teaching English, Spanish, and French, coaching football and baseball, and driving the school bus.

The following year we moved to Rahway, New Jersey, where I taught a special class of seventh graders whose IQ scores ranged from 57 to 122, reading from 0 to tenth-grade level, and arithmetic from 0 to twelfth-grade level. I was responsible for all their learning except for music and art. (See Chapter 6, From Lecturing to Learning, for more details about this experience.) Those two years were a blur of work and graduate studies for Jo and me, with the Christmas holidays and summer in Hancock. There was some time for other activities, and our first child, Alan, was born on May 13, 1954. Multitasking was not part of our vocabulary then, but we certainly epitomized it.

In September, after a summer in Hancock, with infant Alan we moved into Teachers College graduate student housing on 122nd Street to fulfill my year-long residency requirement. I took five courses each semester, created my dissertation proposal, and failed my qualifying exam in the fall. Although I passed the retake for my qualifying exam, my dissertation proposal was turned down. Partly because of my own poor grades, deportment problems, and shaky self-esteem up into college, I wanted to look at the relationships between academic performance and the gap between a student's self-described ideal self and actual self. Although the committee agreed that my hypothesis was sound, they thought that using the difference between two measures as the key variable was unlikely to yield any convincing results. I was determined to go ahead anyway, but I put my proposal on ice until I found work and we got settled.

I started as a school psychologist in the Hewlett-Woodmere school system on Long Island, New York, the week before Labor Day. I was paid $6,000, with time off during the summers. In those days, most school psychologists did diagnostic testing and psychotherapy. The Teachers College doctoral program had a strong clinical orientation. But I was not really interested in being a psychotherapist. Verda

Wentling, my boss, had a preventive mental health orientation, and we spent most of our time working with the superintendent, principals, and teachers trying to improve the mental health climate in the schools. It was a wealthy upper-middle-class community, and getting into the best colleges was the mark of success for students. This competitive environment was tough on students. I worked in the junior and senior high schools, where the competition was severe, and spent most of my time dealing with teachers who were exacerbating that dynamic.

It was a perfect setting to pursue my dissertation topic, and during my first year I did a pilot project that showed a curvilinear relationship between academic achievement and the ideal–actual self relationship. Where the gap between ideal and actual self was large, achievement was poor because students felt doomed to failure; where the gap was small, achievement suffered because they already felt superior. But when it was moderate, achievement blossomed. This was the first time I recognized the importance of having an optimal distance between prior learning and the level of challenge for new work. I shared the results with my doctoral committee and they agreed to let me repeat the study for my dissertation. My PhD was awarded in 1958. That dissertation, and my 3 years as a school psychologist with a preventive mental health orientation, set cornerstones for my future career in higher education studying impacts of diverse college environments, teaching practices, and educational polices on undergraduates and adult learners.

PART TWO

Challenging Higher Education

In 1958, with my PhD and 3 years of experience as a school psychologist, I received a call from a former colleague asking if I would consider a position as director of teacher education at Monmouth College in Long Branch, New Jersey. This was a newly created position, and it started my career in higher education.

To get some perspective on the changes that have occurred during my 55-year career, I e-mailed 19 colleagues whom I have known and worked with in various capacities, asking them to jot down a few of the key changes that have occurred during their careers. Their responses were thoughtful and highly varied; and it was clear I needed to limit my focus to five areas to which I have contributed. Five of these colleagues generously agreed to add their wisdom to my personal experiences and perspectives. I asked them not to comment on the pluses and minuses of my particular work but simply to put it in the context of contributions they and others have made. Believing that we would all be enriched by their diverse approaches, I did not ask them to follow a general format. Thus, each of them responds in his or her own language and style. I end Part Two with some professional reflections.

CHAPTER 4

From Cultivating the Intellect to Civic Learning and Democratic Engagement

With John Saltmarsh

I n March 1958, Bob Allen, a former school psychologist colleague, called my office at the Hewlett-Woodmere High School. A year earlier he had left to become dean of instruction at Monmouth College in Long Branch, New Jersey. We had shared war stories about problematic teachers and administrators damaging students, while we tried to pick up the pieces. I shared my less-than-helpful experiences during my master's degree work at the Harvard Graduate School of Education, and we bemoaned the quality of teacher preparation in general. He asked if I would become director of teacher education at Monmouth, heading up a new department. The salary was $7,500 for a 9-month year and a promise that "the president wants to create the best teacher education program in New Jersey."

"But I've never worked in a college, and I don't know anything about teacher education," I said.

"I never had worked in a college before I took this dean position," he replied. "It's not that hard. You just listen carefully, nod, and keep your mouth shut when you don't know what's going on. Then you ask around, do a little research, and get up to speed. The place is wide open for new ideas. I know you have some and can handle it."

My interview with President Schaefer went well. He emphasized creating the best teacher preparation program in New Jersey. I signed a 1-year contract as director of teacher education, to end June 30, 1959. After a summer of gardening, hiking, swimming, and canoeing in New Hampshire with our three young children, Jo and I moved into our Long Branch house on Labor Day weekend. Thus began one of the most educational years of my young career. By the time Jo and I arrived, Bob had left for a professorial position at Rutgers, replaced by a conservative, traditional dean handpicked by the president. I established an advisory board of local educational leaders and made arrangements for students to be observers in the local public schools as part of each of their courses. Schaefer called me into his office. Red-faced, he said, "Rutgers built all its residence halls on the income from its teacher education program. How the hell am I going to do that with this approach you are taking?"

"You told me you wanted the best program in the state, not that you wanted it mainly to make money," I replied.

On February 2, 1959, I received a letter saying my contract would not be renewed the following July. Our contracts stipulated that faculty members had to be notified in writing by February 1 if they were not to be continued. Using the technicality of the late notification, with the

American Association of University Professors (AAUP) paying for a lawyer, I sued the president. I testified to the board about the apparent reasons for his action and about the ongoing conflicts with other department heads and faculty members. Schaefer offered me $2,000 to go away quietly, but I was too invested in the battle to take the money. That September, 12 department heads submitted their resignations. By October the board made Schaefer president emeritus and the department heads were all retained.

In April 1959, Ron Silva, chair of the Biology Department, told me, "I recently heard about this strange small college in Vermont. It's called Goddard, and the whole program operates based on John Dewey's and William Heard Kilpatrick's progressive education philosophies. You might want to check it out."

Three weeks later I had an interview with President Tim Pitkin at the New York apartment of Elliot Pratt, a major Goddard supporter. Goddard had just received a $450,000 Ford Foundation grant for An Experiment in College Curriculum Organization, a 6-year project to undertake major educational innovations. They were looking for a coordinator of evaluation. I would spend half my time on the evaluation work and the rest teaching a psychology course and meeting individually with 15 advisees each week. The salary was $7,500 for the academic year.

Pitkin described the college. About 120 students lived on campus. There were 32 faculty, staff members, and administrators. Every student worked 20 hours a week on campus, and that work was evaluated. If students completed their first 2 years satisfactorily, they graduated from the Junior Division and applied to the Senior Division by designing their own major, combining further course work and independent studies. Faculty members were expected to be on campus and available to students 5 days a week.

Every Wednesday evening, students and college employees

gathered for a community government meeting, chaired by an elected student. They discussed and acted on a wide range of issues (e.g., pets on campus, residence hall rules, safety and civility problems). The chair and an elected student council met with the president weekly. Every Friday afternoon, all the faculty members and administrators gathered in the Pitkins' living room. They started with sherry from 3:30 to 4:00 and discussed educational issues and other college business until 6:00. The Ford Foundation money would help them create a Learning-Aids Center as a resource for teachers and students, establish stronger relations with nearby schools and communities (so real-life experiences and volunteer work could be integrated with courses), and increase the number of minority and international students. They needed someone who would evaluate Goddard's impact on the students who were experiencing this kind of educational environment.

I was impressed by this small, innovative institution and by the forward-looking project they were undertaking. It seemed to be a tightly integrated application of progressive education principles. I was surprised and relieved that President Pitkin did not ask me about why I might leave Monmouth or about the kind of evaluation program I would design.

"How does this strike you?" he asked.

"It sounds great. I'm really interested."

Pitkin proceeded, "I've looked over your résumé. You sound like a fine person for the job. I have a contract here if you'd like to sign it."

Stunned, I looked down at my hands and rubbed my wet palms together. Pitkin's straightforward look pinned me to the back of my chair.

"I will. My wife and I are ready to move to Vermont and she likes this possibility," I said.

"We do not have tenure," Pitkin said. "Instead, we start with two

1-year appointments, then a 3-year, and, after that, 5-year intervals. You will be evaluated at the end of each time period. So this is a contract starting in September and ending June 30, 1960."

I signed the contract.

"I look forward to having you with us. We begin with dinner and faculty meetings the week after Labor Day," said Pitkin.

"I look forward to being there."

We shook hands and I backed out the door, ready to race back to Jo, share the news, and leave Monmouth. Pitkin's executive assistant, Evelyn Bates, sent me a copy of the Ford Foundation proposal. Here is some of the language that blew me away. (Remember, this was written in 1958, quite a while before we became concerned about sexist language.)

The Goddard philosophy starts with the individual. It holds that each person is truly unique, has his own needs, has to contend with a special set of problems, possesses talents peculiar to him, and is worthy of the respect and love of his fellow men. It assumes that learning is inherent, natural, individual, active, and the means to self-fulfillment. It says that education is the reconstruction of the experience of the individual by himself for himself, but that it is also a transactional process through which the learner is constantly taking something from his environment and giving something to it. It is a social as well as an individual process, and it involves all of the personality, that which we call intellectual, as well as the emotional and physical.

The aim of education is growth, growth as one develops his abilities toward their potential, growth as one seeks and tries to live a good life, growth as one builds his character, growth as one lives intelligently in a present that anticipates the future, growth as one solves the personal and the social problems that he encounters, and growth in self-understanding. To enable each student to achieve the aims of education, the function of the college is to create an environment that is most conducive to learning. This means providing for a variety of experiences, including association and communication with teachers, usually individuals older than the student, in the identification and consideration of community problems, academic problems, and personal problems. It includes working with others at tasks that are essential to the operation and maintenance of the college. It includes individual counseling, involvement, and commitment to group courses, the initiation and pursuit of independent studies, periodic off-campus work as in the nonresident work term, and off-campus experiences in one's study program during an academic semester.

For the student the Goddard philosophy requires a continuing search for and clarification of purposes, assuming responsibility for his own education, exercising freedom and self-control within the limits imposed by membership in the college community and finding world citizenship. It requires a continuing effort to identify, define, and solve problems on his own initiative, accepting responsibility for the welfare of the college community, and the desire to learn for the intrinsic value of the learning rather than for a mark or credit, and the willingness and capacity to make and meet commitments.

For the teacher—and this includes all of the college staff though most clearly those called faculty—the Goddard philosophy requires interest in and dedication to continuing study of the educational process; a desire and determination to engage whole-heartedly in advancing one's understanding of the nature of learning; an eagerness to engage in educational experimentation based on carefully formulated hypotheses regarding the conditions of learning; continuing effort to improve his teaching; interest in and readiness to engage in adult education; investment of a large amount of time and energy working with students on problems of the college community; counseling and study of individual students; imagination and ingenuity in helping students find opportunities for learning through off-campus experience: and recognition that mastery of subject matter is only a means, not the end of education. (Ford Foundation, personal communication, October 1966)

Never before had I read anything that so captured my own emerging sense of what education should be about. This philosophy and its associated values have been the foundation for my career and my life since that summer of 1959.

After conversations with Tim; George Beecher, director of educational experimentation; Forest Davis, academic dean; and Robert Mattuck, director of counseling, and after several drafts, we arrived at the following description of desired outcomes for students:

The Experiment in College Curriculum Organization aims to foster student development in five major areas. First, students are to increase in competence, to become more competent intellectually through increased ability to recognize problems, to think critically about them, to handle abstractions, and to apply knowledge to working situations. They are to develop interpersonal competence through experiences working with peers and adults outside the college on tasks of importance to themselves and others. And they are to become more confident of their own ability to initiate and carry out socially important tasks; they are to develop a stronger sense of their own competence.

Second, they are to become more independent and autonomous. They are to increase in emotional independence so that continued encouragement and support from teachers, peers, or other significant persons is less necessary. They are to develop increased instrumental independence so they can make decisions and cope with problems that arise without continued advice and direction. And most important perhaps, they are to become more cognizant of their interdependence with peers, teachers, the college community, and other cultures.

Third, through examining their own behavior, through studying various aspects of human living, and through continuous exchange with teachers and peers, they are to know themselves better. They are to face themselves and the realities of adult status and thus clarify questions of self and ideal self. In short, the development of identity has to be fostered.

Fourth, they are to become freer in interpersonal relationships. Communication with peers and teachers is to become more wide-ranging and intensive. Experiences with other cultures are to foster increasing ability to relate freely and effectively with persons of different backgrounds. Mutual respect and regard for both peers and adults is to increase.

And fifth, development of purpose is to be fostered. Students are to become more clear about their own motives as the basis for planning and pursuing their learning. Purposes are to be strengthened so effort will be sustained through intermediate steps toward an objective and will persist in the face of obstacles. (Ford Foundation, personal communication, October 1966)

As the experiment progressed, it became clear that two other vectors of change were important. One of these I termed "management of emotions"—developing increased awareness of feelings and impulses, and more effective and fruitful modes of expression and control—and the other, "development of integrity"—clarifying and internalizing a personal value system and increasing ability to behave in ways consistent with that system. Thus, the seven vectors of student development evaluated for the experiment were:

1. the development of competence,
2. the development of autonomy,
3. the development of identity,
4. the freeing of interpersonal relationships,
5. the development of purpose,
6. the management of emotions, and
7. the development of integrity.

Forest Davis suggested the word *vector* because it signifies direction and magnitude. Anyone who has read *Education and Identity* (Chickering, 1969; Chickering & Reisser, 1993) will recognize those vectors as its fundamental framework. I changed the sequence by the time I got around to writing that book 9 years later because it seemed more consistent with emerging student development research. Thus, Goddard's educational philosophy and that first formulation of desired outcomes became the bases for my lifelong career in higher education.

Chapter 5 describes the details of my evaluative research concerning these outcomes and their interactions, as well as how the results were shared and implications for practice discussed with administrators, faculty, staff, and students. This evaluative work at Goddard from 1959 to 1965 provided the basis for the Project on Student Development in Small Colleges from 1965 to 1970, funded by $450,000 from the National Institute of Mental Health (NIMH). Ten colleges, all with enrolments of 1,000 students or fewer, ranged from conservative, church-related institutions to liberal sectarian, with others in between. They each administered a battery of personality inventories, achievement tests, and surveys about the college environments, similar to those I had used at Goddard. I worked with two colleagues and an executive secretary. We received their data at our Plainfield offices, analyzed it, and returned written reports. These reports were followed by weekend workshops at each college discussing the implications for educational practices, student-faculty relationships, and institutional cultures.

I spent most of the time at those workshops dodging bullets and barbs when I argued for more intentional efforts to encourage one or more vectors of student development, even though outcomes like Goddard's were consistent with the glorious language in their bulletins and mission statements. I had the same experiences when I presented results at national and regional conferences. Higher education was about information transfer, dressed up as "cultivating the intellect," delivered by lectures and texts and evaluated by midterm and final exams. There was no language about critical thinking. There was no recognition of the basic elements of Bloom's (1956) *Taxonomy of Educational Objectives in the Cognitive Domain*, which put knowledge and comprehension at the simplest levels, below the higher levels of application, analysis, synthesis, and evaluation. The affective domain was not only terra incognita, it was territory to be ignored and actively avoided. Faculty members were not going to be psychotherapists, counselors, or babysitters. They were experts in their disciplines and these disciplines are what students should learn.

When the American Council on Education (ACE) gave *Education and Identity* the 1969 Eleanor Colford Morris book award "for its outstanding contribution to higher education," I was surprised, given the dominant culture I had been butting up against. That recognition took me out of the woods of Vermont and onto the national scene. Sandy Astin, ACE's director of research at the time, invited me to join ACE as a visiting scholar. Jo and I, with our four kids, enjoyed and learned from the significant cultural changes of living in Bannockburn, Maryland (just outside of Washington, D.C.), and we wallowed in the diverse museums and restaurants in the nation's capital. The ACE work provided me ample time for presentations at national conferences and institutional consultation, making the case for learner-centered education and explicit attention to student development.

During that year, Ernie Boyer, who had become chancellor of the State University of New York system, recruited me to become the founding academic vice president for Empire State College. The position was to serve the diverse educational needs of adult learners throughout the state. (See Chapter 8 for details about the program.) When I wrote the first Empire State College *Bulletin* in July 1971, I described a set of desired outcomes for students consistent with my concern for human development described in *Education and Identity*.

Despite wide differences in age, backgrounds, and special needs or interests, most students of Empire State College will share a number of basic goals: developing competence, increasing awareness, developing purposes, becoming autonomous, understanding oneself, understanding others, and developing integrity. Although at times one goal looms larger than another, they will remain the work of human development throughout life. Because these will be major objectives for many students—though perhaps only dimly perceived by some—they must be served by the policies, programs and practices of the College. (p. 18)

The *Bulletin* described how these developmental tasks were encouraged by our educational policies and practices, and used individual adult students to illustrate how it worked. Those policies and practices were firmly anchored in my Goddard experiences and research.

That evaluation research at Goddard and the subsequent Project on Student Development in Small Colleges provided fertile soil for Kohlberg's (1969) and Gilligan's (1982) stages of cognitive and moral development, Perry's (1968) scheme for ethical and intellectual development, and Loevenger's (1976) ego-development theory. All of these developmental-stage theories hit the streets during the late 1960s and early 1970s. They clearly applied to adult learners and provided the grounds for *A Conceptual Basis for Educational Alternatives at Empire State College* that I wrote and then published in 1976, after I moved from the position of academic vice president to vice president for policy analysis and evaluation, though the paper never drove Empire State's development after I left.

I took a sabbatical from Empire State College during 1966–1967, in part supported by a Danforth Foundation grant through the offices of former vice president Warren Bryan Martin. I had been approached by J. B. Lon Hefferlin to write another book for Jossey-Bass, and *A Conceptual Basis* became the foundation for *The Modern American College* (Chickering, 1981). It was envisioned as a follow-up to Nevitt Sanford's groundbreaking *The American College*, which I devoured when it came out in 1962. I used the opportunity to make the case for higher education and human development and spent much of that year fleshing out the content and recruiting authors. The major sections of the book include different perspectives on human development, authors from varied disciplines who describe how they might encourage one or another developmental dimension, and authors' opinions on the impact of educational policies and practices. When I left Empire State College in 1977 to become distinguished professor and director of the Center for the Study of Higher Education at then Memphis State University, most of the authors had begun writing their contributions to the book. This scholarship occupied much of my time until the book finally came out in 1981. With 42 chapters, Sanford's foreword, the introduction, conclusion, and indexes, this heavy tome was 828 pages of fine print. I suggested to J.B. that they include a dolly in the sale price. I doubt that anyone other than J.B. and I have read the whole thing, but selected chapters continue to be copied.

In early April 1977, a letter arrived from Jerry Boone, academic vice president of Memphis State. Tennessee Governor Lamar Alexander had supported a series of distinguished professor positions for the state universities. Memphis State had been given four, and it wanted to use one of them to expand a Center for the Study of Higher Education in their Graduate School of Education. The center, with a secretary and faculty members on half-time appointments—from the Departments of Curriculum and Teaching, Counseling, Philosophy, and Administration—offered master's degrees for administrators, student services professionals, and faculty members. They wanted to create a doctoral program, strengthen their regional leadership, and become nationally recognized. Would I be interested in a position, either in a professorial role or as center director as well?

Jo and I had spent the year looking for something new and different—different work, a different environment, a different culture. We had never been part of a large state university and my only exposure to a graduate school of education had been my rather unfortunate experience at Harvard University. And we had never lived in the South. There was enough discontinuity with our professional pasts and New England backgrounds for this to be appealing. We made it clear that Jo, with her PhD in counseling and higher education, would be looking for work as well. They agreed to arrange interviews for her at Rhodes and St. Joseph Colleges, as well as with Memphis State administrators.

We landed at the Memphis airport on a hot May day. After we left our suitcase in our room at the Alumni Center, a secretary ushered us into a spacious office where we were greeted by President Billy Mac Jones and Academic Vice President Jerry Boone. Billy Mac, a former University of Texas fullback with a booming voice, towered over us. After admiring Jo, he said they wanted a "stud bull" for this appointment and hoped I would attract strong faculty members and graduate students if I took the position. Tempting as it was, I let the metaphor slide and replied that I thought my national reputation, especially with student service administrators, could be helpful. Jerry was silent through this brief meeting, and then he took us to his office next door. In contrast to the president, he was low-key. He ran through the appointment details. As distinguished professor, I would be paid $45,000 and have a full-time secretary, whether or not I took on the director role. I would be tenured in the Philosophy of Education Department and teach one course each fall and spring semester. The center had its own budget and the director reported to Robert Saunders, dean of the School of Education, and attended weekly meetings with him and the other department heads. They hoped a doctoral program could get state approval so they could build relationships with other colleges and universities in the region and increase enrollments. They expected that the distinguished professor would play a key role in that development, whether or not he was center director. I found the agenda challenging and interesting.

Our other interviews and meetings went smoothly. We were welcomed with the warm Southern hospitality we later learned to enjoy, and there were few sharp challenges or hard-hitting questions. Jo and I were both attracted to this totally new environment. She liked the idea of being a personal counselor in the Student Development Center. The opportunity to expand the Center for the Study of Higher Education with a new doctoral program and learn about state-supported colleges and universities would certainly stretch my professional horizons, and we both looked forward to spending time exploring the region and the Deep South culture.

We drove down to Memphis in late August and moved into a university house we rented next to the campus. I settled into the center and got to work. I knew that a standard higher education doctoral program at Memphis State, still trying to overcome its image as "tiger high" because of its questionable admission standards, could not compete nationally with established programs at institutions such as the University of Michigan, Iowa State University, Bowling Green State University, Ohio University, and the University of California, Berkeley. We would have to create a distinct orientation. Given my background and professional relationships, it was natural to orient the center to prepare administrators, faculty members, and student services professionals to work with the exploding population of adult students. During that fall of 1977, I wrote a $369,000 Fund for the Improvement of Postsecondary Education (FIPSE) proposal called "Higher Learning for Diverse Adults," which would help 13 diverse colleges and universities improve their educational effectiveness with adult students. As soon as funding was approved, I hired Jack Lindquist and Tom Clark as codirectors to come down and run it. They had been close colleagues of mine at Empire State College. Our workshops and interactions with institutional teams built on conceptual materials from *The Modern*

American College (Chickering, 1981) and leaned heavily on Loevenger's (1976) stages of ego development, Perry's (1968) ethical and intellectual development, and Kolb's (1984) experiential learning theory and learning styles, which he was developing throughout the 1970s (see Chapter 6 for further discussion). We argued that institutional initiatives with adult students would be more educationally powerful if they recognized and responded to individual differences in developmental stages and learning styles. By doing so, they would also encourage developmental change along the continua posited by Loevenger and Perry.

Lindquist's (1978) *Strategies for Change*, based on the NIMH project, proposed an adaptive development FLOOR (force, linkage, openness, ownership, rewards) model that was effective with our participating institutions. Catherine Marienau joined us for a year on a Busch Foundation Fellowship to complete her dissertation, which investigated the change processes in our participating institutions (see Chapter 8). Her dissertation, *Bridging Theory and Practice in Adult Development and Planned Change: Case Studies in Higher Education* (1982), received the 1983 Dissertation of the Year Award from the Association for the Study of Higher Education. This scholarly tour de force powerfully amplified both our understanding of planned change in higher education and diverse ways colleges and universities could improve their capacity to encourage adult development. I won't detail all the initiatives attempted here, but I will mention University 101, created at the University of South Carolina, to help adults make the transition into that institution. Subsequently, under the able leadership of John Gardner, former executive director of the National Resource Center, that course became adapted for freshman year programs across the country. As the project wound down, Jack left to become the president of Goddard College, and Tom to be president of Rockland Community College.

During the project's final year, I submitted a $458,055 proposal to NIMH for a 3-year multi-institutional change project called High Education for Adult Mental Health. Ann Lynch came up from the counseling center at the University of Florida to direct it. This project enabled us to keep banging away at helping institutions become more effective with their increasing adult enrollments and deal with personal issues that hamper learning that lasts.

Both of these projects included budgets that supported annual conferences on Higher Education for Adult Development. We typically attracted 350–450 participants, who shared the experiences and learning not only from our project institutions but also from other institutions across the country. Each annual conference began and ended with presentations from myself and other educational leaders, but all day on Saturday and Sunday mornings we had a rich mix of 3-hour workshops. We prohibited talking heads and required that each workshop be designed to include all four elements of Kolb's (1984) experiential learning cycle: concrete experience, reflective observation, abstract conceptualization, and active experimentation. This requirement led to educationally powerful interactions among participants and resource persons and generated high ratings on our evaluations. I set up a foundation account within the center into which we put the registration fees. Inasmuch as project dollars supported most of our expenses, by the end of the Higher Learning for Diverse Adults and the NIMH projects, we had about $85,000 in that account—even after supporting whatever professional travel that center staff could reasonably justify—over and above the very limited university dollars available. We also treated ourselves to fall and spring parties for center faculty, staff, partners, and children.

Each semester during those years, I taught an "Ages, Stages, and Styles" course for doctoral candidates. We reviewed the burgeoning research on the adult lifespan and focused on the developmental tasks associated with various ages. We were enriched by the new developmental-stage literature, principally Kegan's (1982) *Evolving Self;* Gilligan's (1982) *In a Different Voice;* and Belenky, Clinchy, Goldberger, and Tarule's (1986) *Women's Ways of Knowing.* We looked not only at Kolb's (1984) learning style differences but also at other descriptors of individual differences: levelers and sharpeners, field dependence and field independence, and neurolinguistic programming. Together with the literature on developmental-stage differences, this smorgasbord gave us numerous lenses through which to better understand individual differences and respond to them (see Chapter 6 for more detail).

Starting with an exploratory conference at Educational Testing Service (ETS) in September 1973, which included representatives from 22 institutions, I became heavily involved with what became the Council for the Assessment of Experiential Learning (CAEL). Two months later, I represented Empire State at another ETS meeting that included New College at the University of Alabama, Antioch College, San Francisco State University, Thomas Edison State College, El Paso Community College, Florida International University, Framingham State University, and Minnesota Metropolitan State College. In December, ETS submitted a $2.3 million, 3-year proposal to the Carnegie Foundation for the Advancement of Teaching. In late February 1974, Carnegie came through with $821,000 for 16 months. We institutional representatives had our first meeting at ETS on March 7 and 8, where we wisely chose Morris Keeton, professor and former interim president at Antioch, as chair of a steering committee. As a member of the initial steering committee, I argued for assessing Empire State's developmentally oriented outcomes as part of the project. That got some traction with several papers that came out in 1975: "The Learning and Assessment of Interpersonal Skills: Guidelines for Administrators and Faculty" (Breen, Donlon, & Whitaker, 1975a); "The Learning and Assessment of Interpersonal Skills: Guidelines for Students" (Breen, Donlon, & Whitaker, 1975b); and "Interpersonal Skills: Their Identification, Classification, and Articulation in Student Goals" (Whitaker & Breen, 1975). In addition, Mirian Tatzel and Lois Lamdin (1975), two Empire State faculty members, wrote an institutional report titled *Interpersonal Learning in an Academic Setting: Theory and Practice.* These authors continued writing and speaking about interpersonal competence in 1976, 1977, and 1978. At twice-yearly CAEL assemblies, I was making the case for recognizing the implications of developmental-stage theories for teaching and for assessment. In 1976, when CAEL incorporated as the Council for Adult and Experiential Learning, I became a member of the board of trustees, which I chaired from 1980 to 1982.

CAEL's continued interest in developmental aspects of student learning was strengthened by the Student Potential Program, designed to identify students with the capacity for college work even though their grades and test scores indicated otherwise. The "behavioral event interview," developed by David McClelland (1998) at the McBer Consulting Company to select corporate managers, was adapted for use in colleges and universities. This hour-long structured interview asked high-risk applicants to tell detailed stories about things they had done in the last year that pleased them. When the interviews were coded, 10 capabilities emerged: initiative, persistence, creativity, planning skill, critical thinking, restraint, leadership, influence skill, interpersonal diagnosis, and responsiveness. The interview was administered to 600 prospective or enrolled students at a number of diverse colleges and universities between 1982 and 1986. Tapping talents not measured by traditional means, it became used to select students for programs and majors, for advising, and to measure the value added to students' learning and development. In a speech at Empire State in 1983, Keeton described CAEL's vision as including individualization and flexibility of programs, learner self-directedness, and an emphasis on both cognitive and noncognitive achievement.

My relationship with CAEL tapered off in 1987 when I took a half-time position at George Mason University and moved there full time in 1988 as a University Professor. In this position, I reported to President George Johnson half time as an internal resource person for varied institutionwide and more localized initiatives aimed to create a university for the 21st century. I also taught a course on educational leadership in the Graduate School of Education. For 18 months I served as interim dean of the Graduate School of Education while we recruited a replacement for Larry Bowen, who had become ill. These diverse responsibilities were challenging and energizing but provided little opportunity for me to create initiatives that focused directly on student development.

I was drawn back into that arena in 1997, the year after I "retired" from George Mason University and we moved back to Vermont. Tony Chambers, then a Fetzer Institute program officer, sponsored three weekend workshops that brought together diverse, experienced professionals to address issues of authenticity, wholeness, and integrity in higher education. As these workshops wound down, Tony and I, along with Sandy and Lena Astin, Paul Elsner, Cynthia Johnson, Jim and Cheryl Keen, Gene Rice, and Laura Rendon, created a steering committee for follow-up. We invited Jon Dalton, Stuart Hunter, John Gardner, Victor Kazanjian, Peter Laurence, Jenny Lee, and Joe Subiondo to join what we came to call the Collective for Spirituality in Higher Education. The Astins received a small research grant from Fetzer that lead to their book *Meaning and Spirituality in the Lives of College Faculty: A Study of Values, Authenticity and Stress,* which was published in 1999. They then received a major grant from the Templeton Foundation to undertake A National Study of College Students' Search for Meaning and Purpose; a report summarizing the findings of this project was published in 2005.

The collective met periodically during this 5-year project, and I served on the Technical Advisory Committee. With its significant findings and associated publications and workshops, this work put students' spiritual quests on the radar screen of higher education and encouraged institutional responses.

At Jon Dalton's 2002 Institute on College Student Values, he and Lisa Stamm, who had written a literature review on spirituality and higher education for the Templeton Foundation, agreed to join me in writing *Encouraging Authenticity and Spirituality in Higher Education* (2006). Jon and I did a series of regional workshops sponsored by the National Association of Student Personnel Administrators and responded to other requests. With my ongoing collaboration with the Astins, this challenging arena for change was my last crack at calling attention to the affective domain and trying to encourage higher education for human development. Fortunately, others were also working hard to help colleges and universities move beyond simple information transfer and cultivating the intellect.

I became acquainted with John Saltmarsh after he took over as codirector of the New England Resource Center for Higher Education. A student of higher education's recent history, he knows well the kinds of changes in purposes and desired outcomes that occurred during the years of my career and can put my particular contributions in that larger context.

John

There is an important history of American higher education told here, spanning the last half of the 20th century, a history that offers insights for the current civic engagement movement on campuses in the United States and globally. As a younger generation of academic professionals and leaders picks up the mantel of education reform, pedagogical innovation, and the democratic purposes of higher education, this history becomes increasingly important as a guide. Arthur Chickering is part of a community of scholars whose work is grounded in the core democratic purposes of education, aimed at developing holistically educated students who can apply knowledge to solve public problems and demonstrate civic agency through socially responsible action. The kind of education that can achieve these goals is experiential, integrated into communities, and accounts for the psychosocial development of students.

What is particularly interesting about this chapter is that, other than in the title, explicit reference to the language of "civic" is absent. It is not that the civic is absent, but that explicit civic discourse is not used, perhaps because it is not needed. Art's career spanned exactly the period in which the tectonic shift occurred in American culture from the self-evident truth that higher education is a public good to the widespread assumption that higher education is a private benefit. When the civic is self-evident, there is not the compulsion to make it explicit. When the civic is under siege and in crisis, there is the need to raise awareness, to sound the alarm, to issue desperate calls for vigilance. So while the civic is embedded in this chapter, it has yet to be smashed by the wave of privatization and market-driven strategies of neoliberalism crashing down on the academy.

This chapter spans the revival of Dewey through Kolb in the 1980s, and includes the period of the growth of developmental psychology with Perry (1968), Kohlberg (1969), and Gilligan (1982). It covers the flowering of experiential education and the emerging understanding of how students learn—from the growth in the cognitive sciences and the blossoming of service-learning, right up to the present, prefiguring much of *A Crucible Moment: College Learning and Democracy's Future,* a 2012 report by the Association of American Colleges and Universities (AAC&U). As illustrated in this chapter, at the beginning of Art's career, cultivating the intellect through higher education originally meant preparing citizens as actors and agents of democracy; Art's book *The Modern American College* (Chickering, 1981) addressed all the building blocks of the civic engagement movement—moral development, learning styles, the acquisition of purpose through service, field experience, out-of-class activities, and the development of humanitarian concern. Today, for the American scholar, liberal education has become separated from civic purpose; and civic engagement has become a way to reclaim higher education's role in building a wider public culture of democracy.

The opening story of this chapter is particularly telling. It combines Art's attempt to create an innovative teacher-education program at Monmouth College with his retaining the AAUP to defend his faculty rights. The teacher-education program he designed was community based and experiential. He created an advisory board of local education leaders because they had the practical knowledge and experience needed to shape the curriculum, and he had students go into the schools as part of their education. This was good pedagogical practice, drew on the expertise of those other than credentialed academics, met a social need, and served a wider public purpose. When Art needed to defend his position, he turned to the AAUP. Here its founding statement resonates in the background, off-stage. It is the 1915 AAUP statement on academic freedom and tenure that makes the claim for "the social function discharged by the professional scholar" and that boldly and clearly states that "the responsibility of the university teacher is primarily to the public itself" (paras. 18–21). This is at the core of "the nature of the academic calling" (para. 10).

It is certainly at the core of Art's academic calling. Thus, his experience at Goddard as the 1960s opened was powerful. Decades before Barr and Tagg (1995) wrote of a paradigm shift to learning-centered education; well before there was the meta-analysis of educational research by Pascarella and Terenzini (1991) showing the interconnectedness of academic and cognitive outcomes and psychosocial growth, attitude and value change, and moral reasoning; well before there was a literature on asset-based education that values the knowledge and experience every student brings to the education environment, there was the Goddard philosophy. It is a remarkable statement. Art's task was to craft the learning outcomes that would emanate from the philosophy. His focus on competencies resonates strongly with the recent work on assessment and on civic learning outcomes stressing knowledge, skills, values, and actions (see Chapter 5). As he describes in this chapter, students would "become more competent intellectually through increased ability to recognize problems, to think critically about them, to handle abstractions, to apply knowledge to working situations . . . through experiences working with peers and adults outside the college on tasks of importance to themselves and others."

Art's focus on "learning through off-campus experience" and "recognition that mastery of subject matter is only a means, not the end of education," as noted in this chapter, all fed into expanding experiments in both pedagogy and a wave of experimental colleges in the 1960s and 1970s. Focusing on experiential education allowed for attention to process as well as content. For Art, it was the foundation for greater attention to student development; in particular, the linking of affective development to cognitive development. Kolb's (1984) theory of experiential education (grounded in Dewey's [1916/1964, 1933, 1938] philosophy) brought together feeling and thinking, active experience with abstract reasoning, and elevated reflection as a mechanism for creating meaning and understanding. At the same time, pedagogical practice could not be divorced from the institutional environment within which it was practiced. Thus, Art's work always focused on both practice and the kind of institutional change that would allow the practice to thrive. The development of competencies, learner-centered education, experiential learning, reflective practice, and socially responsive knowledge all meant different institutional structures and cultures from what defined traditional academic organizations.

The Modern American College was published at the same time that the civic engagement movement was stirring. College students reacted to the caricature of the "me generation" captured in Christopher Lash's 1979 classic, *The Culture of Narcissism*. In 1984, college students started the Campus Outreach Opportunity League (COOL), a national organization that provided support for student involvement in service and social action. COOL created opportunities for students to engage in public problem solving and to develop as socially responsible citizens. College presidents followed suit in 1985 and formed Campus Compact, led by Frank Newman, whose book that same year, *Higher Education and the American Resurgence*, asserted that "the most critical demand is to restore to higher education its original purpose of preparing graduates for a life of involved and committed citizenship. . . . The advancement of civic learning, therefore, must become higher education's most central goal" (p. xiv). During the 1980s, civic engagement was expressed predominantly though community service outside of curricular connections. By the end of the decade, the institutional change imperative kicked in; if the civic purpose of higher education was going to be central to the undergraduate experience, it would have to be part of the core of the enterprise—the curriculum—and the curriculum would need to be delivered differently. This required a change in practice, as well as institutional change. This was transformative work.

By 1989, Campus Compact had established the national project Integrating Service with Academic Study. In 1990, the National Society for Experiential Education issued its multivolume tome, *Combining*

Service and Learning, edited by Jane Kendall. It was here that Art's influence was especially present. Much of the foundation of the pedagogical practice of service-learning drew directly on the highly influential publication Art wrote with Zelda Gamson in 1987, "Seven Principles for Good Practice in Undergraduate Education." This work reverberated throughout *Combining Service and Learning* and throughout the work on campuses as service-learning took hold across the country in the early 1990s. Throughout the three volumes of *Combining Service and Learning*, Art's scholarship is cited—most notably, "Seven Principles."

The Seven Principles were distilled from a review of the research on education. But they were also based on the practice knowledge of two seasoned practitioners. They were as much drawn from evidence-based practice as from practice-based evidence, which is why they resonated so strongly. The Seven Principles state that good practice in undergraduate education:

1. encourages contact between students and faculty,
2. develops reciprocity and cooperation among students,
3. encourages active learning,
4. gives prompt feedback,
5. emphasizes time on task,
6. communicates high expectations, and
7. respects diverse talents and ways of learning. (Chickering & Gamson, 1987)

The focus on active learning was the opening for the service-learning field, but the other principles also reinforced the collaborative, asset-based, learner-centered, reflective dimensions of community-based experiential education. What was abundantly clear was that education for civic purposes was just good education. It was education that implemented the Seven Principles.

It would be more than a decade before the development of the National Survey of Student Engagement (NSSE) as an instrument to measure students' engagement with learning. NSSE drew on the Seven Principles as well as on more recent research in the cognitive sciences, and found that student engagement with learning was indicated by active and collaborative learning, by contact with faculty outside the classroom, and by educational experiences that provided for interaction with others from different cultures bringing diverse perspectives. The Seven Principles had all these dimensions. By 2002, the annual NSSE report captured precisely the way the Seven Principles spoke to practitioners of service-learning:

> Complementary learning opportunities inside and outside the classroom augment the academic program . . . [and] provide students with opportunities to synthesize, integrate, and apply their knowledge. Such experiences make learning more meaningful and, ultimately, more useful because what students know becomes a part of who they are. (NSSE, 2002, p. 11)

This last finding has a remarkably Deweyian ring to it: Dewey (1927) described what he called "embodied intelligence" (p. 210)—or what he referred to in other writings as "embodied knowledge" (1949/1989, p. 375)—as knowledge that students acquire in such a way that it becomes not only what they know but shapes who they are as individuals. Students are transformed through their education.

The cornerstone of *Combining Service and Learning* (1990) was *Principles of Good Practice for Combining Service and Learning* (Honnet & Poulsen, 1989), which echoed Chickering and Gamson's (1987) "Seven Principles for Good Practice in Undergraduate Education." When I was a young faculty member experimenting with service-learning in the early 1990s, "Seven Principles" and *Principles of Good*

Practice for Combining Service and Learning were tacked to my office bulletin board and to the bulletin boards of hundreds of faculty across the country. Our pathway into civic engagement was through teaching and learning; and in service-learning, done well, we discovered a pedagogy that transformed our teaching practices and how and what our students learned.

"Seven Principles," as a historical artifact, opens at least two related lines of interpretation. The first is that they are principles of good practice in undergraduate education. The focus is on the teaching and learning function of higher education, the pedagogical practice of faculty, and the importance of an education that would actually be effective in cultivating the intellect. "Seven Principles" is part of a wave of critiques, commissioned reports, and studies of the problems with undergraduate education issued from the early 1980s through the mid-1990s, the likes of which is perhaps unmatched in the history of higher education. While "Seven Principles" addressed the problem of undergraduate education, Art's story suggests that there was something else going on that was contributing to the problem. This was also the era of the rise of the high-prestige—always striving for higher prestige—research university. The research university, public or private, gained higher prestige, selectivity, and ranking by amassing research funding, which brought greater capacity to attract more research dollars. The model of excellence across higher education narrowed in this period to a singular aspirational goal of becoming a research university. As Donald Schön (1995) wrote, the detachment of academic expertise in the research university—which separated research from practice—spread across the institutional structures of all of higher education, so that even liberal arts colleges and community colleges became subject to this influence "by a kind of echo effect or by imitation" (p. 32). And when research was prioritized in the reward structure of the faculty culture, then teaching was less valued and undergraduate education suffered. Thus, there emerged a need for principles to ground effective educational practice.

The research university was not Art's world. Look back at his institutional autobiography: Monmouth College, Goddard College, Empire State College, Memphis State University, George Mason University. Art's work is in the teaching and learning function of the college, in improving undergraduate education, and in cultivating the intellect and developing personally and socially responsible individuals.

Funding sources make up the landscape of this chapter. The organizations that funded Art's work include Ford, Carnegie, Templeton, and FIPSE. The organizations that didn't fund him at the time—Pew, Kellogg, Atlantic Philanthropies—collectively poured tens of millions of dollars into improving undergraduate education and building capacity for civic engagement in the 1980s and 1990s. They were committed to higher education as a public good and invested their resources accordingly. By the early 2000s, each and every one of them had shifted their funding priorities away from higher education as a place that educates citizens for a healthy democracy because that self-evident truth had been surpassed by issues of access, affordability, and workforce preparation—predominantly framed as access to the private benefit of higher education. The world of higher education as a place of teaching and learning to cultivate the intellect and develop ethical growth, interpersonal competence, and professional preparation of students as citizens in a democracy was, and is, under siege and highly contested. Civic engagement in higher education is emphasized because it is needed to counter the reductionist trends sweeping across the landscape of high education.

Through to the last project that Art describes in this chapter, in the early 2000s, he pursued a larger purpose for higher education and resisted narrow instrumentalism. His work on spirituality in higher education is representative of his wider efforts to create educational environments where students can find meaning and purpose in life and develop as human beings. Art's work continues in projects like the Bringing Theory to Practice project (BTtoP) as part of AAC&U. BToP combines, in unique ways, the affective and civic domains. The project "encourages colleges and universities to reassert their core purposes as educational institutions, not only to advance learning and discovery, but to advance the potential and well-being of each individual student, and to advance education as a public good that sustains a civic society [by implementing best practices in engaged teaching and learning to support students'] cognitive, emotional, and civic development" (AAC&U, n.d., para. 1). Art couldn't have framed it any better. Projects like BTtoP are emblematic of the legacy of Art's contributions to the civic engagement movement in American higher education.

REFERENCES

American Association of University Professors. (1915). Declaration of principles on academic freedom and academic tenure. Retrieved from http://www.aaup.org/report/1915-declaration-principles-academic-freedom-and-academic-tenure

Association of American Colleges and Universities. (n.d.). Bringing theory to practice. Retrieved from http://www.aacu.org/bringing_theory

Association of American Colleges and Universities. (2012). *A crucible moment: College learning and democracy's future.* Washington, DC: Author.

Astin, A. W., & Astin, H. S. (1999). *Meaning and spirituality in the lives of college faculty: A study of values, authenticity, and stress.* Los Angeles, CA: University of California, Los Angeles, Higher Education Research Institute.

Astin, A. W., & Astin, H. S. (2005). *The spirituality of college students: A national study of college students' search for meaning and purpose.* Los Angeles, CA: University of California, Los Angeles, Higher Education Research Institute.

Barr, R. B., & Tagg, J. (1995). From teaching to learning: A new paradigm for undergraduate education. *Change, 27*(6), 13–25.

Belenky, M. F., Clinchy, B. M., Goldberger, N. R., & Tarule, J. M. (1986). *Women's ways of knowing.* New York, NY: Basic Books.

Bloom, B. S. (1956). *Taxonomy of educational objectives, handbook I: The cognitive domain.* New York, NY: David McKay.

Breen, P., Donlon, T. F., & Whitaker, U. G. (1975a). *The learning and assessment of interpersonal skills: Guidelines for administrators and faculty* (CAEL Working Paper No. 5). Princeton, NJ: Cooperative Assessment of Experiential Learning.

Breen, P., Donlon, T. F., & Whitaker, U. G. (1975b). *The learning and assessment of interpersonal skills: Guidelines for students* (CAEL Working Paper No. 4). Princeton, NJ: Cooperative Assessment of Experiential Learning.

Chickering, A. W. (1969). *Education and identity.* San Francisco, CA: Jossey-Bass.

Chickering, A. W. (1971). *Bulletin.* Saratoga Springs, NY: Empire State College.

Chickering, A. W. (1976). *A conceptual basis for educational alternatives at Empire State College.* Saratoga Springs, NY: Empire State College.

Chickering, A. W. (Ed.). (1981). *The modern American college: Responding to the new realities of diverse students and a changing society.* San Francisco, CA: Jossey-Bass.

Chickering, A. W., Dalton, J. C., & Stamm, L. (2006). *Encouraging authenticity and spirituality in higher education.* San Francisco, CA: Jossey-Bass.

Chickering, A. W., & Gamson, Z. F. (1987). Seven principles for good practice in undergraduate education. *American Association for Higher Education Bulletin, 39*(7), 3–7.

Chickering, A. W., & Reisser, L. (1993). *Education and Identity* (2nd ed.). San Francisco, CA: Jossey-Bass.

Dewey, J. (1927). *The public and its problems.* Chicago, IL: Gateway.

Dewey, J. (1933). *How we think: A restatement of the relation of reflective thinking to the education process.* New York, NY: D.C. Heath.

Dewey, J. (1938). *Experience and education.* New York, NY: Macmillan.

Dewey, J. (1964). *Democracy and education: An introduction to the philosophy of education.* New York, NY: Macmillan. (Original work published 1916.)

Dewey, J. (1989). Philosophy's future in our scientific age: Never was its role more crucial. In J. A. Boydston (Ed.), *The later works of John Dewey* (Vol. 16, pp. 369–382). Carbondale, IL: Southern Illinois University. (Original work published 1949.)

Gilligan, C. (1982). *In a different voice.* Cambridge, MA: Harvard University Press.

Honnet, E. P., & Poulsen, S. J. (1989). *Principles of good practice for combining service and learning.* Retrieved from http://www.nationalserviceresources.org/files/Principles-of-Good-Practice-for-Combining-Service-and-Learning.pdf

Kegan, R. (1982). *The evolving self: Problem and process in human development.* Cambridge, MA: Harvard University Press.

Kendall, J. C. (Ed.). (1990). *Combining service and learning: A resource book for community and public service* (Vols. 1–3). Raleigh, NC: National Society for Experiential Education.

Kohlberg, L. (1969). Stage and sequence: The cognitive-developmental approach to socialization. In D. Goslin (Ed.), *Handbook of socialization theory and research* (pp. 347–480). Chicago, IL: Rand McNally.

Kolb D. (1984). *Experiential learning: Experience as the source of learning and development.* Englewood Cliffs, NJ: Prentice Hall.

Lash, C. (1979). *The culture of narcissism: American life in an age of diminishing expectations.* New York, NY: W. W. Norton.

Lindquist, J. (1978). *Strategies for change.* Berkeley, CA: Pacific Soundings Press.

Loevinger, J. (1976). *Ego development.* San Francisco, CA: Jossey-Bass.

Marienau, C. A. (1982). *Bridging theory and practice in adult development and planned change: Case studies in higher education.* (Doctoral dissertation). Retrieved from ProQuest Dissertations and Theses. (Accession Order No. AAT 8221310)

McClelland, D. (1998). Identifying competencies with behavioral-event interviews. *Psychological Science, 9*(5), 331–339.

National Survey of Student Engagement. (2002). From promise to progress: How colleges and universities are using student engagement results to improve college quality. Retrieved from http://nsse.iub.edu/2002_annual_report

Newman, F. (1985). *Higher education and the American resurgence.* Princeton, NJ: Carnegie Foundation for the Advancement of Teaching.

Pascarella, E. T., & Terenzini, P. (1991). *How college affects students.* San Francisco, CA: Jossey-Bass.

Perry, W. G., Jr. (1968). *Forms of intellectual and ethical development in the college years: A scheme.* New York, NY: Holt, Rinehart & Winston.

Sanford, N. (Ed.). (1962). *The American college: A psychological and social interpretation of higher learning.* New York, NY: Wiley.

Schön, D. A. (1995). Knowing-in-action: The new scholarship requires a new epistemology. *Change, 27*(2), 27–34.

Tatzel, M., & Lamdin, L. (1975). *Interpersonal learning in an academic setting: Theory and practice.* Princeton, NJ: Educational Testing Service.

Whitaker, U. G., & Breen, P. (1975). *Interpersonal skills: Their identification, classification, and articulation in student goals.* Princeton, NJ: Cooperative Assessment of Experiential Learning.

CHAPTER 5

From Myth and Tradition to Evidence-Based Decisions

With George Kuh

The great enemy of truth is very often not the lie—deliberate, contrived and dishonest—but the myth, persistent, pervasive and unrealistic. Too often we hold fast to the clichés of our forebears. We subject all facts to a prefabricated set of interpretations. We enjoy the comfort of opinion without the discomfort of thought.

— President John F. Kennedy, quoted in Schlesinger (1965)

In 1959, when I went to Goddard College as coordinator of evaluation, higher education's policies and practices were largely anchored in myth and tradition. The problem was that we had little evidence about which myths and traditions were consistent with fundamental truths about teaching, learning, human interactions, and educational environments, and which were not.

In *The American College: A Psychological and Social Interpretation of Higher Learning*, Nevitt Sanford (1962) wrote:

99

The explosion in knowledge that is radically reshaping our intellectual, political, industrial, cultural, and military environments has been stimulated largely by research initiated in the universities and colleges. Paradoxically, the colleges and universities have been relative laggards in applying scientific method to the understanding and evaluation of their own functioning. (p. v)

That 1,084-page landmark organized 29 chapters in 9 sections: Introduction, The Entering Student, Academic Procedures, Student Society and Student Culture, Student Performance in Relation to Educational Objectives, Interactions of Students and Educators, The Effects of College Education, Higher Education and the Social Context, and Epilogue. The first paragraph of the Introduction starts:

Practice in Higher Education, as in politics, remains largely untouched by the facts and principles of science. What our colleges do tends either to be governed by tradition or to be improvised in the face of diverse—usually unanticipated—pressures. In the literature of the field there is much partisan argument, and little evidence on the basis of which conflicting claims might be evaluated. Very little is known of what effects, if any, the experience of going to college has on students and less of what particular features of the college environment determine such effects as have been observed. (p.1)

This was the state of affairs in higher education when I tackled the challenge of evaluating Goddard's 6-year Experiment in College Curriculum Organization, supported by the Ford Foundation (and described in the preceding chapter). In 1959 Sanford's comprehensive volume had not yet been published. With my undergraduate degree in comparative literature, a master of arts degree in teaching, and doctoral work in school psychology, I'd never seen any relevant research and theory. And the teacher-education initiatives and political battles that got me fired from Monmouth College took me nowhere near it.

Coordinating the evaluation of this 6-year experiment was a daunting prospect. Fortunately, Ralph Tyler, then an educational evaluation guru at Stanford's Center for Advanced Study in the Behavioral Sciences, was on the Goddard board and a friend of Tim Pitkin. Ralph recommended some good readings and with extended telephone conversations helped me think through how to proceed. First, be clear about the desired educational outcomes for students. Then assess where they are on those outcomes at entrance. Collect rich data about their educational experiences. Retest the students after 2 and 4 years and examine other relevant data to see if any gains have been made. Ascertain which experiences contributed to, or hampered, the desired gains. He also emphasized including faculty members from the outset, not only by sharing reports for discussion but also by involving them in research. It was all pretty simple and straightforward, but easier said than done. At least I had the fundamentals.

As stated in the previous chapter, five key desired outcomes had been specified in the proposal: (a) developing intellectual and interpersonal competence, and an increased sense of competence, (b) increasing emotional and instrumental independence, with more recognition of interdependence, (c) developing identity, (d) freeing interpersonal relationships, and (e) developing integrity. Managing emotions and developing purpose soon became two more desired outcomes. So, that critical first step was well formulated.

The next challenge was generating pertinent data from entering students that would provide benchmarks for assessing gains. There were three critical ingredients that made data gathering and analyses possible. First, *The Goddard Bulletin* in 1958 stated:

> Because Goddard carries on constant research aimed at the improvement of teaching, students are asked to take part in various research studies. A student's participation may involve the filling out of questionnaires or taking of various experimental measures of attitudes, interest or achievement. (p. 7)

Without that stipulation we would not have been able to administer 16 hours of tests and inventories to freshmen during the initial orientation week, and subsequently in 2-year and 4-year follow-ups. Nor would we have been able to get (mostly) wholehearted contributions to other surveys. Second, the work program called for 20 hours a week from each student. I had 5 work-program students helping me week in and week out, year in and year out. They not only provided much-needed assistance in data collection and analysis, they were often useful sources of insight about the data and its implications. Third, I was dealing with small numbers. Goddard's total enrollment in fall 1959 was 121 students; in 1960 it had grown to 157. I had very manageable "universes." Without that institutional policy and without student assistance, that work could never have been done. The small numbers made the whole undertaking quite manageable.

The research had three major elements: (a) a battery of tests, questionnaires, and inventories administered at entrance and at the end of the second and fourth years, (b) questionnaires about their experiences administered each semester to samples of students who entered in 1959 and 1960, and (c) a series of faculty studies.

The following instruments comprised the test-retest battery: Graduate Record Examination Area Tests; Test of Critical Thinking; Test of Critical Thinking in Social Science; Test of Science Reasoning and Understanding; American Council Psychological Examination for College Freshmen; Sequential Tests of Educational Progress–Essay; Sequential Tests of Educational Progress–Reading; Sequential Tests of Educational Progress–Writing; Omnibus Personality Inventory; Stern Activities Index; College Characteristics Index; Survey of Study Habits and Attitudes; and Adjective Checklist for Self- and Ideal-Self Concepts. A Questionnaire for Entering Students was also devised, and administered at entrance. A Career Plans and Aspirations Questionnaire and the Graduate Record Examination Advanced Tests were administered to graduating students.

The Omnibus Personality Inventory, which had just been created by Paul Heist and George Yonge at the Center for Research and Development in Higher Education at the University of California, Berkeley, was the critical instrument for assessing outcomes in the affective domain. It had 14 scales: thinking introversion, theoretical orientation, estheticism, masculinity-femininity, autonomy, practical outlook, impulse expression, complexity, altruism, religious orientation, personal integration, anxiety level, social extroversion, bias. Several of these scales were directly pertinent to Goddard's developmental outcomes. Without this survey instrument I would have been hard put to generate powerful data. The only other possibility was the Minnesota Multiphasic Personality Inventory, but it was unsuitable because of its strong clinical orientation.

In addition to the test-retest program, a sample of students randomly selected from the freshman classes of 1959 and 1960 completed additional questionnaires two or three times each semester. These questionnaires sought four kinds of information: (a) participation in college activities and use of time, (b) relationships with peers, (c) orientations toward various elements of the college philosophy, and (d) general information concerning educational purposes, significant experiences, work program performance, and what they were reading.

During the first 5 years of the Experiment, a series of three inter-related studies was undertaken by the faculty. The first two studies defined in more concrete terms what the faculty meant by "development of independence" and "development of purpose." These studies also made it possible to identify measures from the testing program that differentiated from their peers the students who ranked high on independence or high on purpose, thus providing criterion measures for change in these areas. These two studies were reported in detail in "Dimensions of Independence" (Chickering, 1964) in the *Journal of Higher Education*, and "Does Our Performance Match Our Claims?" (Chickering, 1965a) in *Improving College and University Teaching*. Following these two studies, the entire faculty undertook an intensive study of the 4-year records—narrative evaluations—of the 1964 graduates. This research was based on student self-evaluations plus comments from instructors, work program supervisors, and others. It aimed to assess whether change had occurred on six variables that were identified as part of the development of independence and development of purpose. The variables were: (a) venturing, (b) interdependence, (c) resourcefulness and organization, (d) full involvement, motivation, and persistence, (e) goal directedness, and (f) personal stability and integration. In addition, research was carried out to assess in more detail the 4-year experiences of these students with regard to independent study, use of off-campus resources, experiences with other cultures, participation in the college community, relationships with the faculty, and the kinds of teaching they had experienced.

These three general sources—the test-retest program, the questionnaire study of random samples, and the series of faculty studies—provided the data relevant to the seven major vectors of student development that the Experiment aimed to foster, as listed above: (a) developing intellectual and interpersonal competence, and an increased sense of competence; (b) increasing emotional and instrumental independence, with more recognition of interdependence; (c) developing identity; (d) freeing interpersonal relationships; (e) developing integrity; (f) managing emotions; and (g) developing purpose. For each vector, hypotheses were posited for one or more variables from these three sources. These hypotheses indicated the changes in response that would be taken to represent development in that area. They provided the basis for the hypothetical relationships later proposed in *Education and Identity* (Chickering, 1969).

The findings from these diverse studies were shared in the weekly Friday afternoon faculty meetings and contributed to our ongoing discussions about the elements of Goddard's educational program as spelled out in the Experiment proposal. These conversations led to continuous fine-tuning of existing programs and to further initiatives, some of which became grant funded.

I gave several presentations and authored articles that shared some of the key results of general interest. These included "Faculty Perceptions and Changing Institutional Press" (Chickering, 1965b), published in the *Proceedings of the 1965 Meeting of the Association for Institutional Research*; "How Big Should a College Be?" (Chickering, 1966b), published in *Liberal Education*; and "Talking with College Students" (Chickering, 1967b), published in *Improving College and University Teaching*. I presented a brief paper, "The Development of Autonomy" (Chickering, 1966a), at the 1966 meeting of the Association for Higher Education. I presented a more detailed version at the 1967 meeting of the American Orthopsychiatric Association, and then published the article "Development of Autonomy" in the *American Journal of Orthopsychiatry* (Chickering, 1967a).

Obviously, this research also laid the foundation for *Education and Identity* in 1969. But two of the most important things about this comprehensive 6-year institutional research program were the widespread collaboration with faculty and students and our continuous use of the emerging findings to improve our educational policies and practices. It was that focus on using research to improve education that was the basis for the Project on Student Development in Small Colleges.

On a showery April morning in 1965, Tim walked into my office and asked if I could meet with him at 1:30 p.m. When I showed up, another man about my age was there—Ernest Boyer, a member of the Committee on Innovation of the Council for the Advancement of Small Colleges, which Tim chaired. The National Institute on Mental Health (NIMH) had come through with $450,000 for a 4-year project to start in September. It would use research—similar to that which I was completing at Goddard—to improve the educational effectiveness of participating institutions. Ernie was scheduled to run it, but Sam Gould, chancellor of the State University of New York system, had offered him a vice chancellor position. That offer was too good to turn down. Would I be interested in taking on the project? Participating colleges (in addition to Goddard) were scattered across the country: Earlham in Richmond, Indiana; Malone in Dayton, Ohio; Messiah in Grantham, Pennsylvania; Nasson in Springvale, Maine; New England College in Springfield, Massachusetts; Shimer in Mount Carroll, Illinois; Westmont in Santa Barbara, California; and William Jennings Bryan in Dayton, Tennessee.

There would be a lot of travel. I would do workshops at each institution once a year, have annual meetings with the presidents, and make presentations at professional meetings, including the annual meeting of the Council for the Advancement of Small Colleges, the sponsoring organization. I would have the use of four offices at the Plainfield Inn, an executive secretary, a research assistant, and an experienced college faculty member or administrator still to be selected. The salary was $25,000. I could resume my position at Goddard after the grant ran out. They realized that with my four small children, with moving into a new place out in the country, and with all the travel, it might be more than I wanted to tackle. I could certainly stay in my position at Goddard if I wished.

Seldom speechless, I sat there making unintelligible noises, oohing, aahing, umming.

"We can't wait too long for a decision if we are going to get this up and running in September, as the grant stipulates," Tim said. "You'll need to start recruiting the staff right away and getting in touch with the institutions."

I finally found my voice. "This sounds like a fantastic opportunity. I really appreciate your thinking I can do it. I want to, but I have to talk with Jo before I make a final decision. It sounds like a challenging commitment. I do know about the whole data collection and research part of it, but working with the colleges to use all that is something else again."

Tim replied, "For the last 5 years you've been doing a good job working with us. These are all small colleges, with one thousand or fewer students. Even though they have very different educational philosophies and practices, and range from very conservative to liberal, I think you can handle it."

"Thanks for your confidence. Can I get together with you folks tomorrow?"

"Sure. We can meet again, right here, same time," Tim said.

"Can you give me a copy of the proposal?"

Tim picked up a manila folder from the top of his desk. "Here it is. See you tomorrow."

I shook hands with both of them and tried to walk deliberately out of the office. Once outside of the door, I ran out of the building, jumped into our Volkswagen bus, drove home, and burst into our house.

"Let's sit down, Jo," I panted. "I have great news to share—I think." We went to the living room couch, Jo and I facing each other, the kids on the floor. I told her about the amazing offer, including all the details about travel, staff, offices at the inn, and of course the salary—$10,000 more than I was slated to get in the fall.

"Of course you need to take it," Jo said. "The kids and I will manage."

"Okay," I said. "Let's go get some ice-cream cones to celebrate." The kids cheered. We all walked over to the Red Store, loaded up with double scoops, and came back home to sit on the lawn with our ice cream.

When we finished, I went into the house and called Tim. "Jo is fine with my taking this on. So the answer is yes."

By then I had learned that I grow best, personally and professionally, when I take on things I have never done before, that I don't know how to do, that challenge my prior knowledge and competence, that put me into new environments and new relationships. I'd done that with the Monmouth job. Jo and I had done that saying yes to Goddard and moving to rural Vermont. Despite my initial anxieties and the pressures they created for our relationship, I had learned a lot from these prior experiences, and our marriage was strengthened. I was now comfortable with my varied Goddard responsibilities.

This project presented a whole new set of challenges. It was a voracious beast, gobbling up minutes, hours, and days as I identified and recruited staff; selected and purchased office furniture and supplies; had phones installed; called the college presidents to introduce myself; composed correspondence and materials to describe the project and how we would begin; selected, purchased, and sent off the tests and surveys to be administered to first semester students; found a weekend when the presidents and their chief academic officers could meet with me; and decided on places for those meetings. Somehow it all got done. The week after Labor Day we all moved into four large offices on the top floor of the Plainfield Inn.

Not surprisingly, the tests and surveys used for the project were much more limited than I had been able to use at Goddard. During the first and third years, Dorothy Stockwell from Lyndon State College and Jim McDowell from Earlham College joined me for 3-day site visits to each institution. We visited classes and interviewed students and faculty members. These visits greatly enriched our understandings of the diverse institutional cultures and educational practices. One memory still sticks with me. Jim and I entered a classroom at 8:50 on a sunny fall morning and sat in the last row. At 8:55 a.m. a student walked in and took the middle seat in the front row. Promptly at 9:00 a.m. the middle-aged teacher took his place behind the podium, opened his notes, and lectured for 50 minutes to the young man sitting within spitting distance, and walked out. No hello. No good-bye. It was unabashed delivery, pure and simple; an extreme example of the dominant teaching method of that time.

These data provided powerful evidence concerning highly varied outcomes among these diverse institutions. I won't detail them here. Many of the results are reflected in *Education and Identity* under varied pseudonyms. We mailed comprehensive reports to each institution and scheduled 3-day workshops to discuss their implications for program improvements. It's fair to say that no bells and whistles, trumpet fanfares, or hurrahs greeted me when I showed up. The faculty members and administrators listened politely and some took a few notes. As mentioned in Chapter 4, when I called attention to gaps between the findings and the glowing rhetoric in their catalogs and view books, or the lofty objectives for many of their courses—especially concerning pertinent developmental outcomes—the defensive responses were not always so polite.

In June 1966, I met with all the presidents and the Council for the Advancement of Small Colleges director at Messiah College for a 3-day workshop to review the year and clarify plans for the next. We had a convivial dinner Friday night. When we got settled in for our 9:00 a.m. meeting the next morning, I suggested, "Let's just start by going around the room so each of you can share the kinds of changes that have occurred on the basis of the research results you received." The deafening silence probably only lasted a minute or two but felt like an eternity. Finally, Tim, my staunch ally, stepped in with some of the things Goddard had been doing on the basis of the additional findings. More silence. Then a president, with some emotion, talked about how difficult it was to get the faculty to do anything different from what they'd always done. The floodgates opened. During the rest of that day and most of the next morning I covered the walls with large sheets of paper and listed all the reasons the participants gave as to why the institutions could not really make changes based on the research findings. By now that litany is familiar to many of us. We ended up with ideas for tackling some of that resistance, but as subsequent workshops and reports documented, no real changes occurred that were stimulated by our findings.

The institutional challenges of acting on the research results were compounded by our total ignorance of the complexities of institutional change, particularly in higher education. The dominant model, coming out of agricultural-extension work, was research, development, and diffusion—RD and D. It was not very effective in improving agricultural practices, and our feeble efforts had little impact on our participating institutions. There was no significant research and theory concerning change strategies for colleges and universities. On the basis of that dismal record concerning the use of research findings to make institutional changes, during 1969 I submitted a $395,000 Strategies for Change proposal to NIMH that was funded 2 years later. In that proposal I used the Kennedy quotation that opens this chapter. NIMH ultimately funded the project, and Jack Lindquist's book, *Strategies for Change*, was published by Pacific Soundings Press in 1978. His adaptive development model, FLOOR (Force, Linkage, Openness, Ownership, Reward), was a major contribution to the literature. Unfortunately, it has never received the recognition or application it deserves.

In May 1969 I received a call that changed our lives.

"Hello, Dr. Chickering, this is Logan Wilson, president of the American Council on Education. How are you today?"

"I'm just fine, thanks."

"I'm calling to let you know that your book, *Education and Identity*, has won the Eleanor Colford Morris National Book Award for its outstanding contribution to higher education."

"That's amazing. I didn't know there was such an award."

"Well, there is, and I'm wondering if you would you be willing to speak at the opening session of our national conference in October? Your wife is welcome to join you, and we'll put you both up in a suite at the Sheraton, the conference hotel."

"That's a wonderful invitation and I'll be honored to be there."

"Fine. We'll send you the conference materials and your hotel reservation. I look forward to meeting you."

"Thank you so much."

I was blown into the top of the big tamarack outside the window. The dominant purpose of higher education was cultivating the intellect. My book argued that student development in all its richness and complexity should be higher education's organizing purpose. It described seven vectors for development and recommended significant changes in curriculum, teaching, student services, and institutional size. I knew, from the slings and arrows I had experienced at project workshops and conference presentations, how foreign those ideas were to most college and university faculty members and administrators. It struck me as remarkable that the book had been so recognized.

In February 1970, I got the welcome news from Duane Regan, the program officer at NIMH, that the Strategies for Change project had been funded to start in September. I was on top of the world. My prior work had been nationally recognized, and I had another 4 years of funding to try to help institutions create programs that could put higher education for human development clearly on the map. Then, the first week in April, I got another call.

"Hello, Art. This is Duane Regan at NIMH. I'm afraid I've got some bad news. Our budget has been cut and we're not going to be able to fund your project this year. Your current project has been one of the best we've ever supported. Your proposal to focus on change makes great sense and you'll be at the top of our list to start in fall of 1971. You can count on that."

I took the receiver from my ear and looked at it, trying to see Duane's face at the other end. "So, what do I do for the next 12 months? I have four kids and a wife to support."

Duane said, "I'm terribly sorry and I know this must leave you hanging. There's just nothing I can do about it this year. I'll send you an official letter. You can call me in the fall if you want to be sure how things stand for 1971."

I hung up and turned to look out of my office window at the Plainfield Town Hall next door. It was clear and sunny. No April showers were forecast, but I had been hit by a deluge. I was up the proverbial creek without a paddle. I told Bev, my executive assistant, that I needed to go home for the rest of the day. She looked at me with large question marks in her eyes.

I walked downstairs, out the front door, climbed on my bike, and pedaled the 4 miles home to an empty house. Jo had fled mud season to visit our friends the Robinsons in Wilmington, Delaware. I was holding down the fort with the kids, who were all in school. The ruts in our dirt road were so deep the old Army jeep kept getting hung up on its axles so we had to walk or bike the mile in and out. On a rainy afternoon the week before, as I had walked in with my arms full of groceries, the paper bags dissolved, dropping bread, milk, orange juice cartons, chicken quarters, carrots, and lettuce in the mud. The next morning I picked them up with a bushel basket and rinsed them off as best I could. It was a good time for Jo to be away.

At the house I took out my fly rod and went down to the pond. When I got stuck writing I found that quiet casting, with or without an occasional strike, soothed my turbulent mind and let my unconscious percolate. What to do? My impulse in such situations was to rush into action. Jo's counsel most always was, "Take it easy. Let's just sit on it a while." Even though she was not home, her wisdom was with me, and because she was away I did not have to tell her about the call. Nor did I have to tell the project staff because they were not expecting to stay on anyway. So I kept myself occupied with project details, working around our place, and enjoying the kids while I mulled over what to do.

Three days later, Alexander Astin, director of the Office of Research at the American Council on Education (ACE), called. "We'd like to have you come down to ACE as a visiting scholar for the coming year, from September through June. We can offer you $25,000, plus some help with moving expenses. If you're interested we need a research proposal and you'll have to come down and meet with Logan."

I paused for maybe 20 seconds, long enough to hear a white-throated sparrow call "Old Sam Peabody, Peabody, Peabody" from the ridge behind our house.

"I'm happy to accept, but I'll have to check with my wife, Jo, and get back to you later today."

"That'll be fine. Do you have any thoughts about what you might want to do with our data?"

The whitethroat sang again.

"Well, just off the top of my head, I might like to see what differences there are in educational outcomes for commuters compared with resident students."

"We have a lot of data that could be used for that," he said. "Why don't you write me a brief proposal and we'll set up a date for you to come down?"

"Great. You'll have it next week."

I called the Robinsons to speak with Jo. They had just come back from a visit to Longwood Gardens, where all the spring flowers were blooming. Jo thought a year in Washington, D.C., would be wonderfully broadening for both of us and the kids. She would look for housing while she was down there.

I called Dr. Astin and told him we would be delighted to come and that Jo was looking for housing. We arranged to meet with President Wilson the following Monday. A lawyer friend of the Robinsons came to Washington during the summers and had a house in Bannockburn that he rented during the academic year. Fully furnished, it was all on one floor, with three bedrooms, two baths, kitchen, and dining room—living room. The rent was $320 a month plus utilities. Just over the border in Maryland, it was three blocks from the end of Massachusetts Avenue, where buses ran into the District. The arrangement seemed ideal and a $640 check for the first month's rent and damage deposit sealed the deal.

I flew to Washington, D.C., on Sunday and got a room at the Dupont Plaza Hotel, across Dupont Circle from the ACE offices on the top floor of the National Center for Higher Education building. The receptionist showed me to Astin's large corner office. He was about 6 feet 5 inches tall, fair haired, slim, dressed in a sport coat with a loose tie and an unbuttoned shirt collar. Stacks of computer printouts 3 and 4 feet high were on the floor beside a spacious, well-littered desk and in a closet along one wall.

"Welcome to ACE and to our Office of Research. I'm looking forward to having a good year together."

"It's great to be here. We've found a house and I'm anxious to get started this fall."

He buttoned his shirt collar and pulled up his tie. "Logan's expecting us. Let's go in."

We went by the receptionist into a spacious corner office with an aircraft-carrier desk and a round table off to one side. The large man who had introduced me at the book award ceremony, well buttoned-up in a dark suit and tie, walked around from behind his desk and invited us to sit at the table.

Shaking my hand he said, "Nice to see you again. I'm glad your book seems to be doing well. Sandy tells me you're going to be looking at differences in educational experiences and changes during the college years for commuting and resident students. That's certainly an important issue for us. What are you going to recommend?"

I looked at Astin, hand over his mouth to stifle a smile.

"Well, sir, I guess I'd like to do the research first and then see what to suggest."

"I guess that makes sense. Glad to have you with us. Hope you have a good year." He stood up and walked back to his desk.

Astin and I went to his office. "Logan likes to get right down to business," he said. "He usually knows pretty well what he thinks, whether or not the data are all in. He's fairly conservative but you always know where he stands. Let's go get a cup of coffee and chat a bit before you go to the airport. You can just call me Sandy."

On our way out, he introduced me to some of the other research staff and showed me a small office opposite the elevator that would be mine. Over leisurely coffee at the hotel, he described the data from several hundred colleges that completed their annual Cooperative Institutional Research Program survey, and additional follow-up data from several different cohorts. Those data would be the bases for my comparisons, using "stepwise multivariate analyses." Ever since Monmouth College I had learned to keep my mouth shut when I didn't understand something, so I just said "oh" in response to this last bit of information. My project research had used simple tests for the pretest and post-test data. I was clearly entering a brand-new research world, with totally unfamiliar analytic methods.

He paid for our coffees and told me how to get the subway. I picked up my small bag, found the subway, and made my flights back without any hitches. I wondered why this trip had been necessary just for that small formality, but during the following months I learned a lot about the importance of protocol.

Sandy Astin's invitation to spend that year at ACE as a visiting scholar gave me the opportunity for another applied research project to address what seemed to me to be a critically important issue: the differences in educational outcomes for commuting and resident students. I analyzed ACE's copious data with advice and counsel from Sandy and his sophisticated staff. We had completed some preliminary comparisons as part of the Student Development Project, and the rich ACE data confirmed my hypotheses: there were significant differences between commuting and resident students in student-faculty contact, academic engagement, and participation in on-campus activities—fostering much greater gains for residents. When my book *Commuting Versus Resident Students* was released in 1974, in the Foreword Sandy wrote:

> This major national study of residential living appears at a particularly opportune time in the history of higher education. In contrast to the early 1960s, when generous federal and state subsidies stimulated a dramatic expansion in residential facilities on college campuses, the past few years have been characterized by major cutbacks in dormitory construction, as well as by increasing ambivalence . . . about the usefulness of college dormitories. Arthur Chickering's study raises fundamental questions about the wisdom of these recent trends. (p. ix)

When I went to Empire State College as the founding academic vice president in July 1971, I was determined to have a solid research foundation for our new program. This would help us improve as we went along, and it would also help other state systems and institutions judge whether they wanted to create their own adaptations. I wrote a $500,000, 3-year proposal, "Developing Cost Effectiveness Models for Post-secondary Education," for the Fund for the Improvement of Postsecondary Education (FIPSE). When I met with Virginia Smith, then director of FIPSE, she happily agreed that they should support it. I hired Ernest Palola as project director, Paul Bradlee and Tim Lehman to help with the educational research, and Dick Debus to do the cost analyses. Their surveys and interviews documented the educational power of our program. The most powerful element was the assessment of prior learning based on the students' work and life experiences that were credited toward their individualized degrees. That process helped them realize that they did, indeed, have a lot of knowledge and competence even though many of them had dropped out or failed out of college. The second most powerful element was their relationship with their mentor. Finally, students' learning contracts enriched the academic content of their courses but also deepened students' understandings of those different experiential contexts. These learning contracts integrated a variety of their ongoing experiences at work, at home, and in the community with their reading and writing.

The total cost per student for this individualized educational program was about $2,250; costs at the other State University of New York colleges and universities ranged from about $2,000 to $2,500. Our educational costs per student were also consistent with adult students statewide at other course- and discipline-based traditional institutions.

The Center for the Study of Higher Education at Memphis State University received funding from FIPSE and NIMH for two projects: Higher Learning for Diverse Adults and Higher Education for Adult Mental Health. These projects did not require the participating institutions to collect their own data, but institutional teams relied on research and theory concerning adult development and learning pertinent to their innovations and interventions.

My last effort to help institutions use self-inquiry for program improvement occurred when Zelda ("Zee") Gamson and I created "Seven Principles for Good Practice in Undergraduate Education" in 1987 with the associated faculty, institutional, and student inventories. Zee was one of the authors of *Involvement in Learning* published by the National Institute of Education in 1984. She feared that this report and several others calling for significant reforms in higher education would not reach the faculty members, administrators, and students for whom they were intended. We were both on the board of the American Association for Higher Education (AAHE) and suggested that AAHE sponsor the development of a statement of principles for educationally powerful undergraduate education. Around that time we attended a conference at Wingspread, the Johnson Foundation Center in Racine, Wisconsin, that brought together authors of recent reports on undergraduate education along with other higher education scholars. It seemed to us that a statement of principles could be timed to help drive the reform movement that was sweeping the country.

We wanted the statement to reflect the collective wisdom of those who were most knowledgeable about research on the impact of the college experience and about related organizational, economic, and policy issues. With support from the Johnson Foundation, a small task force met for 2 days in the summer of 1986. This gathering was an extraordinary event. While most of the participants knew one another's work, they had never come together to consider the implications of these works for improving undergraduate education. To start the discussion we presented eight principles and stipulated that we should end up with no more than nine, and preferably fewer. We also insisted that whatever we produced be accessible, understandable, practical, and widely applicable.

We ended up with seven. Good practice in undergraduate education: encourages student-faculty contact, encourages cooperation among students, encourages active learning, gives prompt feedback, emphasizes time on task, communicates high expectations, and respects diverse talents and ways of learning. These principles first appeared as the lead article in the March 1987 issue of the *AAHE Bulletin*. The response was immediate—and was overwhelmingly positive. The principles were republished in the June 1987 issue of the *Wingspread Journal,* and more than 150,000 copies were ordered from the foundation. An unknown number were copied or reprinted in publications such as newsletters of national associations and campus centers for improving teaching.

This enthusiastic response encouraged us to create a faculty self-assessment instrument with examples and indicators of each principle and an institutional inventory with indicators of campus policies and practices that supported the principles. After much testing, dissemination, and feedback, The Johnson Foundation published the final versions of the *Faculty Inventory* and *Institutional Inventory* in 1989. Again, the response was dramatic. Within a week of publication, 40,000 booklets had been distributed. After several printings, their distribution was taken over by Winona State University, which had established the Seven Principles Resource Center. Lou Barsi, then a graduate student at George Mason University, helped us identify items for the *Student Inventory* (Chickering, Gamson, & Winona State University, 1990), which the Winona State Center also distributed.

After my first efforts to use research evidence to improve undergraduate education—with the Experiment in College Curriculum Organization at Goddard from 1959 through 1965—it was most gratifying to have that orientation culminate in such a widely accepted and adapted formulation as the Seven Principles, with its own self-assessment instruments. George Kuh is well positioned to put this work in the context of other changes in this area during the last 50 years.

George

Prior to Chick's Goddard studies and the Project on Small Colleges, culminating in *Education and Identity* (Chickering, 1969), higher education research was mostly about research findings, not necessarily how to use them to improve teaching and learning or inform decision making. Other researchers such as Nevitt Sanford (1962) and some of the contributors to *The American College* were aware, even then, that institutions of higher education were not using information effectively about their core enterprises. And still today, there are few such examples of where the research has directly led to innovations that, once implemented, are linked to improved student performance (Banta, Jones, & Black, 2009; Kuh & Ikenberry, 2009).

In part, the difficulty of using data about student and institutional performance is that intentional, lasting change in colleges and universities often moves at a glacial pace. Few institutionalized innovations, whether based on research or collective wisdom, originate within the academy. Writing across the curriculum is one inside-the-academy innovation that has taken root. Most other changes—from using standardized test scores in admissions to applying electronic technology to teaching and learning—were prompted by calls for more evidence about the quality of student learning and the need to reduce costs. Today's emphasis on obtaining evidence of student accomplishment through systematic assessment of learning outcomes (a logical extension of Chick's work) is due to demands by regional accreditation agencies (e.g., the Higher Learning Commission) and specialized accreditors (e.g., the Accreditation Board for Engineering and Technology) that colleges and universities assess and report student learning outcomes. While there is plenty of such activity underway, this has not brought about the transformation of teaching and learning to foster the holistic student development that is called for by Chick's work and vision.

This is not to say that Chick's voluminous work of over 50 years has gone for naught. His books and papers foreshadowed several major shifts in how we think about and conduct inquiries about the student experience. Among the more influential of such shifts are the perceived legitimacy of assessment today, the demand by policymakers for better and more transparent information about student and institutional performance, the pressure by groups of stakeholders to collect and use student learning outcomes data, and the availability of more and better assessment instruments and approaches.

Because many aspects of the higher education enterprise have changed over the past half century, it is nearly impossible to make legitimate comparisons between the kinds of studies and projects Chick did and what has value today. Student demographics, new providers such as for-profit institutions, and electronic delivery systems are among the most obvious aspects that have changed over time. Although community colleges were on the radar screen in the 1960s and 1970s, their ascendance into policy prominence in the past decade alone has been nothing short of astounding. There are, however, some aspects of today's higher education that are relevant to Chick's interests and work related to using evidence-based decision making to guide institutional improvement.

One of the most significant differences between when Chick was conducting research about the student experience and today is the expectation that the findings from such inquiries will be used both to demonstrate institutional accountability and to guide institutional improvement. Chick blazed a new trail by showing how institutions could systematically collect data about the student experience. Most campuses today have a fair amount of assessment activity underway. But I doubt that Chick had in mind—at least in the early years—that evidence of student and institutional performance would be used to rank colleges and universities (which is a growing cottage industry internationally) or that indicators of the student experience would be employed to make judgments about whether institutions were using their resources responsibly. Worldwide rising enrollments, economic pressures, and other factors make it imperative that postsecondary institutions ensure that their graduates acquire the broad range of skills and competencies demanded in the 21st century. In the past two decades, accreditors and state agencies have increasingly expected colleges and universities to demonstrate their effectiveness, show that they are doing more to help more students succeed and earn a credential or degree, and publicly report the relevant evidence. The vigorous and often harshly critical discussions within the Spellings Commission (Secretary of Education's Commission on the Future of Higher Education, 2006) made it all but impossible for institutional leaders and educational policymakers to ignore calls for more accountability. This, in turn, has made benchmarking (in the form of comparing institutions on various performance metrics) much more common. How to do this in a way that fosters improvement rather than simply compliance is a critical and largely unmet challenge.

In today's climate of accountability, efforts to assess or measure how and to what extent students benefit from attending college are poised to become high stakes if they are presumed to certify (rather than merely represent) specific, predetermined, publicly established attainment standards, thus meeting accountability expectations. At the same time, assessment results amassed and examined over time can reveal observable patterns of institutional and sector strengths and weaknesses in particular competencies or for different groups of students, and these assessment results can inform improvements in curricula or pedagogy. But what seems to be a straightforward process—collect information about the student experience and make the results available to faculty, staff, and external audiences—is more complicated than it first appears.

The task is challenging because of the inherent tensions (Peter Ewell [2009] has sometimes characterized them as contradictions) in the assumptions and uses associated with the twin purposes of accountability and improvement. In the accountability paradigm, evidence about student learning and personal development is intended for external audiences—policymakers, state systems, accreditors, prospective students—who, in turn, use it to make summative judgments about quality and institutional effectiveness. The favored accountability approaches (standardized tests and national surveys) typically yield quantitative data that permit straightforward comparisons between institutions and programs. In contrast, the improvement purpose for obtaining evidence is to enable faculty and staff to form judgments about performance in order to address teaching and learning in ways that will promote higher levels of student engagement and accomplishment. This was the mission and intent of Chick's work in assessment. Often, qualitative information is coupled with quantitative data to help guide program improvements. Much of this information represents authentic student work—captured in portfolios and demonstrations that are often rich with understanding and nuance—which further complicates efforts to compare programs and, therefore, limits accountability uses.

For better or worse (I think the latter), when colleges and universities have options for designing assessment systems, the default tends to favor the accountability purpose because of the pressure placed on these institutions (by external entities) to have comparative data. For this purpose, standardized test scores are attractive. They can populate relatively straightforward templates that display data, such as the average institutional score—a single number—based on students tested with the College Learning Assessment (CLA). Unfortunately, such measures are based on the average performance of (typically) small samples of students.

While these institutional averages are used in contemporary ranking systems, the metrics are inherently flawed in terms of representing student performance because the variation in scores is almost always greater within a given institution than between institutions (Kuh, 2003; National Survey of Student Engagement, 2008). Thus, claims about how an individual student will perform at any given college or university are highly unreliable.

This dilemma is underscored by Thorngate's (1976) postulate of commensurate complexity, whereby an empirical observation can simultaneously represent only two out of the three virtues of being general, accurate, and simple. This means that efforts to assess student learning using, for example, a simple approach such as a single standardized measure to make general claims about the performance of multiple institutions will likely not be accurate.

To respond to the accountability and improvement challenges, universities must forge tools sensitive to individual institutional contexts and a wide array of desired learning outcomes. They must also report the results in ways that are understandable and meaningful to external audiences and helpful for informing internal improvement efforts. Courses, credits, certificates, and degrees are traditional proxies for student accomplishment, but they are only proxies. For these reasons, the performance-based tasks instructors assign to students—in courses and in field-based learning—must be the centerpiece of quality assurance in terms of student learning. This means, among other things, that the higher educational enterprise must become better at assessing student learning outcomes, using the resulting data to inform resource allocation and other decisions, and communicating to their constituents about how well students are performing.

The good news is that there are many more assessment tools and approaches now available than just a decade ago. In Measuring Quality, an online inventory of assessment resources, Borden and Kernel (2009) summarized 250 instruments; software tools and platforms; benchmarking and information resources; and projects, initiatives, and services for assessing program and institutional effectiveness. A decade earlier, Borden and Zak Owens (2001) did something similar and found only about two dozen such products and services. The proliferation of instruments and vendors during the last decade was undoubtedly spurred by regional and specialized accreditors' requiring that institutions have evidence about student learning and that such evidence be used to guide change. One wonders what Chick thinks about having such a proliferation of tools to choose among. At the least, that many more instruments are available acknowledges both the importance of measuring student learning and the complexity of the task. At the same time, the number of holistic inventories such as Chick used in the Goddard and Small College Study has not kept pace with the development of more narrowly focused tools. I have occasionally talked with colleagues, Ernie Pascarella among them, about revising a tool like the Omnibus Personality Inventory, which was one of the instruments Chick used in the Goddard studies.

Although there are now many assessment tools, consensus about what the critical outcomes are to measure remains elusive. Considerable progress has been made on this front through Liberal Education and America's Promise (LEAP), a 10-year effort started in 2007 by the Association of American Colleges and Universities to sharpen the focus on the areas of student attainment demanded by the 21st century. There are four broad categories of outcomes featured in LEAP: knowledge of human cultures and the physical and natural world; intellectual and practical skills; personal and social responsibility; and deep integrative learning. These are happily aligned with Chick's holistic view of what should be privileged in the undergraduate experience and are consistent with the orientation of the developmental vectors described in *Education and Identity* (Chickering, 1969) as well as with the views of what constitutes an educated person as put forth in *The Modern American College* (Chickering, 1981).

A relatively new learning-outcomes framework may bring a more coherent understanding of the skills and competencies demanded of educated people in a global society. In January 2011, the Lumina Foundation released a beta version of the Degree Qualifications Profile (DQP). Its purposes are to challenge faculty and academic leaders in the United States to think deeply and concretely about aligning expectations for student learning outcomes across higher education and provide a framework for documenting the proficiencies students should master. The DQP has jump-started discussions about what post-secondary degrees granted by U.S. colleges and universities really mean with respect to what graduates know and can do. The DQP describes the specific proficiencies that graduates receiving a particular degree must exhibit. The DQP presents proposed competencies in five areas of student learning—specialized knowledge, broad integrative knowledge, intellectual skills, applied learning, and civic learning; and it addresses three degree levels—associate's, bachelor's, and master's.

It remains to be seen whether the DQP turns out to be transformative. At the least it may be a much-needed counterpoint to the shrill voices that are demanding colleges focus more narrowly on skills and competencies that are presumed (not always accurately) to be valued by employers.

Chick's Goddard studies were not the first to incorporate a longitudinal research design. Ted Newcomb's Bennington College studies, for example, were well known to the handful of scholars involved in studies of the student experience. However, Chick's mixed-method design employing multiple instruments was most unusual, as was its wide-angle view of the college experience. Chick credits Ralph Tyler for conceptualizing the research design of the Goddard studies. But however important project design is, the real work—including managing unanticipated challenges—comes later. A. A. Milne, best known for his books about Winnie-the-Pooh, put it this way: "Organizing is what you do before you do something, so that when you do it, it is not all mixed up" (Brainy Quote, n.d.). By all accounts, Chick deftly organized and managed a very complex research undertaking!

Reading Chick's description of the Goddard research effort seems almost surreal by today's context. Try to imagine what would be required these days for a team of investigators to recruit substantial proportions of first-year students and have each of them complete 16 hours of inventories and tests while motivating them to do their best work; this is something that plagues contemporary assessment efforts (Liu, Bridgeman, & Adler, 2012). Assuming all this can be handled logistically, it is even more difficult to entice the same groups of students to participate multiple times during their college experience, to complete similar batteries of tools, and to participate in interviews. Finally, there was the nontrivial matter of involving Goddard's faculty in the research program, which added an unusually rich perspective on the student experience and institutional functioning.

Chick had the advantage of small scale and a relatively compliant pool of participants, students and faculty alike. Even so, the management of such an effort over an extended period of time set a new standard for longitudinal research. The field has benefited from the work of other scholars who have conducted several additional major studies in this tradition. These include federally funded national centers that produced dozens of research papers about the undergraduate student experience (among other topics), many of which are summarized by Pascarella and Terenzini (2005). The Wabash National Study has since produced a treasure trove of more recent findings (Pascarella & Blaich, 2013). However, none of them demanded the amount of time from either students or faculty members that the Goddard project demanded.

Chick's 1974 book, *Commuting Versus Resident Students*, was one of the first to empirically demonstrate the meaningful differences in how types of students experience college, and to distill policy and practice implications from the findings. Prior to this work, most of the research on undergraduates' experience focused on full-time students living on campus. Of course, full-time students were still in the majority at that time, comprised of captive audiences who generally were willing to participate in surveys and other data-collection approaches. Many such studies drew on participants enrolled in introductory general education courses, especially psychology or sociology. Pat Cross (1971) was another of Chick's contemporaries with an interest in and writings on adult learners, a group about which Chick also had firsthand knowledge and experience.

As mentioned earlier, data use remains the continuing challenge. When describing the Goddard project, Chick briefly refers to "the weekly Friday afternoon faculty meetings.... These conversations led to continuous fine-tuning of existing programs and to further initiatives, some of which became grant funded." It is hard to imagine anything akin to that happening anywhere today! Despite considerable effort on the part of Chick and his colleagues, the research findings led to few substantive changes at Goddard. Moving from data to action remains a major challenge even today, as determined by studies of assessment practices (Kuh & Ikenberry, 2009). "Seven Principles for Good Practice in Undergraduate Education" (Chickering & Gamson, 1987) is the conceptual foundation of the National Survey of Student Engagement (NSSE). In large part, this is because these seven principles had been documented as effective educational practice by other studies. For example, among the participants in the 1987 Wingspread Conference Center meeting, where these principles were originally hammered out, was C. Robert Pace. Pace had already incorporated, in some form, the student experiences representing good practices in undergraduate education in the College Student Experiences Questionnaire (CSEQ) (Pace, 1980, 1984). He was an informal advisor to, and Chick was a member of, the design team that helped develop NSSE in 1998 (Kuh, 2009)—another reason that this widely used instrument focuses to a large extent on the kinds of educationally purposeful activities represented in "Seven Principles," which to my knowledge is the single most widely distributed document in American higher education. The principles became so popular and offered so much promise to improve teaching and enhance learning that Winona State University established an office to encourage faculty and staff to apply the ideas to their work and to distribute products toward this end.

As Jon Dalton explains in Chapter 7, student development remains an important focus of student affairs. But since the mid-1990s, ushered in by *The Student Learning Imperative* (American College Personnel Association [ACPA], 1994), the concept of student learning, broadly defined, was later adopted and championed by national student affairs associations such as ACPA and NASPA (Keeling, 2004). Chick and I were members of *The Student Learning Imperative* writing team, along with Charles Schroder, who initiated the work when he was ACPA president, Lena and Sandy Astin, Patricia Cross, Pat King, Susan Komives, and Patrick Terenzini. Our meetings, some of which were at Schroeder's mountain home in Estes Park, Colorado, were intellectually stimulating and personally rewarding. (One irrelevant, irreverent memory from one of these gatherings was my dropping a huge pan of lasagna and Pat Cross's scooping it off the kitchen floor and back into the pan within seconds. No one complained!) Fortunately for the field and for higher education in general, Chick insisted that cultivating the dispositions and attributes of the whole student had to be a core underpinning of *The Student Learning Imperative*.

The report was a call to arms that had "legs": for several years it was an organizing framework for national and regional meetings and for journal articles. Especially helpful to the movement was a courageous, forward-looking, and statesmanlike decision by then NASPA president-elect, Jon Dalton, to feature *The Student Learning Imperative* at NASPA's 1995 Annual Conference. In those days, such interassociation collaborations and cooperation were all too rare. ACPA's magazine, *About Campus,* was introduced in 1995 in large part to promote

the vision of *The Student Learning Imperative* and subsequent congenial documents by featuring efforts to translate theory and research into
practical actions that campuses can take to foster learning and success.
Chick was a member of the inaugural *About Campus* editorial board of
contributors.

Chick's early work was mostly grant funded, a testament to the
timeliness and quality of his ideas, scholarly acumen, and research
expertise. If Chick was running the project, his track record made it
a good bet that the work would be rigorous and of interest and use to
the field. This is another aspect of the postsecondary landscape that has
changed over the past quarter century in that there is less government
funding for innovative inquiries such as Chick designed. The federal
government has continued to make research and development dollars
available through competitions hosted by the U.S. Department of
Education. But in recent years the strong preference has been for quasi-
experimental designs, which are extremely difficult and costly to implement. FIPSE, once an incubator of innovation, was either defunded in
some years or its resources used to fulfill political ends.

Private foundations also favored Chick's work, and they have—for all
practical purposes—at the present moment replaced the federal government for sponsoring research with a focus on undergraduate education.
After a period of relative inattention during the 1980s (there are exceptions, with periodic forays into higher education by the W.K. Kellogg
Foundation, Lilly Endowment, and the Carnegie Corporation of New
York), The Pew Charitable Trusts, under the leadership of Russ Edgerton,
former president of the American Association for Higher Education, initiated a series of targeted grants, many of which were focused on the quality
of undergraduate education. NSSE and CCSSE (Community College
Survey of Student Engagement) were two of the projects launched with
Pew support. But Pew's involvement was short-lived.

Campuses vary in their capacity to effectively use published research or their own outcomes-assessment results on teaching and learning to inform improvement efforts and adapt good practices to their local circumstances. Scholars, institutional leaders, governing board members, and policymakers share some of the responsibility for shortfalls in this arena. Researchers often use indecipherable prose, mistakenly presuming that the best research is that which informs other scholars and adds to the knowledge base, rather than writing for the people who need the information to guide their efforts. For these reasons, just as institutions have outsourced functions such as food service, bookstores, and housing operations, increasing numbers are turning to for-profit venders to help with analytic efforts to better understand student persistence and other features of the student experience. Some enrollment management firms historically focused on admissions issues have expanded their missions to include retention. A spate of new groups and consultants with similar aims has recently appeared. These organizations provide data collection and analysis services, which Chick did himself at Goddard and later, and that institutional researchers at many colleges and universities once did.

Institutions of higher education need to do at least two things to achieve the progress that Chick was hoping for in enhancing student learning and increasing student persistence and graduation rates. First, faculty and staff must become familiar with and figure out how to productively *use* the available information about effective educational practices. Governing boards need to evaluate senior administrators in part on whether they are implementing—throughout the institution—empirically derived, effective educational practices and continuous quality improvement processes. Boards must also mandate annual reports that feature these indicators. At the end of the day, incentive structures need to change if more students—especially those from historically underserved backgrounds—are to survive and thrive in college.

One advance that we will hear more about is using software to identify and support students who need or can benefit from additional structure, typically early in the college experience. Such systems, when coupled with a demonstrably effective coaching system, can produce a win-win: More students overcome obstacles and persist. Persistence rates tick upward, which results both in increased completion rates and more tuition dollars. Institutions then realize a break-even return on their investments in student success interventions.

Unlike the situation Chick faced in the 1960s, most colleges and universities today are awash in data. Converting these data into meaningful information that can be acted on is a daunting task. Fortunately, data analytics are now available that make it possible to aggregate and examine information about student and institutional performance from different parts and levels of the institution. This allows institutions to make sense of complex environments and to base their decisions on the more fulsome, nuanced understandings that emerge. For example, one software product enables higher education administrators to gain insight into institutional effectiveness and student success from their computers, tablets, or smartphones.

But using analytics requires careful thought—both about what we need to know and about what data are most likely to tell us what we need to know. Imagine being able to integrate the results—from a student engagement survey, from student performance represented in portfolios of authentic student work and internship supervisor evaluations, and from educational costs—by major field or some other relevant variables to determine the relative return on institutional investment to student learning and personal development! Or, imagine being able to choose among the following applications:

- Course level: learning trails, social network analysis, discourse analysis
- Educational data mining: predictive modeling, clustering, pattern mining
- Intelligent curriculum: development of semantically defined curricular resources
- Adaptive content: adaptive sequence of content based on learner behavior, recommender systems
- Adaptive learning: adaptive learning process (social interactions, learning activity, learner support, not only content)

Although their promise is yet to be fully realized, it is likely that the capacity to use analytics and apply findings in the cause of enhanced student learning will distinguish high-performing and low-performing institutions.

Much in the higher education landscape has changed since Chick conducted his landmark studies at Goddard and the Project on Small Colleges. The groundbreaking work comparing the educational outcomes of commuter and residential students provided an indication of the tradeoffs in educational benefits for the half of all undergraduate students today who start at 2-year colleges in order to live at home or continue to work. Chick's enduring focus on creating teaching and learning conditions that foster the development of the whole student has never been more relevant than now, when an increasingly popular view of the academy's future role is to deliver general education and introductory courses online to thousands of students simultaneously, none of whom is required to be in the same place at the same time with their peers.

One wonders what all this will produce. And the only way to produce periodic answers to that question is to obtain evidence about student accomplishment and use it to make wise decisions about what to invest in. Thanks to Chick, we know a lot more today about why and how to do so.

REFERENCES

American College Personnel Association. (1994). *The student learning imperative*. Washington, DC: Author.

Association of American Colleges and Universities. (2007). *College learning for the new global century: A report from the National Leadership Council for Liberal Education and America's Promise*. Washington, DC: Author.

Banta, T. W., Jones, E. A., & Black, K. E. (2009). *Designing effective assessment: Principles and profiles of good practice*. San Francisco, CA: Jossey-Bass.

Borden, V. M. H., & Kernel, B. (2009). *Measuring quality in higher education: An inventory of instruments, tools and resources*. Retrieved from http://apps.airweb.org/surveys

Borden, V. M. H., & Zak Owens, J. L. (2001). *Measuring quality: Choosing among surveys and other assessments of college quality*. Retrieved from http://www.airweb.org/images/measurequality.pdf

Brainy Quote. (n.d.). A. A. Milne quote. Retrieved from http://www.brainyquote.com/quotes/quotes/a/aamilne166124.html

Chickering, A. W. (1964). Dimensions of independence: The findings of an experiment at Goddard College. *Journal of Higher Education, 35*(1), 38–41.

Chickering, A. W. (1965a). Does our performance match our claims? *Improving College and University Teaching, 13*(1), 35–37.

Chickering, A.W. (1965b). Faculty perceptions and changing institutional press. *Proceedings of the 1965 Meeting of the Association for Institutional Research*, Stony Brook, NY.

Chickering, A. W. (1966a). *The development of autonomy*. Paper presented at the 1966 meeting of the Association for Higher Education, Washington, DC.

Chickering, A. W. (1966b). How big should a college be? *Liberal Education, LII*(3), 1–12.

Chickering, A. W. (1967a). Development of autonomy. *American Journal of Orthopsychiatry, 37*(2), 7–15.

Chickering, A. W. (1967b). Talking with college students. *Improving College and University Teaching, 15*(1), 30–32.

Chickering, A. W. (1969). *Education and identity.* San Francisco, CA: Jossey-Bass.

Chickering, A. W. (1974). *Commuting versus resident students.* San Francisco, CA: Jossey-Bass.

Chickering, A. W. (Ed.). (1981). *The modern American college: Responding to the new realities of diverse students and a changing society.* San Francisco, CA: Jossey-Bass.

Chickering, A. W., & Gamson, Z. F. (1987). Seven principles for good practice in undergraduate education. *American Association for Higher Education Bulletin, 39*(7), 3–7.

Chickering, A. W., Gamson, Z. F., & Winona State University. (1990). *Student inventory: 7 principles for good practice in undergraduate education.* Winona, MN: The Seven Principles Resource Center, Winona State University.

Cross, K. P. (1971). *Beyond the open door: New students to higher education.* San Francisco, CA: Jossey-Bass.

Ewell, P. T. (November 2009). *Assessment, accountability, and improvement: Revisiting the tension* (NILOA Occasional Paper No.1). Urbana, IL: University of Illinois and Indiana University, National Institute for Learning Outcomes Assessment.

Goddard College. (1958). *The Goddard Bulletin.* Plainfield, VT: Author.

Johnson Foundation. (1989a). *Faculty inventory: 7 principles for good practice in undergraduate education.* Racine, WI: Author.

Johnson Foundation. (1989b). *Institutional inventory: 7 principles for good practice in undergraduate education.* Racine, WI: Author.

Keeling, R. P. (Ed.). (2004). *Learning reconsidered: A campus-wide focus on the student experience.* Washington, DC: National Association of Student Personnel Administrators & American College Personnel Association.

Kuh, G. D. (2003). What we're learning about student engagement from NSSE. *Change, 35*(2), 24–32.

Kuh, G. D. (2009). The national survey of student engagement: Conceptual and empirical foundations. In R. M. Gonyea & G. D. Kuh (Eds.), *Using NSSE in institutional research* (New directions for institutional research, No. 141, pp. 5–20). San Francisco, CA: Jossey-Bass.

Kuh, G. D., & Ikenberry, S. O. (2009). *More than you think, less than we need: Learning outcome assessment in American higher education.* Urbana, IL: National Institute for Learning Outcomes Assessment.

Lindquist, J. (1978). *Strategies for change.* Berkeley, CA: Pacific Soundings Press.

Liu, L. O., Bridgeman, B., & Adler, R. M. (2012). Measuring learning outcomes in higher education: Motivation matters. *Educational Research, 41*(9), 352–362.

Lumina Foundation. (2011). *The degree qualifications profile.* Indianapolis, IN: Author.

National Institute of Education. (1984). *Involvement in learning: Realizing the potential of American higher education.* Washington, DC: Author.

National Survey of Student Engagement. (2008). *Promoting engagement for all students: The imperative to look within—2008 results.* Bloomington, IN: Indiana University Center for Postsecondary Research.

Pace, C. R. (1980). Measuring the quality of student effort. *Current Issues in Higher Education, 2,* 10–16.

Pace, C. R. (1984). *Measuring the quality of college student experiences: An account of the development and use of the College Student Experiences Questionnaire.* Los Angeles, CA: Higher Education Research Institute.

Pascarella, E. T., & Blaich, C. (2013). Lessons from the Wabash National Study of Liberal Arts Education. *Change, 45*(2), 6–15.

Pascarella, E. T., & Terenzini, P. T. (2005). *How college affects students: A third decade of research.* San Francisco, CA: Jossey-Bass.

Sanford, N. (Ed.). (1962). *The American college: A psychological and social interpretation of the higher learning.* New York, NY: Wiley.

Secretary of Education's Commission on the Future of Higher Education. (2006). A test of leadership: Charting the future of U.S. higher education. Retrieved from http://www2.ed.gov/about/bdscomm/list/hiedfuture/reports/pre-pub-report.pdf

Schlesinger, A. M. (1965). *A thousand days: John F. Kennedy in the White House.* New York, NY: Houghton Mifflin.

Thorngate, W. (1976). "In general" vs. "it depends": Some comments on the Gergen-Schlenker debate. *Personality and Social Psychology Bulletin, 2*(4), 404–410.

CHAPTER 6

From Lecturing to Learning

With Gene Rice

During the spring semester of 1951 at Harvard's Graduate School of Education, I was assigned to Mrs. Lawrence to complete a practice-teaching requirement. She had been teaching senior English courses at Newton High School in Newton, Massachusetts, for many years. She was about 5 feet 4 inches tall, round, with gray hair, a jolly spirit, and lots of energy. Most of the kids liked her and did their homework. They were working their way through George Eliot's *Silas Marner.* On a Friday afternoon, after a week of observing, she asked me to take over the following Monday. I spent most of the weekend doing careful reading and preparing my lesson plans for the coming week. When I walked into class on Monday morning, I was ready and eager to show off my literary prowess. I was about 15 minutes into describing and diagramming the plot on the board when she rocketed up from the chair at her desk. Jumping up and down in front of me, punching her right fist in the air, she said, "No, no, no. Telling is not teaching!"

She told me to sit down, erased my diagram, and began asking the class pointed questions. Who were the main characters? What three words would describe each one? What single sentence captured the essence of their different relationships? What were the they doing? Why were they doing those things? Do you see any similarities among the characters and your friends, parents, school authorities, or church members? The students had good ideas and were eager to share them. By the end of that hour, Mrs. Lawrence had elicited from the students much richer insights and ideas than had occurred to me. More importantly, they had made connections with their own experiences and relationships. She then asked me to go home and rethink my lesson plans for the following days. I did so, and with her guidance during subsequent weeks, I started to learn how challenging good teaching can be.

"Telling is not teaching" has been the single most important lesson of my 55-year teaching career. I was lucky to get it right at the outset. All my courses at Wesleyan University had been taught traditionally— 50-minute lectures, midterm and final exams, and occasional "pop" quizzes. The only exception was geology, where field trips took us to the surrounding countryside to look at phenomena we were learning about. It is unfortunate that none of those professors, highly knowledgeable and experienced though they were, had ever been exposed to Mrs. Lawrence. I am sure I would have come away with much more learning if they had possessed her teaching skills.

Two years later, during the 1952–1953 academic year, I had the most challenging and formative teaching experience of my young career. Jim O'Brien, principal of Rahway Junior High School, had created a special class of 25 seventh-grade boys and girls whose IQ scores ranged from 57 to 122 whose reading scores ranged from 0 to the tenth-grade level, and whose arithmetic scores ranged from 0 to twelfth-grade level. Among the students were two pre-pubescent, short, skinny, Black, 13-year-old boys; a 14-year-old Italian girl who had a perfect read on me (I can still see her grin when I would explode after she perfectly imitated and ridiculed my efforts to create some order and encourage some learning); a 16-year-old White girl who was the perfect cross between the beauty of Hollywood stars Betty Grable and Marilyn Monroe; and two 16-year-old boys, Rich, White, and Benito, Italian, who enrolled in the Marines when school ended the following June (after spending 9 months honing their capacity to frustrate authority—me—they must have found the Marines to be a cinch). In contrast to Rich and Benito, the boy with an IQ score of 57 was sweet, happy, and totally amenable to what I set him to do. But of course none of these young men could pay attention to much of anything other than the Betty Grable/Marilyn Monroe look-alike.

By collecting all these kids in one class, Jim had made life much easier for numerous other teachers. He gave me a room large enough for different subgroups and a generous budget so I could buy a wide range of workbooks and other materials. These kids were with me all day, every day, except when the circulating music and art teachers came to the school. Then I would get a 50-minute breather while those teachers tore out their hair. I had total control over our schedule. We could go out for recess when the weather was decent and whenever we all needed a break. When the weather was bad we could play basketball, dodge ball, and other games in the gym.

During that year, I often woke up screaming with nightmares, mainly about Rich and Benito. A hug and a pat from Jo would calm me down, and I would wake up again a few hours later, ready for the next day's battles. I could not help liking Rich and Benito, despite their attention deficit disorders, as their behaviors were later labeled. They really did like "Mr. Chickering," no matter how often I sent them down for time-out in the assistant principal's office or threatened them with expulsion. I heard from each of them for several years while they were in and out of the Marines.

I did not realize it then, but these experiences laid the cornerstones of what later became the basis for my future teaching, for my design of Empire State College, and for the subsequent "Seven Principles for Good Practice in Undergraduate Education" (Chickering & Gamson, 1987). I could not ignore the critical importance of being sensitive to individual differences, respecting them, and trying to find or create helpful environments and activities for different individuals or subgroups. I managed our time on task in ways that fit the subject matter and the teaching, rather than forcing all activities into the prescribed 50 minutes that characterized the daily schedule. Using their out-of-class experiences with the school, their peers, their parents, and the community helped the learning become real and pertinent to their daily lives. Having two or three or four students work together on problems or with their workbooks foreshadowed the learning teams and cluster contracts I used with graduate students. This was 20 years before congressional legislation mandating appropriate educational services for all children and before individualized and experiential education was part of secondary or higher education. But it certainly had become powerfully etched on my mind. So I am indebted to Jim and to these "educationally challenged" boys and girls for providing one of the most powerful learning experiences of my professional life.

When I moved to Goddard in 1959 I taught Personality Theory in the fall and Introduction to Psychology in the spring. Classes met for 50 minutes three times a week. It was easy to keep students engaged and active in Personality Theory by having them look at their own prior experiences and their current personal characteristics through the lenses of Freud, Jung, Adler, Horney, and Sullivan. Introduction to Psychology was a different matter. Students came in expecting to learn how to read each others' minds, psych each other out, and be successful participants in Goddard's sexually active culture. Instead, they found laboratory research, mostly with rats, about learning theories, perception, physiology, and motivation. The first time I taught the course I used Krech and Crutchfield's (1958) *Elements of Psychology*, a solid standard textbook. We worked our way through it, chapter by chapter, with quizzes and exercises that we discussed in class. No one worked beyond the minimum. I had given them a pretest when the course started. When I gave it again at the end, the results showed little learning.

I decided to take a dramatically different approach the following spring. That summer I sent for sample copies of 12 different introduction to psychology textbooks. After quick reviews, I put them all on a reserve shelf in our small library. Early in the fall semester I posted a brief course description in the community center. Each student who decided to take the course during the spring semester needed to select and buy a text during the fall. I wrote a one-pager suggesting how to choose their text by comparing the tables of contents and indexes, and reading a chapter or two to see which author they liked best. I also said that they should keep Wednesdays free. We would meet as a group from 8:30 a.m. to 11:30 a.m., and then we would break for lunch and use the rest of the time for individual work until 3:30 p.m.

The 23 students who enrolled had chosen 11 of the 12 textbooks. During our first class meeting, after completing the same pretest I had used before, we compared the tables of contents to see what these varied authors included. Of course, there was a lot of overlap. We created a course outline on the board, listing the topics we would cover and how many sessions we would devote to each. For each topic we would use class sessions (a) to identify the concepts or principles that all the texts agreed were well established, and (b) to identify those points on which texts differed or where prior research was unclear. Participants selected one of those points and looked at pertinent journals to see whether research since the book was written provided further clarification. They prepared brief summaries to share in the following class. Because Goddard's small library had a limited set of journals, most of the students and I traveled to the University of Vermont's Bailey Library on Wednesday afternoons to do this work. Some went there on other days. We concluded each topic area by creating a group summary of how recent research updated the areas of disagreement or uncertainty among the authors.

This whole process created active engagement and participation by all the students—and by me. I was a much more interested teacher and learner and so were all the others. The post-test showed learning gains of 1.5 standard deviations. For readers who are not statisticians, that is an exceptionally large gain. The American Psychological Association Division of Teaching Psychology, where I was an active member, subsequently invited me to present this work in a plenary session for their 1962 annual meeting in Montreal.

I repeated this approach for three additional semesters and my enrollments grew to 35–45 students from among the 200–280 then at the college. At these class sizes, I created learning teams of six or seven, where the members had different texts and each team did what the whole group had done when I had only 23 students.

These experiences enriched my learning about teaching in several important ways. Giving students responsibility for selecting their texts and using texts by diverse authors with their different emphases brought the field alive. Using large and flexible time blocks enabled diverse class activities and much wider participation. Combining both group and individual work—where each person chose a topic of interest and made a clear contribution to the collective effort—strengthened motivation and the quality of individual and team products. Most important, perhaps, I came to realize that my own enjoyment and active engagement made me a much better teacher.

There were two other powerful educational activities at Goddard that enriched my thinking about teaching and learning: weekly faculty meetings and winter weekend workshops. Every Friday afternoon during the fall and spring semesters, all faculty, staff members, and administrators—about 30 of us—gathered in President Tim Pitkin's living room. Sherry and snacks were served from 3:30 to 4:00; then from 4:00 to 6:00 we talked about various educational issues. Tim defined teaching as "creating the conditions for learning." This definition meant that no aspect of the institution was unimportant. Tim led the discussion with sharp Socratic questions. General policies and practices were debated. Results from my evaluative research were questioned and the implications examined. We discussed teaching and learning, experiential programming, advising problems, community government, and the general culture. These conversations were freewheeling and wide ranging. Everyone participated. Their breadth and depth made these the most powerful professional development activities I have ever experienced.

During January and February, while students were on their work terms, Tim, with help from Evelyn Bates, George Beecher, and Forest Davis (academic dean), invited diverse educators from the Northeast to three weekend workshops. These workshops started with dinner on Friday and went through lunch on Sunday. There were typically 25 to 35 participants, who came by train and car.

One workshop always focused on the behavioral sciences and education. For 4 consecutive years it was called the Rogers Conferences. Carl Rogers (1951) developed client-centered therapy (CCT) during the 1940s and 1950s, which is a nondirective approach to therapy. CCT is anchored in the belief that all persons tend to move toward growth and healing, and have the capacity to find their own answers. Above all else, the therapist seeks to provide an accepting and understanding climate. This nondirective approach is very appealing because clients control both the content and the pace. The therapist isn't evaluating them in any way, trying to figure them out, or provide advice. This orientation was totally consistent with Dewey's (1938) view that learning is reconstructing experience, and with Goddard's learner-centered approach. Carl came for each weekend, and we wrestled with the implications of his therapeutic approach for higher education and for Goddard.

Another weekend focused on psychoanalytic concepts and education, where we examined the implications of the work of Freud, Jung, Adler, Sullivan, and others. The third was called Current Educational Issues. Those weekend immersions, filled with frank exchanges among diverse, experienced administrators and teachers, expanded my conceptual horizons and deepened my awareness of the complexities and potentials of my chosen career.

The Project on Student Development and my year as Visiting Scholar at the American Council on Education (ACE) took me out of active teaching for 5 years, from 1964 to 1969. But I spent the 4 project years looking closely at the educational policies and practices, institutional cultures, teaching practices, and consequent outcomes at diverse institutions. I was heavily immersed in reading pertinent literature and studying the limited impact of teaching through lectures, texts, midterms, and final exams. I reported on that research in a variety of journals and at diverse professional meetings. Pulling my ideas together for *Education and Identity* (Chickering, 1969), with its seven vectors for student development, created a theoretical framework—and implications for higher education policies and practices—that has supported my work for the more than 40 years since then.

By 1971 Ernie Boyer had become chancellor of the State University of New York (SUNY) system. The British Open University had brought higher education to England's taxi drivers, farmers, and housewives 2 years earlier. Ernie hired me as the founding academic vice president to create a new SUNY college—Empire State—to serve the diverse educational needs of adults throughout the state. Based on the experiences I shared above, my orientation was anchored in four critical propositions. Learning that lasts and attendant personal development require: (a) respecting and responding to individual differences, (b) giving students responsibility for designing their learning and pursuing it, (c) letting students use flexible time frames appropriate to their purposes, and (d) providing support from a well-informed, concerned teacher.

I was convinced that the British Open University approach of correspondence courses designed by faculty experts and driven by weekly television programs would not well serve the diverse learners across the state of New York. That conviction was confirmed when Jo and I spent a week visiting the institution, hosted by Chancellor William Perry. By 1971, the University Without Walls movement that Tim Pitkin had helped start, based on Goddard's low-residency adult-learner programs, was growing rapidly across the country. In fact, there was a unit at Skidmore College in Saratoga Springs, New York, where we set up Empire State's home offices in a former Skidmore library. The varied University Without Walls programs gave us a short history of experiences to build on, in addition to my own principles.

With President James Hall, with some strong faculty members whom I had come to know from the small Project colleges and elsewhere, and with John Hall and Forest Davis, former Goddard administrators, we created an institution authorized to offer an associate of arts and sciences degree, a bachelor of arts degree in science, and professional studies degrees. Each person designed an individual degree program, pursued through individual learning contracts that could range in length from 1 to 6 months, full or half time. Each contract called for responses to four questions: What are your purposes? What learning activities will you pursue? What resources will you use? How will you evaluate whether you have achieved your purposes?

We did not award credits. Students enrolled either full time or half time, avoiding the totally ambiguous and variable convention of allocating academic credit. We also awarded up to the equivalent of 3 years toward a BA degree or 1.5 years toward an AA degree for learning based on prior work and life experiences. Students could leave and return with minimal red tape. We were regionally accredited by the Middle States Association of Colleges and Schools in our fourth year. Our degree completion rate at the end of 5 years was 93%.

We required that the president mentor at least three students and that the academic vice president and the vice president for financial affairs each mentor five, so that all of us top administrators had direct experiences with our students and with this new educational approach. I thoroughly enjoyed working with my learning-contract students. I had worked with Goddard's traditional-aged undergraduates designing and pursuing independent studies, so I had relevant prior experience. But these adult Empire State students, whose average age was 35, broadened the kinds of prior experiences and ongoing work, community, and family contexts they brought to their studies, which enhanced how conceptual material could be applied and processed. This let us design educationally powerful contracts directly relevant to their ongoing, real-life situations. The most challenging part of creating a learning contract was, and remains, articulating the evaluation criteria against which judgments would be made as to how well the purposes have been achieved. This complex issue still plagues all kinds of teaching. You can read many syllabi and find no publicly stated criteria for evaluation. "I know it when I see it," is the dominant faculty response.

In 1977, I left Empire State. Jo and I went to what was then

Memphis State University in Tennessee, she to work as a counselor in the Student Development Center and I to direct the Center for the Study of Higher Education and teach in the graduate program. I taught one course each semester: Comparative Higher Education in the fall semester; Ages, Stages, and Styles in the spring semester. This teaching built on the four principles I had articulated for Empire State—with one important addition.

In response to a request from Jossey-Bass Publishers, I was putting together a book titled *The Modern American College*. In doing so, I had run into David Kolb's (1976, 1984) experiential learning theory and his *Learning Styles Inventory* (1976). His thinking and research were based on Dewey's progressive education. I reached Kolb at the Massachusetts Institute of Technology (MIT), and he agreed to contribute a chapter. His "experiential learning cycle" starts with concrete experience. Then come reflective observation, abstract conceptualization, and active experimentation. When you have completed this cycle, you are ready to address new experiences with increased knowledge and a wider repertoire of behavioral alternatives (Kolb, 1976). Kolb's research, with his *Learning Styles Inventory,* had shown that persons differ in their preferred styles and, further, that preferred styles differ with various professions. For me, this clearly was a domain of individual differences that I needed to respect and recognize in my teaching. It also provided a useful heuristic for the general design of my courses and for designing particular units within the larger whole. Equally important, it provided a basis for designing the professional development workshops I was doing at diverse colleges and universities in the United States and abroad.

Now I had the basic elements that governed my last teaching assignments, not only at Memphis State but also at George Mason University, where I moved in 1987 as a University Professor. In that role I reported to the president and served half time as an internal consultant for varied innovative programs. Because of those responsibilities, I taught only one course each semester, Leadership and Organizational Behavior in Higher Education. The two courses at Memphis State and the one course at George Mason shared several basic characteristics. I combined group work and individual learning contracts. The learning contracts gave me a way to recognize and respect individual differences in prior learning, in special interests and motives, in working contexts, and in learning styles. The group work dominated the first half of the course while learning contracts were being designed. It tapered off as the learning contracts took more time and effort. At both institutions, I could almost feel these advanced graduate students pursuing doctoral degrees sweating and shaking when they first confronted the learning contracts. This was the first time, after 8 or more years of higher education, they had been asked to articulate purposes for their own learning, describe the resources and activities they would use, and evaluate how well they achieved their purposes.

We used large time blocks. At Memphis State we met from 5:30 p.m. to 9:00 p.m. on Friday nights and from 8:00 a.m. to 12:00 p.m. on Saturdays. In the Deep South, in the fall, nothing happened on Saturday afternoons except football. At George Mason, in northern Virginia, we met from 8:30 a.m. to 4:30 p.m. on Saturdays. We had five of these long sessions every 3 weeks after an initial evening meeting. These large chunks of class time let us do interactive and reflective exercises, watch films and listen to tapes, and hear individual and group reports. The 3-week intervals gave ample time for extensive preparation and a wide range of experiential and reflective activities.

During our opening 3-hour session, everyone took Kolb's Learning Styles Inventory, and I posted each person's preferred style on a single sheet of newsprint so we all could see the diversity. Then I explained how my general course design, combining readings, field observations, and application activities, encompassed the full cycle and responded to their diverse learning styles. I also distributed the learning-contract forms and discussed its parts, giving examples and soliciting some of their own ideas. I emphasized that these contracts served two purposes: each person could pursue in depth some particular aspect of the course that was of special interest, and each could design activities and resources either to fit his or her preferred learning style or to strengthen some other approach to learning. If an individual found another person or two who shared the same interest, together they could create a cluster contract where each participant's work would be spelled out and its contribution to the whole made clear.

After a short break, we leafed through a 93-page course workbook I had made available at nominal cost through the university bookstore. The workbook described my purposes for the course, the basic principles behind its design, the readings required for each session, the exercises, field observations, and reflections that were to be submitted for evaluation with the criteria and score ranges I would use. Anyone who met those evaluative criteria for all the exercises, and whose learning contract fulfilled its purposes, would get an A. There was no grading on a curve.

After clarifying any questions, I indicated that I would be creating learning teams that would include persons with (a) diverse learning styles and (b) similar learning-contract interests. These teams were to serve three purposes. Members would (a) share substantive suggestions for resources and activities as learning contracts were being designed, (b) help each other with the preparatory exercises and activities if some member needed assistance, and (c) be a source of emotional support to the extent that was needed. Time was set aside for team meetings during our Saturday sessions, but the teams were free to work together between classes if they wished. To end this first session, I distributed 3-by-5-inch cards and asked them to give me their contact information and their initial thinking about a learning-contract topic. I used this information and their learning style scores to create the initial learning teams and distributed the team member assignments at our next meeting. Both the learning team composition and the learning-contract topics were open to change if further experience warranted.

Obviously, numerous details varied as this basic approach played itself out at Memphis State and at George Mason. The readings, field observations, reflective activities, exercises, and class sessions differed for each course workbook. Changes also occurred as a function of group dynamics among these experienced professional men and women. Over time, I learned better what worked and what did not, and was able to sharpen my own ability to implement my basic underlying educational principles. For two successive semesters, I co-taught the Leadership and Organizational Behavior course with a doctoral student who was the human resources development director for a large Virginia corporation. Her corporate leadership and organizational development perspectives expanded the range of potential applications and practices for the other students, most of whom were in schools or colleges.

I taught my favorite course of all time in the spring of 1989—Strengthening Adult Motivation to Learn—with a sharp young woman who was a vice president at Northern Virginia Community College. It was designed primarily for community college faculty members, and we had 24 students from diverse Virginia and Maryland institutions. As with my other courses, after an initial evening meeting, we met five times on Saturdays during the semester. This enabled faculty members distant from George Mason to take the course. They often drove up Friday night and stayed with a friend, and stayed over Saturday night to work in the library or pursue other activities. Participants selected a course they were teaching. We worked our way through Ray Wlodkowski's (1985) book, *Enhancing Adult Motivation to Learn*, for which the course was named, sharing ways in which the beginnings, middles, and endings of their courses could be revised to increase and sustain motivation, not only throughout the course but also to continue learning afterward. For their learning contracts, each participant selected a course to teach the following summer or fall and redesigned it in the light of their experiences during the semester. The evaluation section of their contracts described the data they would collect and the criteria they would use to judge whether these new motivational strategies actually increased student motivation and performance. And the part I liked best was that all students got an incomplete grade that would stand until after they had taught the course and submitted their contract with its evaluation. Needless to say, George Mason's registrar was not delighted by this strategy, but with a nudge from the dean and provost, the registrar put up with it. Everyone completed the course and almost all earned A's. Over the next few years, I ran into some of those students at local, regional, and national conferences. They all testified as to the enduring impact of that experience on their teaching. What more could a devoted teacher ask?

Now, after all those experiences, I would not say that I have learned to teach. I would not claim that I have mastered the complexities of this rewarding and exciting mix of intellectual, interpersonal, and emotional challenges. But if I were asked to teach a group of students again, I would use this basic approach.

Gene Rice, through his own teaching and administrative roles in experimental programs, his research and writing, and his being director of a national forum on faculty roles and rewards for 10 years under the aegis of the American Association for Higher Education, is well positioned to put my particular teaching journey in the context of the wide range of changes that have occurred during the last 50 years.

Gene

If I were to choose a title for this chapter of Arthur Chickering's professional life, I would take it from the words of Chick's practice-teaching supervisor at Newton High School, Mrs. Lawrence: "No, no, no. Telling is not teaching!" Chick entered American higher education just at the time when the whole focus was on faculty—on what they know, who they are, and what they do. This was *The Academic Revolution* that Jencks and Riesman wrote about in 1968. The last four decades of the 20th century, when Chick's leadership was so critical, was the time when American universities and colleges struggled with the shift from a concentration on faculty to the centrality of students—their development and learning.

Chick's professional story is a powerful statement of how his influential intellectual constructs (theory) grew out of lived experience. When I see these connections sketched out, I'm not only moved, but I'm also convinced of what a vital contribution they are to the theory-practice debate intensifying in American higher education. They provide support for John Saltmarsh's contention in Chapter 4 that the "Seven Principles for Good Practice in Undergraduate Education" (Chickering & Gamson, 1987) are "as much drawn from evidence-based practice as from practice-based evidence."

My own attempt to put Chick's account into a larger context is also grounded not only in my intense interest in social theory and the contemporary history of American higher education, but also in my own experience, which in many ways paralleled his, although a few years later. In this chapter Chick writes about the impact of his early teaching experience at Goddard, his explicit devotion to progressive education, the influence of Dewey, and Dewey's (1938) principle tenet— learning is the reconstruction of experience. During that same period, I was in an experimental college in California—Raymond College at the University of the Pacific. In the mid-1970s, when Chick was the founding academic vice president at Empire State, I was the program officer at the Danforth Foundation assigned to monitor the grant to Empire State that contributed to the establishment of its Center for Individualized Education. Later, I was dean of the faculty and vice president for academic affairs at Antioch College. The parallels between my experiences at Raymond and Antioch and Chick's work at Goddard and Empire State are, in detail, striking. I remember sitting in Provost Warren Bryan Martin's living room (Raymond College) having a long faculty conversation with Goddard President Tim Pitkin—drinking sherry just as Chick had—talking about the reform of higher education: learning communities, community government (colleges as laboratories for democracy), independent study, work-study programs, and holistic education. In many ways, Chick not only contributed to shaping the reform period of the latter part of the 20th century, but was profoundly shaped by the changes taking place—his telling the unfolding of his life's story helps us see this interaction.

In their study of experimental colleges, titled *The Perpetual Dream*, Grant and Riesman (1979) argued that colleges like Goddard, Raymond, Antioch (and this applied later to Empire State) were telic in nature. They challenged the emerging purposes of the research university model and proposed instead to focus on what was happening to students—undergraduate education, particularly. Chick's work and the large cadre of institutions he influenced were *not* revolutionary; they were counter-revolutionary. They came into being in opposition to the growing strength and influence of the larger research universities.

Chick's orientation to learning and the kinds of institutions that were attracted to it were shaped against a rapidly rising academic hegemony dominated by an increasingly professionalized, research-oriented, discipline-driven, specialized faculty being produced by the rapidly expanding graduate programs of the postwar, post-Sputnik era.

During the period of prosperity in higher education—particularly the 1960s and early 1970s—the growth of graduate programs affected both undergraduate students (herded into large lecture halls staffed by one faculty member) and a cadre of exploited teaching assistants—an especially effective business model. As Mrs. Lawrence told young Chick: "Telling is not teaching!"

The higher education that emerged in the United States from that yeasty period following World War II contained deep structural contradictions. Burton Clark (1987), one of several talented sociologists devoted to understanding this period, wrote of the "paradox of academic work" (p. 98). On the one hand is the structural hierarchy and competition leading to a higher education system that depends on research and comes to be regarded as the envy of the world; and, on the other, is an intentionally diverse and inclusively open system that requires that attention be paid to the quality of teaching and student learning. Clark's conclusion borders on the cynical—"This is the way the system operates." Clark warned:

> Statesmen bent on major repairs soon find that their categorical imperatives, couched in the "musts" and "shoulds" of the rhetoric of reform, stumble over an inability to state "how" the incentives that decisively affect the behavior of institutions and professor might be changed. (p. 100)

Chick is one of those statesmen and there were musts and shoulds aplenty in his work, but he went on to address the organizational- and professional-development implications of his reform commitments. From Tim Pitkin and others, Chick had learned well that learning is by design. Nowhere was this more evident than in his work at Empire State, where he and his colleagues pioneered in structuring a program in individualized learning for adults. The Danforth grant that I monitored at Empire State focused on preparing faculty to teach in a context where learning contracts were central—theory and practice came together. Because Chick continued to write and teach while he was working as an administrator, his thought and practice had a major impact on developing movements, not only on student affairs (see Chapter 7), but also organizational and professional development, as well as what was also known as adult development. The influence on the emergence of the Professional and Organizational Development Network in Higher Education (POD) was especially important.

The significance of Chick's leadership in bringing together the compilation *The Modern American College* when he did—1981—can hardly be overstated. Chick provided intellectual support for a budding transformational period in American higher education. His publication of Bill Perry's (1981) chapter, "Cognitive and Ethical Growth: The Making of Meaning," breathed new life into the Perry work. The volume introduced Carol Gilligan to higher education and reignited the interest in moral development. David Kolb's (1981) essay "Learning Styles and Disciplinary Differences" arrived just when the emphasis on adult learning began to take off; re-entry women—as they were called at that time—were flooding into weekend colleges; and different ways of knowing were being widely debated. Kolb provided a theoretical framework for dealing with practical differences in modes of learning, and Chick and his colleagues at Empire State and Memphis State demonstrated how this approach could be built into an individualized and experience-based curricula. They also experimented with organizational structures needed to support such an approach.

Standing behind so much that Chick accomplished in his practice—institution building—and his reflection on theory is the influence of John Dewey. Throughout his career, Chick continued to raise the larger question of the relationship between education and democracy. Again, his early teaching experience at Goddard had a lasting impact. At Goddard, as at other experiments in progressive education, the ideas of Dewey were resuscitated—at Antioch this was very explicit and intentional. Dewey had taken the key elements of democracy—freedom and equality—and given them new meaning. Freedom became not just freedom *from* (e.g., tyranny, oppression) but freedom *to*—freedom to grow and develop, freedom to learn as individuals, as institutions, and as a society. Dewey also gave new meaning to equality: not just to be the same, but to celebrate our differences and learn in community, to confront our differences and build a rich mosaic that strengthens our democracy and our humanity. Whether it was at Goddard, ACE, Empire State, Memphis State, or later at George Mason, this orientation to learning was central.

In shifting the focus from faculty to student development and learning, Chick continued to maintain a balance between substantive intellectual content and process. The temptation—to which many in the education reform movement yielded—was to demean faculty and their insistence on the driving force of disciplinary expertise. Often on campus, a wedge was driven between student affairs (the process of learning) and academic affairs (intellectual content). Chick resisted this enticement and built the integration of content and process into both his writing—*The Modern American College* (Chickering, 1981)—and his campus-based practice. In fact, Chick helped pave the way for the pivotal work of Lee Shulman and the Carnegie Scholars Program when Lee became president and moved the Carnegie Foundation to Stanford University. This work fundamentally challenged the split between pedagogical process and intellectual content that for decades was the albatross around the necks of schools of education. Teaching and learning, for a time at least, was transformed into a serious scholarly enterprise and in some institutions was honored and rewarded as such. Chick had a role in the transformation of this basic approach to teaching and learning.

In 1998 the National Conference of Higher Education, of the American Association for Higher Education, chose as its theme "From Taking Teaching Seriously to Taking Learning Seriously." Conference organizers asked Patricia Cross, who was a professor of higher education at the University of California, Berkeley, to address the question: "What do we know about student learning and how do we know it?" Much of this plenary presentation was structured around Chickering and Gamson's (1987) "Seven Principles for Good Practice in Undergraduate Education." Toward the close of the 20th century and the opening of the next, Chickering and Gamson's list became the starting point for a robust agenda on the research and assessment of undergraduate learning.

In 1995 Robert Barr and John Tagg published an article in *Change* magazine tracing the movement "from teaching to learning" and identifying the components of a new paradigm for undergraduate education. The article identifies major movements driving this transition, and makes clear that the theory and practice that Chick fostered through his life and work are being taken seriously. The learning communities movement that Chick's work encouraged is flourishing. It is not surprising that it rose out of, and continues to have its grounding in, an experimental college—The Evergreen State College—and the leadership there.

The experience-based learning to which Chick was so committed has taken a variety of forms. First, the most influential is the focus on the engagement of the learner, which has been most fully developed by the National Survey of Student Engagement under the leadership of George Kuh (see Chapter 5). The second-most-influential form is the focus on community engagement, a movement that is most broadly identified as service-learning, championed by Campus Compact and best represented by John Saltmarsh (see Chapter 4). These movements are flourishing and well represented in this book. Chick also had a significant impact on the earliest stages of the focus on leadership—a movement that has grown in significance and that took on special importance for Chick while he was teaching at George Mason.

Chick's dissertation topic had a significant impact on his subsequent intellectual development and later contributions to higher education. In his dissertation he explores the gap between the ideal self and the actual self and its influence on academic achievement. Chick notes Piaget's (1954) concept of optimal distance, applied to the balance between challenge and support and contends that this optimal distance leads not only to gains in cognitive learning but to personal transformation. Chick goes on to assert that this principle of optimal support became the cornerstone of his educational orientation. The theme that Chick chose can be traced through the recent leadership literature; for instance, the thesis is central to Mihaly Csikszentmihalyi's work. Csikszentmihalyi has become a kind of intellectual guru for the leadership movement through his work *Creativity* (1996) and his seminal book, *Flow* (1990), which became a bestseller when President and Mrs. Clinton took it on their summer vacation. More recently, Csikszentmihalyi has collaborated with Howard Gardner, of Harvard University, on books concerning business leadership and the making of meaning, and one book on organizational ethics. The interest in leadership has spread widely across professional endeavors, and Chick's early concern for the balance between challenge and support and his concern for developmental readiness have been key principles for higher education. Chick also anticipated the assumption of Csikszentmihalyi (1990) and others in the leadership movement that "repression is not the way to virtue" (p. 115) and, I'm sure, would agree with Csikszentmihalyi's influential statement that "when people restrain themselves out of fear, their lives are by necessity diminished" (p. 115).

At present, Chick's lifelong preoccupation with student learning outcomes has found its most vocal and active advocate in the American Association of Colleges and Universities through Liberal Education and America's Promise. This program brings together the expanding global interest in essential learning outcomes. It now encompasses George Kuh's (2008) important work on student engagement in high-impact practices and has recently initiated the Degree Qualifications Profile, supported by the Lumina Foundation (2011). The whole endeavor is having a major impact internationally on the vigorous quest for quality assurance and transferability.

The public discussion of undergraduate learning is currently dominated by the emergence of massive open online courses (MOOCs). Some have referred to the offering of these courses by the nation's leading universities—e.g., Stanford, Harvard, MIT—as a campus tsunami. It is being seen as both the ultimate in democratizing education and as a possible financial bailout for universities suffering from a devastating recession. In this vigorous, contentious debate, which is becoming increasingly globalized, Chick's earlier work will take on new relevance. His grappling in the early 1960s with the impact of the residential experience on student learning—which led to *Education and Identity* (Chickering, 1969)—his research at ACE, and especially his efforts at Empire State to honor individual differences in the learning process and prepare faculty (mentors) to take student learning seriously have, in recent years, become more important, not less. I anticipate that interest in the individualized learning contract will be resurrected. At least I hope so. In one form or another, the future of online learning is already here. The quality of that future depends in large measure both on how vigorously we press the questions that absorbed Chick throughout his life and on how seriously we take the concern for individual student development and learning to which he gave priority.

The purpose of this reflective addition to this chapter is neither to laud Chick's many contributions—although there is ample opportunity for that—nor to assess the importance of his achievements. The intent of this effort is to place his work in context. Chick and others of us who are in his age cohort were enormously privileged—structurally and demographically advantaged. The vision of America as the land of opportunity is borne out in Chick's story, and it is an inspiring one.

To begin one's life in the Depression was, ironically, a gift for those of us who were White and male. There were fewer babies born during that time than at any other in the 20th century. We had what business people call a competitive advantage. The United States, following World War II, entered a period of rapid growth and prosperity, with higher education's being a major driving force. The role of the GI Bill, the education available—Mt. Hermon, Wesleyan, Harvard, Columbia (who could ask for more?)—and the role of mentors who intervened in the life of Chick as a young man were beneficial, indeed. Then in mid-career, at just the most propitious time, higher education expanded with the support of the government (e.g., New York State and FIPSE) and private foundations (Danforth, Ford, Kellogg, Lilly—this list goes on). Add to that the jobs that were available, the publication opportunities, and the vitality of the associational life—we lived privileged lives. The professional advantages of our age cohort were structural, rooted in longstanding social injustices. Young men and women coming along today, particularly contingent faculty who aspire to a life in higher education, will read some of this with a touch of envy and resentment. We can never use the phrase "when I was your age" around young academics without some qualification.

In closing, I want to say a word about Chick's most recent venture: the exploration of the place of spirituality and religion in higher education. He joined a number of others led by Sandy and Lena Astin in generating a national discussion of this controversial issue. I bring this up, in part, because I was privileged to participate in this endeavor, but, more important, because Chick's involvement in this inquiry was an extension of his career-long effort to understand the way college students make meaning of and with their lives.

This inquiry took Chick into yet another group of colleagues and a growing body of literature—another movement. In their empirical work, the Astins demonstrated a growing spiritual hunger emerging among college and university students across the nation and a reluctance on the part of faculty to respond. What emerged was an alternative epistemology, which builds on the assumption of a postmodern academy that was beginning to see that every perspective is rooted in particular personal, social, and cultural conditions. This different approach to knowing—old hat to Chick—realigns the relationship between the academy and the larger questions of meaning. As Sharon Daloz Parks (2000) argued in *Big Questions, Worthy Dreams*, this alternative perspective invites the academic community to bring the strength of contemporary scholarship to the struggles to create a meaningful faith in an openly pluralistic world—a world where every human perspective is incomplete and certainly not value-free. This perspective was fully congruent with Chick's lifelong approach to learning and not only gives voice to racial, ethnic, gendered, and class perspectives that have so often been marginalized by the dominant approach to knowing, but also recognizes the legitimacy and importance of the spiritual and religious dimensions of inquiry—the power of community and commitment in the lives of all of us. The centrality of holistic education that Chick picked up in his early days at Goddard informed, in a new way, this later-life agenda.

When one reflects on Chick's life and work and its close identification with Vermont, it's hard to resist quoting from the memorable lines of Robert Frost's (1936) "Two Tramps in Mud Time":

Only where love and need are one,
And the work is play for mortal stakes,
Is the deed ever really done
For Heaven and the future's sakes. (p. 18)

Art Chickering's life and his important contributions to our understanding of how we learn are mirrored in those lines.

REFERENCES

Barr, R. B., & Tagg, J. (1995). From teaching to learning: A new paradigm for undergraduate education. *Change, 27*(6), 12–25.

Chickering, A. W. (1969). *Education and identity.* San Francisco, CA: Jossey-Bass.

Chickering, A. W. (Ed.). (1981). *The modern American college: Responding to the new realities of diverse students and a changing society.* San Francisco, CA: Jossey-Bass.

Chickering, A. W., & Gamson, Z. (1987). Seven principles for good practice in undergraduate education. *American Association for Higher Education Bulletin, 39*(7), 3–7.

Clark, B. R., (1987). *The academic life: Small worlds, different worlds.* Princeton, NJ: Carnegie Foundation for the Advancement of Teaching.

Csikszentmihalyi, M. (1990). *Flow: The psychology of optimal experience.* New York, NY: Harper & Row.

Csikszentmihalyi, M. (1996). *Creativity: Flow and the psychology of discovery and invention.* New York, NY: HarperCollins.

Dewey, J. (1938). *Experience and education.* New York, NY: Macmillan.

Frost, R. (1936). *A further range.* New York, NY: Henry Holt.

Grant, G., & Riesman, D. (1979). *The perpetual dream: Reform and experiment in the American college.* Chicago, IL: University of Chicago Press.

Jencks, C., & Riesman, D. (1968). *The academic revolution.* Chicago, IL: University of Chicago Press.

Kolb, D. A. (1976). *Learning styles inventory.* Boston, MA: McBer.

Kolb, D. A. (1981). Learning styles and disciplinary differences. In A. W. Chickering (Ed.), *The modern American college: Responding to the new realities of diverse students and a changing society* (pp. 232–255). San Francisco, CA: Jossey-Bass.

Kolb, D. A. (1984). *Experiential learning: Experience as the source of learning and development*. Englewood Cliffs, NJ: Prentice Hall.

Krech, D., & Crutchfield, R. S. (1958). *Elements of psychology*. New York, NY: Alfred A. Knopf.

Kuh, G. (2008). *High-impact educational practices: What they are, who has access to them, and why they matter?* Washington, DC: Association of American Colleges and Universities.

Lumina Foundation. (2011). *The degree qualifications profile*. Indianapolis, IN: Author.

Parks, S. D. (2000). *Big questions, worthy dreams: Mentoring young adults in the search for meaning, purpose, and faith*. San Francisco, CA: Jossey-Bass.

Perry, W. (1981). Cognitive and ethical growth: The making of meaning. In A. W. Chickering (Ed.), *The modern American college: Responding to the new realities of diverse students and a changing society* (pp. 76–116). San Francisco, CA: Jossey-Bass.

Piaget, J. (1954). *The construction of reality in the child*. New York, NY: Ballantine Books.

Rogers, C. (1951). *Client-centered therapy*. Cambridge, MA: Riverside Press.

Wlodkowski, R. J. (1985). *Enhancing adult motivation to learn*. San Francisco, CA: Jossey-Bass.

CHAPTER 7

From Student Services to Student Learning

With Jon Dalton

I n contrast to my work as a teacher, administrator, and researcher, I have never been a student affairs professional. Whatever contributions I have made to that professional domain rest primarily on publications, supplemented with conference presentations, workshops, and institutional consultations. Goddard had no student services professionals, no residence hall assistants, no formally organized student activities. There was a community government, with an elected student council that met with President Tim Pitkin weekly. The elected student chairman presided over the Wednesday evening community meetings, which included students, faculty, administrators, and staff. All faculty members and administrators met weekly with up to 15 advisees and more frequently if called for by the students, or if necessary at the advisor's initiative. During the years I was there Robert Mattuck was director of counseling and we called on him if we needed help. During the Project on Student Development in Small Colleges, from 1965 to 1969, I do not recall any specific meetings with student affairs professionals at participating institutions.

My first formal contact—indeed, my first awareness that there was a student affairs profession—occurred when I spoke at the 1966 annual meeting of the National Association of Women Deans, Administrators, and Counselors (NAWDAC). In the Goddard research and with the project, I used the Omnibus Personality Inventory (OPI). Paul Heist, a creator of OPI and a professor at the University of California, Berkeley, had become a good friend and source of wisdom about higher education research and evaluation. I had shared the powerful test-retest results at Goddard and the dramatic differences among entrants at the diverse colleges participating in the project. He also was aware of the seven vectors that were providing the conceptual framework for my research. In the spring of 1966, he suggested my name to the NAWDAC conference organizer and I accepted an invitation to share my research. My presentation was well received and published in their journal under the title, "The Young Adult: A New Course for the College Personnel Curriculum" (Chickering, 1967c).

I had no further contact with student affairs professionals until I was given the Outstanding Service Award from the National Association of Student Personnel Administrators (NASPA) and was invited to speak at the 1972 annual conference. By then, *Education and Identity* (Chickering, 1969) had become pretty well known to student affairs professionals. With NAWDAC's warm reception and subsequent publication, I felt more comfortable arguing that student services professionals, even more than faculty members or administrators, needed to be knowledgeable about student development so they could respond more effectively when problems occurred and help young adults cope with the challenges of late adolescence. The NASPA audience of mostly older men responded with polite applause. Of course, I had no idea where they were coming from professionally, what their responsibilities were, what kind of graduate programs for these professionals were currently in place. I had not read any of their professional literature, so my comments were grounded in total ignorance. I was just making my pitch, unable to connect it to their work, their administrative responsibilities, or their prior learning. Fortunately, we quickly adjourned to good food with plenty to drink and that conviviality got us through the evening without embarrassment.

Following that conference, I was invited to meet with faculty members and administrators at a few higher education centers—University of Michigan, Bowling Green State University, The University of Iowa, and University of California, Berkeley—to discuss the implications of my work for both their curricula and their research. This was another whole new world for me. I did not know such graduate centers existed, except for my personal interactions with Paul Heist at Berkeley. Totally ignorant about their students or their curricula, once again I found myself at a loss to know what to suggest or how to be useful. I learned much more about the range of services and activities they provided and their substantial history than they learned from me.

During this period, *Education and Identity's* seven vectors had become a useful way for student affairs professionals to frame their roles beyond simply providing services. They began thinking about ways in which student government, residence hall programming, clubs, and other activities could be designed to encourage new dimensions of student development. When I was invited to consult with particular institutions, I always asked to see the annual reports that presented data about their varied programs. I was struck that the only data they reported described the number of programmatic activities and the number of students participating. There were no data about the educational or developmental impact of the programs. I pointed out that this was like evaluating faculty teaching based on seat time for the numbers of students who came to class, without regard to whether any learning occurred. Their challenge was to articulate hoped-for educational or developmental outcomes for the varied program interventions and try to get some data as to whether these were achieved. These outcomes should be associated with the espoused educational goals of the particular college or university. The data could also be used as a framework for collaboration with faculty members: the programmatic activities could provide experiential contexts for the academic work in particular courses and classes.

A weekend workshop I led at Bradford College in the late 1970s illustrates my approach. Then president Art Levine invited me to work with the student affairs professionals to help them better contribute to Bradford's "Practical Liberal Education." Under his leadership, the institution articulated a core that included shared languages (words and numbers), common institutional experiences, common work experiences, common ethics, common planet, and common aesthetics. During the morning session, I shared David Kolb's (1984) experiential learning cycle with its sequence of concrete experience, reflective observation, abstract conceptualization, and active experimentation. We discussed how that conceptual framework might be applied to their key programs. After a lunch break, I listed Bradford's core across the top of a sheet of newsprint and drew lines down the page to create columns. Down the side of the page we listed all the student activities, residence hall programs and such, and drew lines across the sheet to create a matrix of boxes. Next, we discussed which programs and activities might contribute to which elements of the core and checked the appropriate boxes. By the end of the afternoon we had a mix of potential relationships that could guide thinking about how to intentionally use their programming to strengthen one or more of the core elements. As we adjourned, their overnight homework was to think about which academic departments or courses offered content pertinent to the core and which faculty members might be recruited to start integrating the work of one or another course with the varied experiences that student affairs programs provided.

The next morning we distributed copies of Bradford's course catalog to stimulate our thinking and to jog our memories. With the matrix of boxes that associated activities and outcomes, the task was to write in courses, classes, or faculty members who could enrich those varied combinations of activities and outcomes with pertinent reading, writing, reflective journals, and active experimentation. With this conceptual clarification before us, we turned to candid discussion of the political and interpersonal complexities involved in pursuing those potential collaborative relationships with departments and faculty members. Clearly, it made sense to start small, with just a few faculty members who were interested in strengthening their teaching by integrating the experiences that student affairs programming could offer. We shared our thinking with President Levine during the last hour of the morning. He supported this approach and, with his blessing, concrete action planning could begin. Unfortunately, Bradford went broke soon after, and President Levine went to the Harvard Graduate School of Education, so I never learned how that approach turned out. But it has proven useful in workshops with other colleges and universities and in conference presentations.

Prior to publishing *Education and Identity,* I published two articles of interest to student services professionals: "College Residences and Student Development" (Chickering, 1967a), and "Talking with College Students" (Chickering, 1967b). *Education and Identity* triggered a number of my other publications: "College Advising for the 1970s" (Chickering, 1973) and "Education and Identity: Implications for Residence Hall Living" (Chickering, 1974). Presumably on the basis of this work and professional presentations at their annual meetings, in 1980 I was honored to receive the Contribution to Knowledge award from the American College Personnel Association (ACPA).

Further publications resulted in my receiving ACPA's Senior Scholar award in 1984: "Potential Contributions of College Unions to Student Development"(Chickering, 1981); "The Critical Role of Value Development in Student Development"(Thomas, Murrell, & Chickering, 1982); "Education and Identity Revisited"(Thomas & Chickering, 1984a); "Comprehensive Counseling and Support Programs for Adult Learners: Challenge to Higher Education" (Lynch & Chickering, 1984); and "Foundations for Academic Advising" (Thomas & Chickering, 1984b).

After being recognized in "An Interview with Arthur W. Chickering" (Krivoski & Nicholson, 1989), I continued to plug away and published the following articles: "Empowering Lifelong Self Development" (Chickering, 1994); "The University Learning Center: A Driving Force for Collaboration" (Chickering & O'Connor, 1996); "Academic and Student Affairs, Collaboration to Strengthen Liberal Education" (Chickering, 1997); and "Why We Should Encourage Student Activism" (Chickering, 1998). I offer this list of publications to give a sense of my work beyond my initial *Education and Identity*.

When Jo and I moved back to Vermont in 1996, after I retired from George Mason University, my publications pertinent to student affairs ceased for a few years. I took a visiting professor position at the Vermont College campus of Norwich University in Montpelier, just 6 miles from our house. Norwich had purchased Goddard's low-residency programs, the faculty had moved, and Jack Kytle had left the

Goddard presidency to become dean. He employed me part time to lead a task force to design a new doctoral program that would build on their low-residency bachelor's and master's degrees. That work kept my professional juices running for 2 years until the doctoral proposal was ultimately turned down by the Norwich faculty.

In 1995, before we moved back to Vermont, Jon Dalton, vice president for student affairs at Florida State University, had invited me to open his Institute on College Student Values, then held at Wakulla Springs, Florida, a beautiful state park near the coast, not far from Tallahassee. Immersed as I was in the implications of developmental stage theories for higher education, I gave a talk there titled "Moral Responsibility, Human Development, and Higher Education." In 2002, Jon invited me to give another keynote, "Reclaiming Our Soul: Democracy and Higher Education." That year began one of the most enjoyable and productive working relationships of my career. It was during that conference that Jon, Leisa Stamm, and I decided to write a book, *Encouraging Authenticity and Spirituality in Higher Education,* published in 2006.

From 2002 until 2009, Jon invited me to participate in the annual Institute on College Student Values as faculty in residence. In that capacity, I attended and sometimes commented on plenary presentations and workshop presentations. Jon also organized 7:00 p.m. meetings with their student affairs graduate students, in which our conversations were enriched by local pizzas and soft drinks. I also usually offered brief wrap-up comments at the end of the closing institute lunch. With help from the John F. Templeton Foundation, Jon started the *Journal of College and Character* in 2004. Ably edited by Pamela Crosby, it publishes Institute on College Student Values presentations and articles submitted by student affairs professionals, faculty members, and administrators. As is quite apparent by now, I like to write, so the journal became a good outlet for some of my thinking and professional concerns. My curriculum vitae at the end of this book contains a complete list of articles published in the *Journal of College and Character*. A selected list of my articles includes: "Encouraging Authenticity and Spirituality in Higher Education" (Chickering, 2003); "Curricular Content" (Chickering, 2004a); "Policy Issues: Legislative and Institutional" (Chickering, 2004b); "Authenticity and Spirituality in Higher Education: My Orientation" (Chickering, 2006a); "Strengthening Spirituality and Civic Engagement in Higher Education" (Chickering, 2006b); "On What Basis Do You Vote? Developmental Perspectives for a Pluralistic Democracy" (Chickering, 2007).

"A Retrospect on Higher Education's Commitment to Moral and Civic Education" (Chickering, 2010b) is an edited version of the opening keynote celebrating the 20th anniversary of the institute. In my judgment, the institute has been one of the most powerful forces for keeping character development—historically one of the key purposes of higher education—alive in colleges and universities throughout the country. My comments were titled "Honoring Jon Dalton." I said, in part:

> During its 20 years, for many of us, working in less than en-
> thusiastic or hospitable home environments, this annual
> event has provided not only intellectual stimulation and use-
> ful contacts. More importantly perhaps, it has provided emo-
> tional support to sustain the cool passion we need to tackle
> the forces of institutional and systemic inertia, and in some
> cases, active opposition. . . .

> I would like to close these opening comments on a personal
> note. In my now 51 years of work in higher education, argu-
> ing for greater attention to "the affective domain" for help-

ing students address issues of purpose and meaning, integrity and identity, and spiritual growth, I have never felt as strong a sense of urgency about the values orientation and potential impact of this institute as I do now. (Chickering, 2010a)

I feel that sense of urgency as strongly now as did then.

After that anniversary celebration, Jon handed off the administration of the institute to colleagues at Florida State in the Division of Student Affairs. Jon and I keep in touch, and I cannot think of a better person to put my work in the context of changes in student affairs during the last 50 years.

Jon

Education and Identity (Chickering, 1969) influenced the three major conceptual paradigms that have shaped the modern mission of student affairs: student services, student development, and student learning. Student affairs administration is still a relatively new professional field in American higher education, although its primary functions are rooted in some of the earliest American and European colleges. The profession emerged in America in the late 19th century at a time of changing priorities in colleges (Sandeen, 2011). College faculty members were increasingly preoccupied with teaching and research and no longer had time to attend to the personal concerns of students. The public, however, and parents in particular continued to feel a need for colleges to care for students' welfare and to intervene when student problems arose. Consequently, colleges accepted an in loco parentis responsibility for guiding and nurturing students as a necessary requisite of their mission. In response to the growing need to care for students' personal welfare, a new category of college staff emerged that came to be identified as *student affairs*.

The concern for serving the welfare of students developed over time into a wide range of institutional services led by student affairs staff whose primary focus was serving students' needs and welfare in ways that enhanced their overall educational experience. The earliest conceptual paradigm for the work of student affairs was *student services*, a loosely framed philosophy that emphasized a concern for the holistic needs and well-being of students in all areas of college life not directly affiliated with the academic functions of the institution.

Despite its growing presence and influence in American colleges (and increasingly in colleges and universities in other countries), the field of student affairs initially struggled to clearly define its central mission and relevance in higher education, especially when much of higher education moved away from an in loco parentis relationship with students. The field matured significantly during the last half of the 20th century, and its evolution as a profession was advanced considerably by the intellectual contributions and personal leadership of Arthur Chickering. In the remainder of this chapter, I will explore several pivotal changes in the intellectual frameworks used by student affairs and suggest how the conceptual contributions of Chickering, especially in his seminal work *Education and Identity*, served to promote these critical developments.

When I began work in student affairs at the University of Kentucky in 1963, not many of my colleagues had student affairs professional degrees. At that time, student affairs departments in most colleges and universities were loose confederations of services organized around a common connection to serving students. There was little in the way of an integrating philosophy or intellectual paradigm that defined student services and connected student affairs staff to each other and to the educational mission of the university. Student services were usually organized as independent service delivery operations that were clearly important to students but regarded by many, if not most, faculty and administrators as peripheral to the central educational functions of the institution. The specific student services included in student affairs departments varied considerably from campus to campus depending upon how presidents and other institutional leaders chose to package them.

Few individuals who worked in student services in the 1950s and 1960s had professional graduate training in programs of higher education or student affairs administration. Many individuals came to student affairs work from the three M's: military, management, and ministry. Perhaps the most important credentials these early student affairs leaders possessed were their ability to relate to young people and their expertise as program leaders and managers. Student affairs as a professional field of study did not fully emerge until the last half of the 20th century. Michigan State University, for example, had one of the early graduate programs in student affairs administration—and this was not founded until 1949. Most student affairs professional degree programs evolved during the last half of the 20th century.

Over the past 50 years, many new and diverse student affairs programs and services have evolved, including women's centers, computer centers, child care programs, civic education and service programs, fitness centers, diversity programs, research and assessment programs, living-learning centers, and development offices, to name a few. New student affairs titles, programs, and services have regularly appeared on the scene and many traditional services have been renamed, reframed, and reorganized in an ongoing process of updating and adjustment. Consequently, the field of student affairs has developed through a constant process of evolution, and these persistent changes have made it difficult to clearly define and promote a core of essential professional functions and roles that are shared by all practitioners (Dalton & Crosby, 2011).

Student services was the earliest paradigm used to describe the collection of institutional programs and activities loosely organized around the purpose of serving student welfare. These services evolved over time in response to critical student needs such as housing, health, spiritual guidance, counseling, financial aid, recreation, and social life. They were justified as necessary support for students to facilitate their success in the rapidly changing higher education environment. The values associated with the student services paradigm emphasized benevolence and care for students, advocacy of students needs, and affirmation of students' holistic development.

Student support, welfare, and needs were at the core of the student services movement and helped frame and define the earliest intellectual paradigm of student affairs work. The student services paradigm gave a useful practical focus to the work of student affairs, but it had one serious limitation: it had little grounding in educational theory or research. This lack of a commonly accepted theoretical framework and research literature hampered the development of the profession and weakened the impact of its contributions to higher education.

The second student affairs paradigm took shape out of the transition from student services to *student development*. Chickering noted earlier in this chapter that he was almost completely unaware of the student affairs profession when he published *Education and Identity* in 1969. His lack of awareness about student affairs staff and functions on campus was not unusual, especially for faculty members. Student affairs staff and programs were often invisible to faculty, whose focus centered largely on their academic discipline, teaching, and research responsibilities. My own recent experience illustrates this point. When I moved from the role of vice president for student affairs to a full-time faculty position, I observed that the domain of student affairs I had left behind dropped almost immediately from my personal radar screen. From the vantage point of my faculty duties—teaching, research, writing, grading, and attending faculty meetings—I had very few encounters with student affairs programs and services. Little if any attention was given to student affairs functions or activities in the routine of faculty life. It was stunning for me to recognize how completely the world of student affairs I had just left behind had evaporated from my landscape. I experienced in a more visceral way how and why faculty members so often fail to understand and appreciate the educational contributions of student affairs. The *silo* effect created by institutional bureaucracy, academic specialization, and the compartmentalization of student services on campus promotes separation and isolation. This is especially a problem for student affairs, which has long been viewed as operating on the periphery of the academic mission of the academy.

Despite Chickering's unfamiliarity with student affairs, his *Education and Identity* fortuitously provided one of the most important conceptual cornerstones for the development of contemporary student affairs work. Almost immediately, it helped to move student affairs from a services paradigm to a student development orientation. The theoretical framework of *Education and Identity* succinctly described the development of young adults in higher education settings and provided student affairs staff with much-needed conceptual tools for their work. Nothing before *Education and Identity* had so clearly described, with such straightforward and accessible language, the educational and personal development of students during college. The seven-vector theory fit the practical work of student affairs, and staff seized upon it because it offered them a practical blueprint for the purposes and practices of the profession.

Education and Identity helped to move the student affairs profession from an orientation of a disconnected delivery of diverse student services to a much more educationally centered and connected role. Chickering's seven vectors accurately described the most important and characteristic struggles of students in the college environment. They portrayed student development as a flexible process of growth and maturation in which students progressed at their own pace in response to the conditions they encountered. The tasks, or vectors, that Chickering used to describe students' development in college rang true for student affairs staff; they confirmed the behaviors they witnessed among students. Consequently, the theoretical framework conveyed in *Education and Identity* enabled student affairs staff to see the evidences of student development in more practical ways than they had been able to observe before.

One of the virtues of the vector model of development was that it provided a flexible construct for understanding the many variables that influenced students' development in college. The vector model focused specifically on students in the college environment and provided sufficient flexibility to be applicable across the many individual differences increasingly found in college populations. *Education and Identity* was also published at a historically opportune time of expanding diversity in American higher education. Affirmative action, the women's movement, and the gay rights movement all brought to colleges and universities an agenda of concern for the rights, welfare, and representation of diverse students on campus. Student affairs professionals were often the front-line staff in higher education who were called upon to respond to civil rights issues and take the lead in advocating for a more pluralistic campus. The vector model of student development was timely in that it provided a conceptual framework for student affairs work that recognized individual student differences and described an open, nonlinear process of change and growth during the college years.

Education and Identity likewise contributed to the development of the student affairs profession by helping to lay a foundation for a more formal student affairs research agenda on student learning and development. The vector theory helped to provide a very useful rubric for research; its theoretical framework and constructs helped to provide groundwork for the scientific study of college student experiences, especially the importance of out-of-class experiences to the overall learning and development of college students.

Student affairs had already formalized its commitment to the holistic development of students in *The Student Personnel Point of View* (American Council on Education, 1937), one of the most important foundational documents of the student affairs profession. That document asserted: "The concept of education is broadened to include attention to the student's well-rounded development physically, socially, emotionally, and spirituality, as well as intellectually" (p. 1). Commitment to the holistic development of students had been a consistent core value of the student affairs profession and may be one of its most important contributions to contemporary undergraduate education in America. This concern for holistic student development was embodied and promoted in the values framework of Chickering's vector theory.

Higher education has been good at disseminating disciplinary knowledge but has paid far less attention to how students use what they learn to create personal meaning and positive social structures (Chickering, Dalton, & Stamm, 2006). For much of the history of higher education in America the college campus was divided into two separate worlds of classroom and extra-curriculum. *Education and Identity* documented the importance of including personal values, meaning, and purpose as part of educational experiences. Chickering's description of student development recognized the implicit connections between students' academic preparation and their individual searches for meaning and purpose that often occurred in campus settings outside the classroom. His view of student development also stressed the need to integrate both of these domains of students' lives in order to enhance the educational impact of college. Student development theory helped to connect these two worlds for student affairs staff and to make the case that all of the campus is important for learning. It incorporated the core value of holistic education and provided a conceptual framework for integrating the cognitive and affective dimensions of students' learning in college.

The growing recognition of the powerful educational influences of out-of-class college environments also helped validate the educational role of student affairs staff. That staff recognized very early in the development of the profession that the collegiate social involvement—friendships, faith, fun—all play important roles in the academic success of students. These diverse experiences, many of which occur outside the classroom, contribute to the holistic development of students (Chickering, Dalton, & Stamm, 2006).

Chickering's vector theory did much to "connect the dots" of integrated learning, to show that higher education works best when it creates an "intricate system of interlocking arrangements" for students that reinforces and enhances learning (Chickering, 1969, p. 323). It demonstrated that the experiences college students have in nonacademic arenas such as residence halls and social peer groups can influence the development of intellectual competence by "setting the context" for learning (Chickering, 1969, p. 221). Thus, Chickering recognized very early what we have come to accept as a cornerstone of undergraduate education: that effective higher education requires a whole-campus approach to student learning. This recognition of the interconnectedness of learning experiences in college was an important influence in creating greater acceptance of the educational contributions of student affairs in the higher education setting.

That increased acceptance lead to the third paradigm, to a shift from student development to *student learning*. While student development theory provided useful conceptual frameworks for understanding and explaining the challenges and tasks that most students confront during the college years, there were difficulties in substantiating empirically many of its descriptions and claims. The concept of development, for example, was so encompassing in its reach and so indeterminate in meaning that researchers and practitioners found it difficult to translate into discrete, measurable outcomes. Practitioners found the language of student development to be useful in understanding the "big picture" of their efforts with students, but in practice it was difficult to use the theory to measure specific outcomes of their developmental efforts. Faculty found the language of student development hard to understand and often accused student affairs staff of using a special kind of jargon that seemed to have little direct connection to students' academic work or formal educational development.

Consequently, the use of student development theory attracted some influential critics, including Bloland, Stamatakos, and Rogers (1994) who argued persuasively that developmental theory was fatally flawed and should be abandoned by student affairs practitioners. The authors argued that "we have cultivated an expertise that was not requested, is not sought out, and for which there is little recognition or demand" (p. 4). Critics also claimed that an expertise based on a foundation of developmental theory had limited practical value in the everyday work of student affairs staff and was little understood and valued by colleagues in higher education. These criticisms, combined with a powerful new movement of educational accountability and outcomes assessment in the 1980s and 1990s, led to a shift in focus in student affairs from student development to student learning.

The intellectual shift from student development to student

learning was an important transition for a student affairs profession that sought to build on its past knowledge base. In *Learning Reconsidered: A Campus-wide Focus on the Student Experience* (Keeling, 2004), this transition was described not as a departure from past student affairs paradigms but as an evolution to a fuller and more complete expression of student affairs' historical focus on the whole student.

Learning Reconsidered defined learning as a "comprehensive, holistic, transformative activity that integrates academic learning and student development processes that have often been considered separate, and even independent of each other" (Keeling, 2004, p. 4). Proponents of this new paradigm argued for the "integration of all of higher education resources in the education and preparation of the whole student" (p. 3). The new conceptual focus on *student learning* accomplished two objectives that were historically important to the student affairs profession: (a) it married academic learning and student development, two goals that had often been considered separate, into one integrated, holistic educational process; and (b) it provided a strong conceptual rationale for student affairs as a formal partner in the collegiate educational process. By placing the student squarely at the center of collegiate educational efforts, it both reaffirmed student affairs' enduring concern for the holistic welfare of students and provided a powerful rationale for connecting the work of student affairs to the broader campus curriculum. It sought to shift the mission and focus of student affairs work to the central learning enterprise of higher education. The new paradigm had the advantage of positioning the work of student affairs within the mainstream educational mission of higher education. It stressed the critical role of student affairs programs and services in involving and engaging students in ways that helped them invest themselves more strategically in the learning process and integrate the full range of their educational experiences.

Notwithstanding the strengths of the student learning paradigm, it has not been without its critics. Some opponents, especially from the faculty ranks, continue to argue that student affairs is not a legitimate partner in student learning (National Association of Scholars, 2008) and that the training and expertise of student affairs staff do not equip them for educational leadership. This type of criticism of student affairs is likely to continue, especially by those who regard learning as primarily a cognitive process that can and should only be cultivated in formal academic settings. But this more narrow and limited view of learning is challenged by contemporary research that finds the greatest gains in student learning are facilitated by the integrative and holistic approach of the student learning paradigm.

Just as Chickering's vector theory helped to lay the groundwork for student development theory, it also has been influential in promoting the learning paradigm by the manner in which it connects personal and intellectual development in the formulation of the vectors of student development. For example, the first vector, *competence*, directly links the cognitive and affective domains of student learning. The competence vector includes the three developmental dimensions of intellectual, physical, and social abilities. Here we see how Chickering connects intellectual tasks such as acquiring knowledge and critical thinking to the broader personal-growth concerns of students. The competence vector explicitly recognizes that the personal and social concerns of students can directly enhance or detract from their intellectual development.

In his research for *Education and Identity*, Chickering recognized that at that time there was little evidence about the relationship of intellectual development and other aspects of student change in college. He found few theories about relationships between intellectual development and other components of student development. Then, the primary focus of most research on student development was on intellectual competence, and few formal research efforts had been made to relate it to other aspects of change. In *Education and Identity* Chickering illustrates how intellectual competence interacts with and is affected by other aspects of student development, particularly interpersonal competence and physical and manual skills. He argued that the development of intellectual competence varies "with the particular requirements and conditions set for students" (p. 24). The abilities to write and communicate more effectively, for example, can enhance students' feelings of autonomy and self-direction. Likewise, improvement in interpersonal competence can help students become more engaged in classroom discussions and more confident in expressing themselves.

In essence, *Education and Identity* argues for an integrated system of learning that builds upon the interaction between intellectual development and other aspects of student development. It is a call for active learning that engages students in a holistic manner and that calls upon colleges and universities to use the resources of student affairs and other aspects of student life to make learning a truly transforming experience.

> In most colleges, intellectual activities are restricted to manipulation of abstractions and symbols. In most colleges, awareness of feelings and expression of them in thought and action are to be tempered in the service of propriety or simple self interest. In most colleges learning is more passive than active. (Chickering, 1969, p. 31)

This pivotal recognition of the inseparability of the intellectual and personal domains of students' lives in college became a cornerstone of the student learning movement.

The student affairs profession has evolved considerably over the past 50 years, such that today it encompasses a surprising variety of institutional student services on college and university campuses. Most of these student services and programs have become an integral part of the higher education milieu and an essential part of the contemporary college experience (Dalton & Crosby, 2011). The many changes in student affairs over the past half century have been accompanied by reformulations in our mission, with the result that today the profession finds its purpose much more squarely within the mainstream educational purposes of higher education. The evolution of the profession over the past 5 decades has incorporated past conceptual paradigms and integrated them into an intellectual framework more fitting for the challenges of contemporary higher education.

This evolution benefited significantly from the theoretical framework and practical applications of *Education and Identity.* This seminal work has been a pivotal influence in shaping the growth of student affairs work and its intellectual paradigms over the past 50 years. Chickering's contributions to the literature of student affairs, however, go far beyond *Education and Identity.* Many of his student affairs-related publications are listed earlier in this chapter. But it was *Education and Identity* that provided one of the first and most fruitful conceptual models that prompted a reconceptualization of the role and mission of student affairs. It opened the way for greater intentionality, reflection, planning, and assessment in student affairs programming. It was updated in 1993 and continues to be an important foundational work in understanding the educational and personal needs of college students and the role of student affairs in contemporary higher education.

Finally, the spirit of *Education and Identity,* its holistic vision of students' learning and development during their college years, its sympathetic understanding of the struggle of youth to gain a sense of purpose and meaning, and its recognition that transformative education must integrate learning and experience are reflected in

Chickering's own life. It has been his cool passion, reflected in his writing, speeches, mentoring, and collaborations over the past half century, that has helped to shape our understanding of the essential work of student affairs today.

REFERENCES

American Council on Education. (1937). *The student personnel point of view: A report of a conference on the philosophy and development of student personnel work in college and university.* Retrieved from http://www.myacpa.org/pub/documents/1937.pdf

Bloland, P. A., Stamatakos, L. C., & Rogers, R. R. (1994). *Reform in student affairs: A critique of student development.* Greensboro, NC: ERIC Counseling and Student Services Clearinghouse.

Chickering, A. W. (1967a). College residences and student development. *Educational Record, 48*(2), 170–186.

Chickering, A. W. (1967b). Talking with college students. *Improving College and University Teaching, 15*(1), 30–32.

Chickering, A. W. (1967c). The young adult: A new and needed course for college personnel administrators. *Journal of the National Association of Women Deans and Counselors, 30*(3), 98–11.

Chickering, A. W. (1969). *Education and identity.* San Francisco, CA: Jossey-Bass.

Chickering, A. W. (1973). College advising for the 1970s. In J. Katz (Ed.), *Services for students* (New directions for higher education, No. 3, pp. 69–80). San Francisco, CA: Jossey-Bass.

Chickering, A. W. (1974). Education and identity: Implications for residence hall living. In D. A. De Coster & P. Mable (Eds.), *Student development and education in college residence halls.* Washington, DC: American College Personnel Association.

Chickering, A. W. (1981). Potential contributions of college unions to student development. In W. M. Klepper (Ed.), *College unions at work: The impact of college unions and their programs on today's students* (pp. 23–27). Stanford, CA: Association of College Unions-International.

Chickering, A. W. (1994). Empowering lifelong self development. *NACADA Journal, 14*(2), 50–53.

Chickering, A. W. (1997). Academic and student affairs: Collaboration to strengthen liberal education. In Charles E. Coombs (Ed.), *Proceedings, fourth annual general education symposium.* Boston, MA: Berklee College of Music.

Chickering, A. W. (1998). Why we should encourage student activism. *About Campus, 2*(6), 2–3.

Chickering, A. W. (2003). Encouraging authenticity and spirituality in higher education, introduction. *Journal of College and Character, 4*(8), 1–15.

Chickering, A. W. (2004a). Curricular content. *Journal of College and Character, 5*(1), 1–20.

Chickering, A. W. (2004b). Policy issues: Legislative and institutional. *Journal of College and Character, 5*(1), 1–9.

Chickering, A. W. (2006a). Authenticity and spirituality in higher education: My orientation. *Journal of College and Character, 7*(1), 1–5.

Chickering, A. W. (2006b). Strengthening spirituality and civic engagement in higher education. *Journal of College and Character, 8*(1), 1–5.

Chickering, A. W. (2007). On what basis do you vote? Developmental perspectives for a pluralistic democracy. *Journal of College and Character, 9*(1), 1–8.

Chickering, A. W. (2010a, February 8). *Honoring Jon Dalton.* Keynote presented at the Institute on College Student Values, Tallahassee, FL.

Chickering, A. W. (2010b). A retrospect on higher education's commitment to moral and civic education. *Journal of College and Character, 11*(3), 1–6.

Chickering, A. W., Dalton, J. C., & Stamm, L. (2006). *Encouraging authenticity and spirituality in higher education.* San Francisco, CA: Jossey-Bass.

Chickering, A. W., & O'Connor, J. (1996). The university learning center: A driving force for collaboration. *About Campus, 1*(4), 16–21.

Dalton, J. C., & Crosby, P. C. (2011). A profession in search of a mission: Is there an enduring purpose for student affairs in U.S. higher education? *Journal of College and Character, 12*(4), 1–7.

Keeling, R. P. (Ed.). (2004). *Learning reconsidered: A campus-wide focus on the student experience.* Washington, DC: American College Personnel Association and National Association of Student Personnel Administrators.

Kolb, D. A. (1984). *Experiential learning: Experience as the source of learning and development.* Englewood Cliffs, NJ: Prentice Hall.

Krivoski, J. G., & Nicholson, R. M. (1989). An interview with Arthur W. Chickering. *The Journal of College and University Student Housing, 19*(2), 6–11.

Lynch, A. Q., & Chickering, A. W. (1984). Comprehensive counseling and support programs for adult learners: Challenge to higher education. In H. B. Gelatt, N. K. Schlossberg, E. L. Herr, A. Q. Lynch, A. W. Chickering, G. R. Walz, & L. Benjamin (Eds.), *New perspectives on counseling adult learners* (pp. 45–73). Ann Arbor, MI: ERIC Counseling and Personnel Services Clearinghouse.

National Association of Scholars. (2008). *Rebuilding campus community: The wrong imperative.* Retrieved from http://www.nas.org/articles/Rebuilding_Campus_ Community_The_Wrong_Imperative

Sandeen, A. (2011). Does student affairs have an enduring mission and purpose? *Journal of College and Character, 12(4),* 1–8.

Thomas, R. E., & Chickering, A. W. (1984a). Education and identity revisited. *Journal of College Student Personnel, 25*(5), 392–399.

Thomas, R. E., & Chickering, A. W. (1984b). Foundations for academic advising. In R. B. Winston, Jr., T. K. Miller, S. C. Ender, & T. J. Grites (Eds.), *Developmental academic advising* (pp. 89–117). San Francisco, CA: Jossey-Bass.

Thomas, R. E., Murrell, P., & Chickering, A. W. (1982). The critical role of value development in student development. *NASPA Journal, 20*(1), 3–13.

CHAPTER 8

From Traditional Students to Adult Learners

With Catherine Marienau

My first experience with alternative programs for adult learners was with the Goddard Experimental Program in Further Education (GEPFE). It started in 1967 as a weekend program specifically designed for Headstart workers from Vermont and New Hampshire. Once a month the workers came to campus Friday evenings and left Sunday mornings after being immersed in workshops and meetings with faculty members to plan and pursue their individually designed educational programs. They were all women, diverse in socioeconomic status and educational backgrounds. They were program directors with college degrees, teachers with some or no postsecondary experiences, and cooks with no high school diplomas. True to Goddard's basic educational principles, each person designed and carried out her own program with an advisor. Jo's doctoral dissertation with the Union Institute and University, *Six Years in the Lives of Six Women* (Chickering, 1974),

191

documented the profound impact the GEPFE program had on these predominantly working-class participants.

My next experience came with the Adult Degree Program. In 1997, Richard Hathaway wrote *The Friendly Pioneer: An Informal History of the Adult Degree Program.* Richard, an historian, was a much-beloved Goddard faculty member from the program's early years and its director from 1970 to 1972. He was also a good friend, a staunch member of our Plainfield Friends Meeting, and a local hero to us unabashed liberals. Following are excerpts from his history. I quote at length because this pioneering program triggered the University Without Walls movement that swept the country during the 1970s and also was the basis for my approach to creating Empire State College. There have been many adaptations, so perhaps it is useful to record the basics of this first initiative.

> Goddard's pioneering Adult Degree Program (ADP) was a radical departure from traditional educational patterns. It drew from a variety of practices to establish a substantially new educational design for adult students aged 26 or above. Instead of defining a prescribed curriculum, ADP asked its students to design semester-long independent study projects that reflected their own passions and interests. Instead of lengthy campus residency requirements, the program expected twelve days of intensive residency twice annually, wherein students would initiate and conclude their half year study projects. Instead of faculty as fountains of wisdom from whom students gratefully drank, faculty worked as knowledgeable facilitators and mentors, helping the students accomplish what they aspired to achieve. . . . This stance was congruent with the view of faculty as adroit senior partners in learning espoused by Goddard's energetic founder, Royce S. ("Tim") Pitkin.

This design was not for everyone. Students accustomed to prescribed curricula sometimes found ADP's expectation of autonomy uncomfortable. Those used to traditional, often compartmentalized, learning found it necessary to stretch their academic imagination as they discovered the most compelling questions in the liberal arts required transdisciplinary explorations in their monthly communications with faculty guides.

Yet from its modest beginnings in August, 1963, when nineteen students and three veteran faculty members gathered in Kilpatrick Lounge to inaugurate the program ADP's model of educational enterprise began to make its distinctive mark in American higher education. . . .

From the start, about three quarters of the ADP's population was made up of women, with an average age of 39. . . . By 1972 the Program had divided its nearly 400 students into eight groups averaging about fifty students each. Faculty members worked with six to eight adult students per group, while teaching in the regular undergraduate program as well. By 1975 the ADP had grown to 520 students.

As the program developed, in 1970 full time ("core") faculty who worked exclusively (in ADP) were added. These newly professional adult educators also worked with the director of the program to develop policies, and in hiring and in retention, and considered changes in program design . . .

Although the residency over the thirty-three year history of the program has been shortened from twelve to eight days, the ADP's basic calendar has endured to the present: (1) the exploration phase, wherein students explore potential faculty mentors and refine their study proposals; (2) the start-up advisory group sessions in the second half of the residency, wherein more precise study plans are formulated and agreed upon by students and faculty advisors; (3) the crucial five and one-half months off campus wherein books are read and evaluated, essays, reports, and critical annotations are composed and practical experiences integrated into regular faculty/student exchanges; and (4) the final evaluation phase, wherein students return to campus, report on their process and products, and complete their critical evaluations of the study with faculty.

Letter grades were rejected in favor of extensive critical narrative evaluations which served as the official transcripts of student work. Thus, persons reviewing students' records learned not only the faculty's judgment about the quality of the work but some of its contents as well. (pp. 3–4)

Most of these basic elements still persist in Goddard's varied low-residency undergraduate and master's degree programs. I experienced its educational power personally when I spent from 2009 to 2012 completing Goddard's Master of Fine Arts in Creative Writing degree. That learning stimulated this professional memoir and informed my attempt to create it.

During the year I was a visiting scholar at the American Council on Education (ACE), Ernie Boyer, who had become chancellor of the State University of New York (SUNY) system, and I met for lunch or dinner two or three times when business brought him to Washington, D.C., and when we were at the same conferences. He told me about his failed attempt to create an alternative institution with a new campus in Old Westbury on Long Island. In late January, his office called, inviting me to a day-long meeting in Albany on February 9, 1971. Merton Ertell, a SUNY administrator, chaired the meeting. Other participants included Alan Pifer, then head of the Carnegie Foundation, Calvin Lee, an academic administrator from a Maryland university, and Stephen Bailey from Syracuse University. We responded to a prospectus formulated by top SUNY staff during the fall of 1970. It said, in part:

> [The College] will seek to transcend conventional academic structure which imposes required courses, periods of time, and residential constraints upon the individual students. [The college] will rely on a process rather than a structure of education to shape and give it substance as well as purpose. This emphasis will place the central focus upon the individual student learning at his own pace with the guidance and counseling of master teachers.
>
> This process will place the responsibility for learning on the student in return for his freedom to pursue his education according to his individual needs and interests.
>
> Through appropriate counseling and advisement, a program of study will be designed for each student to meet the individual's particular educational objectives, taking into account fully his then current educational experience. (Bonnabeau, 1996, pp. 18–19)

It was a fascinating and challenging day. The student-centered educational orientation was highly consistent with my Goddard experiences and an organizing principle for my book *Education and Identity* (Chickering, 1969). I was able to chip in here and there on the basis of those prior experiences and my research for the Project on Student Development. The day ended with a strong endorsement from all parties for going ahead.

About a month later, Jo and I were in Estes Park with a small group of educational leaders for a Danforth Foundation-sponsored workshop discussing needed changes in higher education. I was pulled out of a morning session by a call from James Hall, a SUNY central staff member, who had helped organize the February 9 meeting.

"Dr. Boyer wonders whether you would be interested in becoming the academic vice president to help create the new institution we discussed on February 9. You would start full time July 1 after your year at ACE is up. If you can meet with us occasionally before then, it would be helpful."

Bright sun bounced off the snow outside the windows and lit up the peaks against a clear blue sky. A small herd of elk was pawing for grass on a hillside field across the valley.

"That's a generous invitation. I assume it will involve moving to New York. I'll need to discuss that with Jo and the kids. There is another complication. The National Institute of Mental Health [NIMH] will be funding my Strategies for Change Project starting August 1. If I accept this position, I'll need to figure out what to do about that project. It's an important follow-up for my institutional change work and I'd not want to drop it."

"I understand this is an important decision. Just give me a call when you're ready," replied Hall.

"I will."

I rejoined the meeting but was so preoccupied the issues escaped me. Jo had questions in her eyes. During lunch we moved to a table away from the group and I told her about the offer. As usual, when any new challenges came along, she was enthusiastically supportive. We were not enthusiastic about moving our kids off the farm and out of the small rural schools where they were doing so well. Neither of us thought well of the New York schools with their statewide Regents Examinations and competitive environments. We did not like putting our kids in suburbs where adolescent drinking and drugs were much more common than in Vermont. We decided to mull it over and call the kids the next evening.

Both of us were pretty distracted during the afternoon's discussion.

Though I know we all dream, I seldom remember mine, but I woke up the next morning emotionally moved by a vivid experience during the night. I was seated at a large oval banquet table replete with delicious Indian food. Ernie was sitting at the head of the table holding a large platter filled with poppadums—delicious round, thin, crusty wafers about four or five inches in diameter. The platter went around the table, but when it got to me, there were just crumbs. Was this a forecast of what this offer would turn out to be? When I told Jo about it as we were dressing, she reassured me.

"Don't worry. You're always good at turning lemons into lemonade."

At suppertime we called the kids—Alan, Susan, Peri, and Nancy. They had been looking forward to getting back to Vermont and, as we had expected, did not like the idea of leaving our wonderful place. A new regional high school was just getting started, and they were looking forward to going there. The kids asked what would happen with our dog, Poppy; our cat, Marshmallow; Susan's and Peri's horses, Gold and Silver; plus their gerbils and hamsters. We did not have any good answers and hung up after telling them we were still thinking about it.

That night I had another dream, still vivid when I woke up. I was standing on a high bluff looking down on a broad beach filled with bright umbrellas, picnic baskets, and sunbathers, with swimmers enjoying the gentle surf. Suddenly, a huge wave washed the people and all their belongings up close to the top of the bluff where I was standing. I saw their arms waving and heard terrified screams. Then the water receded. They and their possessions littered the beach. Powerfully moved by the scene, I stood above it, unharmed. Jo's reaction was, "See, whatever happens you'll be all right. Why don't you at least meet with Ernie and see what this will involve?"

I called Hall and told him we wanted to explore this further. We scheduled a meeting with Ernie for the following Friday afternoon. It was a sunny spring day with tulips and daffodils blooming and trees full of tiny green leaves. Ernie's secretary greeted me warmly. Not surprisingly, he was on the phone. He had told me about his 180-plus phone calls and messages each week that interfered with sustained thinking and getting important things done. When the secretary showed me in, Ernie came out from behind his big desk and shook hands warmly.

"How about going out for a walk while we talk?" I asked.

"Great idea!" he replied.

We spent 45 uninterrupted minutes strolling in the warm sun in a small park next to his office complex. He told me about his hopes for this brand-new free-standing institution and commented on how my Goddard and Project on Student Development experiences fit nicely with what they wanted to do. It would be a year-round job, accompanied by a tenured appointment as a professor. The salary would be $30,000, plus health and retirement benefits. Our moving expenses would be covered once we found housing and Jo and the kids could come down. Jim Hall and Bill Dodge, SUNY's vice president for continuing education, would join me for initial planning as often as I could come up until July 1, when I would start full time. My total lack of administrative experience, except for supervising the small student development project staff, was not discussed. I didn't really have any questions for Ernie, partly because I was totally ignorant about public higher education, and partly because I was nonplussed about the whole situation. It sounded like a once-in-a-lifetime opportunity—for which I felt entirely unprepared. As we walked back into his office, I accepted the position. The chance to help create something so consistent with my own educational orientation, and that appeared to be just what higher education needed for returning adults, seemed much more important than the Strategies for Change Project. I told him I would be in touch with Jim

Hall about coming up for early planning and to look for housing as soon as I made some holes in my ACE schedule.

Outside, I sat down on a bench under the trees. My mind was spinning, as it had when Tim Pitkin and Ernie approached me about the Project on Student Development. I was anxious and full of self-doubt. The shaky self-esteem that plagued my growing up and college years came flooding back. Despite my success at Goddard and with the Project on Student Development, during my months at ACE I had seen enough to realize that although Goddard and the small private colleges I worked with served their students well, they played limited roles on the national stage of higher education. Now I was being asked to play in the majors, and not just as a faculty member or junior administrator in an existing institution. Ernie and the SUNY system were asking me to lead the creation of a brand-new kind of college. Sure, I had done some useful original research and written an award-winning book, and I had been invited to be a visiting scholar at ACE's Office of Research. But maybe I was just a "supernova"—a flash of light with a black hole in the middle. As a longtime tennis fan, I had watched a few one-slam wonders—players who had a lucky draw and peaked just enough to win Wimbledon or the French or U.S. Open, and rapidly dropped off the charts. And what about those two vivid dreams? What did they foretell?

My mind wandered through dense woods and briar thickets during the flight back to Washington National Airport and on the drive back to Bannockburn. I wondered about the new job and what it would mean for my family and my career; I felt as if I was making my way through one of those pea-soup fogs Jo and I had endured living in South Jersey and Long Beach 15 years ago. Jo was enthusiastic when I told her I'd accepted. The kids tried to congratulate me but could not really hide their ambivalence. We all happily headed back to Vermont. The family would stay there while I looked for housing in Saratoga Springs. A whole new set of challenges was just over the horizon.

Meanwhile, I accepted the NIMH grant for the Strategies for Change project. I found office space in Saratoga Springs and hired Bill Hannah, who had worked on the student development project with me, as administrative director. I placed an ad in *The Chronicle of Higher Education* and asked Bob Blackburn at the University of Michigan's higher education graduate program to recommend candidates for the two other staff positions. I had admired Bob when he was the academic vice president at Shimer College, one of participating institutions in the student development project. He recommended Jack Lindquist, a former University of Michigan star fullback, top student, and excellent writer, who had just completed his doctoral degree. When Jack and his wife, Shari, flew in for an interview, I knew he was just what we needed. I offered them our upstairs apartment while they looked for housing. I also hired Larry Bemis, a bright young anthropologist. By the end of July, the project was staffed and ready to hit the ground running under Bill's able leadership. I remained as project director and joined weekly staff meetings.

For me, the key challenge, articulated by Ernie, was to create an institution that would serve adults throughout the state of New York. That was our mission. We were authorized to grant associate in arts, associate in science, bachelor of arts, bachelor of science, and bachelor of professional studies degrees. With those degree authorizations, and with potential enrollees diverse in race, ethnicity, national origin, and prior learning, it was clear that a batch processing, one-size-fits-all approach would not work. We needed individualized degrees pursued with individual learning contracts, just as Goddard had for its undergraduate majors and in its adult degree program. With New York's diverse population and with the range of studies they would pursue, a norm-referenced, grading-on-a-curve approach to evaluating students' contracts also would not work. Goddard used narrative evaluations, and there was a small consortium of colleges that did so as well. That was the only way to capture the richness and complexity of the work undertaken in a learning contract.

It also would be foolish to assume that all learners came with the same levels of competence and knowledge in relation to the areas of learning they wanted to pursue. It was likely that many already had substantial learning from prior work and life experiences. We needed to devise a way to evaluate and recognize that prior learning so their Empire State studies could build on it, avoid redundancy, and be challenging enough to sustain interest and motivation. Traditional college courses forced all content and desired outcomes onto a Procrustean bed of 15- or 16-week semesters, typically delivered with 50-minute classes 3 times a week, or occasionally 3-hour classes once a week, for a total of 45 contact hours. It made much more sense to have the time fit the students' purposes, content, and learning activities, so contracts could be half time or full time and range from 1 to 6 months. Twenty hours per week was expected for half-time contracts and 40 hours for full time.

We were an open-enrollment college. Interested students were asked to answer five questions on their application: What do you want your life to be like 5 years from now? What do you want to learn? How do you learn best? What resources work best for you? What prior learning is pertinent to your purposes? We knew these would be challenging questions for our applicants and did not expect sophisticated answers. But we wanted potential students to begin thinking about themselves and their education in ways consistent with our approach. After being accepted for admission, 20 to 25 students were invited to an orientation workshop from 6:00 to 9:00 Friday evening, 9:00 a.m. to 5:00 p.m. Saturday, and 9:00 a.m. to 12:00 p.m. Sunday. These workshops aimed to help students understand Empire State College's educational approach and ascertain whether their purposes would be well served if they enrolled. Their responses to the questions on their application were the starting points for the workshop. Faculty members responded to their questions and suggested how each person might proceed. A $50 fee included Saturday lunch, and they did not make a final enrollment decision until after the workshop. The big question was often whether to enroll full time or half time. To aid participants in making the decision, we gave them each a blank calendar of the past 2 weeks and asked them to fill in how they had spent each day. Then, if they intended to enroll full time, we asked them to cross out activities to free up 40 hours, and if half time, 20 hours. We knew that time on task would be critical and we wanted these busy, ambitious adults to be realistic. Many students changed from assuming full-time to half-time enrollment, and some half-time students said they would come back after they were able to reorganize their lives to free up the expected hours. We ran these workshops monthly to build enrollments in our forthcoming learning centers. These were the key responses to the educational challenges set forth in Boyer's prospectus.

Then there was the organizational challenge of serving adults throughout the state. We needed small, human-scale units, where faculty members would know each other well enough to work together and where administrators would have close relationships with them. Roger Barker and Paul Gump's (1964) research for *Big School, Small School* documented the educational power of small schools, in the range of 200–300 students, especially for students who were not the best and the brightest. Goddard had 121 students on the Greatwood main campus in fall 1959, when I arrived. When the student population reached 250, we started a second Northwood campus. With teaching loads of 25 full-time-equivalent students per faculty member, a learning center of 250–300 students could support 10–12 faculty members across disciplines in science, social sciences, and humanities, with a dean and associate dean. This was consistent with Barker and Gump's research. So that's how we started, with learning centers in Albany, Rochester, and Long Island. We were also asked by the New York Central Labor Council to start a unit in the International Brotherhood of Electrical Workers building on 25th Street in New York City, a request we could not refuse. After starting additional units at SUNY Rockland Community College, SUNY Purchase College, and in Buffalo, we created a statewide center based in Saratoga Springs. That center coordinated work by smaller units of one or two faculty members in a variety of other locations in the state of New York: Binghamton, Plattsburgh, Oneonta, and Watertown.

We soon had several thousand diverse students enrolled in all these varied locations, pursuing creative degree programs and learning contracts. Their work not only included their own reading and writing, but also courses at other institutions and systematic use of ongoing experiential contexts that were part of their families, jobs, or community activities. It became readily apparent that quality assurance across all this diversity was necessary—the diverse student population, diverse educational contracts and programs, and diverse locations. To oversee this, we hired Al Serling to direct the Office of Program Review and Assessment; Al had been at Educational Testing Service. Myrna Miller, a former faculty member, became the associate director. Their job was to review the degree programs and learning contracts that came to our central records office. If blatant problems recurred for particular faculty members, they called the appropriate associate dean and raised the issue. They could not second-guess or turn back approved contracts, but they could flag them and share the questions they had. This delicate and sensitive work helped even out the expectations across the institution without intruding heavily on local judgments by the deans and faculty members. These were the basic elements of Empire State College during the early 1970s.

With the NIMH Strategies for Change project, and getting Empire State conceptualized, staffed, and underway, my workload was the most intellectually and emotionally challenging I had ever experienced. Even with my Monmouth College baptism, I was totally unprepared for the political maneuvering and infighting. With all this going on, being alone all week had its advantages. I was at the office by 6:30 or 7:00 in the morning and worked as long into the night as I could manage. I ate simply and quickly, with working lunches Monday through Thursday. Most weekends I went to Vermont on Friday afternoons and left Monday mornings at 5:00 a.m. to be back at Empire State in time for our 8:00 a.m. presidential administrative council meetings. I strapped a steno pad filled with scribbled notes to my left thigh with rubber bands. While I steered with my right hand, my left held a small recording machine so I could dictate short memos and letters I had saved specifically for those 3-hour drives. Once a month or so, Jo joined me. We took in a concert or show at the Saratoga Performing Arts Center, or a good movie, and made up for the weeks apart with leisurely lovemaking. She cooked tasty meals for me to have during the week that were a welcome alternative to the simple food I fixed for myself.

Weekends in Vermont were a welcome change from the all-consuming workload in Saratoga Springs. When the weather permitted, I walked in the woods with one or another of the kids to hear how things were going. Somehow it was easier for them to share their adolescent problems with friends, school, or at home when we were among the trees, flowers, and wildlife. We paused to watch a bird, a squirrel or chipmunk, an occasional deer, or we bent over to examine a flower. Silences were not as loaded as they could be when sitting inside.

But I was heavily preoccupied with the intellectual, interpersonal, and political complexities of Empire State. I stopped going to the Quaker meeting on Sunday mornings because I could not quiet my mind and avoid stewing about some educational issue or interpersonal dynamic. I needed to be actively engaged with something physical or interactive to keep those ruminations at bay. Sometimes they generated something useful, but usually my mental rowboat floated round and round in a maelstrom, sucked deeper and deeper into conflicting feelings and speculations, as Empire State's internal political and interpersonal conflicts heated up. I tossed and turned, waking up during the night disturbed by some problem. When that happened in Saratoga Springs, I often got up and read a bit or made some notes, but during weekends in Vermont I did not want to disturb Jo and the kids. Monday mornings, not really refreshed from that break, tears flowed as I kissed Jo on the cheek, quietly rose, and drove away. I sobbed out loud in our Plymouth as I blasted through Montpelier and down Interstate 89, the speedometer at 85 or 90, until I finally went back to the dictation I had not finished on the way up. By the time our Monday morning administrative council meetings were over at 9:30 or 10:00 a.m., I was fully absorbed by the college and all its challenges.

In fall 1975, I agreed to surrender the vice president for academic affairs position to John Jacobson, whom I had hired to be the first dean of our Rochester Learning Center. I became vice president for policy and planning without day-to-day line responsibilities. I was burned out. Empire State had been hammered out on the anvil of conflicts between Loren Baritz and me. Jim Hall had hired Loren as provost to address issues of academic content and balance my learner-centered focus on process, and he was caught in the crossfire. As dean of our Rochester Learning Center, Jacobson had been one of my stalwart supporters. I felt good about having him move into my position. In my new role, learning center deans no longer reported to me and I had no operational responsibility for all the administrative decisions and details concerning the academic program—budgets, enrollments, staffing, promotion and tenure, quality assurance, and such. Nor was I responsible for getting ready and implementing our first accreditation visit by the Middle States Association. Theodore Mitau, chancellor of the Minnesota State higher education system, who had initiated their University College with a learner-centered approach similar to Empire State's, chaired the accreditation team and we were fully accredited without reservation.

With the heavy workload and emotional demands off my shoulders, Jo and I enjoyed leisurely dinners, often followed by Performing Arts Center concerts and shows. We especially savored strawberry and cream breakfasts at the track during the August racing season, admiring Secretariat's gait and demeanor while trainers exercised him. I also enjoyed quiet times in Vermont without stewing about Empire State. There was plenty of time and energy for Jo, the family, and our rich, loving relationships.

I obtained a sabbatical leave for 1976–1977. Hall and Baritz were glad to have me out of their hair. Jo and I had sold our second house in Saratoga Springs and moved into a small apartment. We happily left Saratoga Springs during the summer of 1976 and began a wonderful year together on the old farm we loved so much. I was ready to move on and Empire State's top administrators were ready to have me leave. Empire State was well launched. As "Mister Empire State," as I came to be called, I was invited to give plenty of domestic and international presentations and had many consultations with organizations and individual institutions interested in this new model for adult learners as an alternative to the British open university.

My heavy involvement with the Council for Adult and Experiential Learning (CAEL) continued when I moved to the Memphis State

Center for the Study of Higher Education in the fall of 1977. While Jack Lindquist and Tom Clark were leading the Higher Learning for Diverse Adults project from 1978 to 1981, and Ann Lynch the Higher Education for Adult Mental Health project from 1981 to 1984, my time was divided between functioning as a resource person for their workshops and institutional consultations and being actively involved with CAEL. With W. K. Kellogg Foundation support, CAEL's Project Learn strengthened a national network of regional managers. Jacqueline Wright, a doctoral student and graduate assistant in the center, moved into that role when Charles Claxton decided to vacate it. We had a large region: Alabama, Mississippi, Louisiana, Tennessee, Oklahoma, and Texas. Jacque and I worked closely together, sponsoring and implementing workshops and creating networks of professionals working with adults and promoting the assessment of prior learning. As chair of the CAEL board, I also attended the twice-yearly regional managers' meetings as well as the board meetings and annual assemblies. I continued to write and preach about adult development and learning in varied CAEL contexts as well as elsewhere. CAEL recognized this work when it gave me a CAEL Guru Award at its 10th anniversary celebration in New Orleans. My contributions were also recognized later when I was given CAEL's first Morris Keeton Award in 1990.

Of course, I continued a good bit of writing, usually with colleagues in the center and elsewhere. Here is a list of some of my writings from 1979 to 1989: "Adult Development—Implications for Higher Education" (Chickering, 1979); "Adult Development: A Workable Vision for Higher Education" (Chickering, 1980); "Adult Development and Learning" (Marienau & Chickering, 1982); "Comprehensive Counseling and Support Programs for Adult Learners: Challenge to Higher Education" (Lynch & Chickering, 1984); "Model Programs for Adult Learners in Higher Education" (Lynch, Doyle, & Chickering,

1985). Much of this work was pulled together in *Improving Higher Education Environments for Adults: Responsive Programs and Services from Entry to Departure* (Schlossberg, Lynch, & Chickering, 1989).

Catherine Marienau has been a stalwart colleague and close friend since she spent 1980–1981 with us at the Center for the Study of Higher Education. She has also been active in CAEL, a president of the Adult Higher Education Alliance, a scholar, professor, and innovator at the DePaul University School for New Learning. I can think of no one better positioned to put my particular contributions to the recognition and education of adult learners in the larger national context and to address the progression and current state of adult learning.

Catherine

A large volume, with many pages flagged, sits prominently on my bookshelf, within easy reach. The inscription from the author reads:

> For Catherine,
>
> You are such a fine addition, it's great to have you with us. I hope we can struggle together with these issues in the future. I doubt we'll settle them all this semester.
>
> Chick

The book is *The Modern American College*; the editor is Arthur W. Chickering (1981). The setting is the Center for the Study of Higher Education at then Memphis State University, where I was serving a one-year stint (1980–1981) as professional-in-residence. Chick's seminal work placed adult learners and their developmental growth on the agenda for higher education. Indeed, Chick and his associates "argued that research and theory concerning human development and the life cycle can provide a unifying vision for higher education and lifelong learning" (p. 773). For someone like me, who was at that time gaining some understanding about adult learning while administering and mentoring in an individualized, criterion-referenced adult degree program (University Without Walls/University of Minnesota), this book was a fundamental resource for ideas and practice. For someone like me, who has been an advocate of change and innovation for more than 40 years, Chick's advice to "apply cool passion to reform" (p. 783) has helped to maintain a steady fire over the long term. Clearly, we did not settle all the issues concerning adult learners in 1981 or even in the 20th Century.

I will highlight significant advances that hold promise to foster full potential for learning, development, and life advantages for adult learners, as well as discuss aspects of serving adult learners that have persisted across the last 4 decades. My comments will flow between now and then, with brief glimpses into the foundations that were built in the intervening years.

Who are the adult learners of today? During the early years, adult learners were grouped under the umbrella of "nontraditional students." Today, *adult learner* has become the predominant nomenclature. And, as more of our military servicemen and servicewomen and their families seek higher education, many institutions are adding *military* as a distinguishing mark alongside *adult learner*.

In certain respects, the demographic profile of adult learners hasn't changed much from Chick's description of the diverse clientele served in the early adult degree programs. Now, as then, central characteristics of adult learners include a mix of ages (24 and older), life responsibilities beyond school, limited access to higher education, constraints of time and money, and wide-ranging individual differences as learners. Something I learned during my early studies of adult development has stayed with me—the notion that adults grow more different from one another as they grow in age and maturity. Today these individual differences still include varying motivations, learning styles, and barriers to overcome. The age range of adult learners is still wide, from mid-20s to 70s. Female learners continue to be the majority in undergraduate adult degree programs, where they can comprise up to 75% of the population. A more balanced ratio between females and males is found in graduate programs, although women are tipping the scales in once male-dominated professions such as law and medicine.

Now, as in the early days of the adult learner movement, many adult-centered programs intentionally try to close the gap between those who have and have not. These programs know first-hand the challenges of overcoming deeply embedded institutional and social barriers. Many adult-centered programs reach out and are attractive to persons of color, to first-generation college attendees, to people in lower economic brackets, and to those committed to social service and social change. These dimensions of diversity enrich the cultural experiences of all involved. These dimensions also raise the bar for creating learning environments that embody cultural awareness and inclusion, and avoid microaggressions with regard to gender, race, class, and other socially constructed -isms.

While advances in technology-assisted learning offer a tremendous boost to adults' access to higher education, these advances also can advantage those with technological savvy over those without—for example, older learners in the nonprofit sector. As more higher education institutions go online with delivery and require use of technology within on-ground courses, adult learners of all ages and incomes are pressed to invest in, and learn how to use, up-to-date technology. The range of individual differences among adult learners argues against the temptations of batch processing (i.e., to prescribe content and timelines in order to increase access and completion time). New technologies dramatically increase capacities to respond to some, but not all, individual differences. We must keep watch on to what extent the payoffs for batch processing are at the expense of developmental outcomes and learning that lasts.

Clearly, the landscape of higher education for adults is changing—some spokespersons claim the institution itself is transforming. A major force is the avalanche of online learning, which burst onto the large stage starting in the mid-1990s, providing unparalleled access to college courses and other ways of packaging information. Paul LeBlanc (2013), president of Southern New Hampshire University, predicts that "historians of this period, possessing the clear-sightedness that only time provides, will likely point to online learning as the disruptive technology platform that radically changed [higher education]" (para. 2). Included in this new wave of innovation are the rapid growth of for-profit institutions and free online courses taught by big names at prestigious institutions (MOOCs—massive open online courses). While online learning is the new wave, the concept of distance learning is not new to many adult degree programs, which have been serving adult learners at a distance, even before fax machines and the Internet. For example, at University Without Walls/University of Minnesota, we served students—one by one, letter by letter—who resided in prisons, rural areas, and countries such as Zambia and India. Now, technology enables access to information about anything, any time, for anyone who can access the Internet.

Another force that is driving changes in higher education is the growing presence of adults in both on-ground and online environments. Since the 1970s, more than 40% of all college enrollments now are students over the age of 25. Currently, the fastest growing population of adult learners is 24–29 year olds, who are extending time in school to mix in work and family responsibilities, to add more credentials, or to prolong entering the fray of the highly competitive job market.

However, hundreds of thousands of older adults are still in the pipeline for higher education. The current Complete College America initiative, funded at the national level and implemented at the state level, recognizes the need to reach and serve adults who started and have not completed their college degree. Increasing access, lowering costs, and shortening time to completion are three mandates of this initiative.

Colleges and universities are recognizing the growing population of adults and the enrollment potential, and, noting society's need for a better-educated citizenry; the call is to become more adult-learner friendly. This modest phrase rests on the shoulders of decades of innovations—successful and failed—and represents a dizzying number of adaptations of the basic educational tenets that Chick articulated at the beginning of this chapter.

A phrase that Chick and his colleagues used in the early 1980s was "turning colleges toward adults." During my year as professional-in-residence at the Center for the Study of Higher Education, Jack Lindquist and I studied 13 colleges and universities that participated in the Higher Learning for Diverse Adults project, funded by FIPSE (Fund for the Improvement of Postsecondary Education). Our monograph, *Turning Colleges Toward Adults* (1981), chronicled the practices and principles that were guiding institutions in their intentions to serve adult learners well. What we found in 1981 was congruent with CAEL's nine principles of effectiveness for serving adult learners (Marienau, 1999). The CAEL nine principles address these areas:

- Reaching out to adult learners in ways that overcome barriers of time, place, and tradition to promote lifelong learning;
- Helping adults align career and life aspirations with educational goals;
- Providing options for financing education that are equitable and flexible;

- Assessing outcomes of students' learning, whether obtained through formal or informal means, with award of college credit;

- Engaging in teaching-learning processes (e.g., experiential, problem-based) that promote integration of concepts and application to students' lived contexts;

- Providing academic and student support systems that promote learners' self-agency;

- Using technology as a tool to increase access to information and enhance learning experiences;

- Engaging in strategic partnerships with employers and other organizations to increase learners' employability; and

- Guiding students in strategic application and integration of their learning to achieve educational and career goals.

In keeping with CAEL's principles, the field of adult learning/education hosts a variety of successful models and good practices for serving adult learners. In his book, *Lifelong Learning at Its Best: Innovative Practices in Adult Credit Programs,* Bill Maehl (2000) championed our nation's need for lifelong learning. He highlighted four innovative responses to learner needs: individualization and self-directed learning; learner-centered design; competence-based focus; and advanced professional development that can include sponsors outside the academy. These are the same basic tenets that Chick and other pioneers were articulating and advocating in the late 1960s through the early 1970s.

Current higher education institutions that implement these principles are called Adult Learning Focused Institutions (ALFIs). They have used the ALFI assessment tools to assess and improve adult student services. An adult learning-focused institution excels in areas such as outreach, life and career planning, assessment of learning outcomes, teaching-learning process, and student support systems (for details on ALFI, see the CAEL website and Klein-Collins, 2011).

The time is ripe to merge the aims and traditions of innovative adult higher education with what many thought leaders see as a new system for all of higher education. Given the drivers of an unstable economy, both nationally and internationally, and the need for a more educated workforce, it is urgent to reach and serve adults now. It is worth paraphrasing the points of current thought leaders Johnstone, Ewell, & Paulson (2010) to help us recognize that their vision is highly compatible with a vision for adult learning that has persisted for the past 40-plus years. Their points are well worth noting to underscore the enormous challenges that still need to be conquered, and to feel encouraged where there is promising movement.

- Academic awards (credits, certifications) should be structured in terms of outcomes or competencies, rather than courses and seat time.

- Academic awards should be based on demonstrated achievement of competencies through sound assessment practices.

- Early assessment of outcomes or competencies should be used to determine individual gaps in current abilities that can guide subsequent learning experiences for students.

- Opportunities for learning beyond formal coursework should be encouraged that include certifying learning obtained on the job or through other life experiences (e.g., credit for learning from experience, including prior learning assessment).

- The role of mentors and advisors should be elevated in helping individuals shape paths of learning toward established competencies.

- Verification of attainment of competencies/outcomes through third parties—such as professional organizations (e.g., American Society of Training and Development, Society for Human Resource Management, Project Management Institute), consortia of institutions (e.g., Adult Learning Consortium–University System of Georgia), or other providers—should be accepted.

Out of these actionable ideas, I emphasize that competence-based learning and assessment are powerful partners. This is where innovation and tradition in adult higher education can inform a new vision for higher education and guide colleges and universities in making the right decisions in regard to adults.

As noted, competence-based learning arose in adult degree programs in the early 1970s. In a survey of 137 adult degree programs in the United States (Eldred & Marienau, 1979), only a few reported having competence-based programs. Some of these programs were housed within institutions, such as: University Without Walls/ University College/University of Minnesota; Adult Degree Program/ Goddard College; and the School for New Learning Individualized BA Program/DePaul University. Others were institutions devoted to competence-based education; for example, Empire State College (where Chick played various key leadership roles) and Metropolitan State University. Some 20 years later, Maehl (2000) showcased competence-based programs that blended, in holistic fashion, liberal education with professional orientation or specialization. Among these institutions are: Alverno College; Regents College (now Excelsior); the School for New Learning at DePaul University—individualized BA program; Rio Salado College—Law Enforcement Technology program; and Antioch University—MA with Professional Preparation for Teacher Certification. I would add to this list the Master of Arts in Applied Professional Studies (MAAPS) program at the School for New Learning at DePaul University. Launched in 1984 with support from FIPSE, this program attracts entrepreneurial learners who design their own areas of focus around eight areas of competence. Students' customized professional cores are supplemented with liberal learning seminars that address effectiveness in these domains: personal, inter-personal, organizational, global, and inquiry. All students engage in self-assessment throughout their programs with regard to continuous development of skills and habits in agency, flexibility, and reflection (DePaul University, 2012).

This program and 12 others (representing associate through master's levels) are featured in CAEL's report "Competency-Based Degree Programs in the U.S.: Postsecondary Credentials for Measurable Student Learning and Performance" (Klein-Collins, 2012). The report is based on a year-long study funded by the William and Flora Hewlett Foundation. Given the array of models and practices, even among only 13 institutions, Klein-Collins grappled with how to catego-rize the competence-based programs. She settled on two categories: (a) competency frameworks within traditional course-based programs (e.g., Alverno College, Brandman University, Marylhurst University); and (b) competency frameworks that drive curricular redesign (e.g, Southern New Hampshire University, Westminster College, Western Governors University, School for New Learning (BA and MAAPS programs at DePaul University).

At a convening held in Indianapolis in September 2012, hosted by the Lumina Foundation and the Bill and Melinda Gates Foundation, many of these institutions were at the table to advise on and advocate for new models for higher education (i.e., competence-based learning and assessment). Forty-three 2-year and 4-year public and private institutions participated, but no for-profit institutions. In a report to my colleagues at the School for New Learning at DePaul, I categorized the participants as follows:

- Early pioneers in competence-based learning, 3 to 4 decades of experience (Alverno College; Empire State College; School for New Learning at DePaul University)
- Current pioneers, 1 to 2 years of experience (Westminster College; Kentucky Community and Technical College System; Brandman University, using Liberal Education and America's Promise (LEAP) and the Lumina Foundation's Degree Qualifications Profile)
- Long experience with adults—now turning to competence-based programs (University of Maryland, University College; Sinclair Community College; Charter Oak State College)
- Piloting programs: Southern New Hampshire University (College for America—low-cost, online associates degree); Colorado Community College System (competence-based college); Northern Arizona University (personalized learning)

The concept of competence continues to resist a universally accepted definition, although we seem to be getting closer. As we can see from the examples above, the variation in terminology is no deterrent to the current proliferation of competence-based models and practices. Chickering and Claxton first addressed this issue in 1981, as Chickering describes in the next chapter. Over the intervening years, many have deliberated the meaning of competence and its manifestations (see Klein-Collins, 2012, for brief review). On April 17, 2013, Carol Schneider, president of the Association of American Colleges and Universities (AAC&U), was quoted as saying, "We don't have agreement on what we mean by the term competency" (Fain, 2013).

Only a few days later, on April 24, 2013, the U.S. Department of Education, as reported by a program officer at Lumina Foundation, offered this definition:

> Competency-based education is an outcomes-oriented approach that is not dependent on seat time measures of learning. Instead, student achievement of learning outcomes is assessed and certified through observational methods, such as task performance, exams, demonstrations, or other direct measures of proficiency, and credentials are awarded based on successful demonstration of competence. The emphasis of this approach is on the mastery of specific competencies as demonstrated through performance-based assessments. (M. Offerman, personal communication, April 24, 2013)

Perhaps we are getting closer to an inclusive enough construct for competence-based learning that makes room for multiple approaches and delivery formats, that attends to individual differences among increasingly diverse learners, and that accommodates varying levels of higher education. Let us also advocate for definitions that invite integration of, rather than division among, liberal and professional/vocational learning; prior and current learning; formal and informal settings; theory and application; and education and employability.

A unifying thread that must be woven across all competence-based approaches is assessment. In assessments lie the challenge and the promise of education's being able to meet the standards of higher learning and the needs of adult learners—indeed, all learners. We owe much to the prior learning assessment (PLA) movement that began with CAEL in the mid-1970s. CAEL's founder, Morris Keeton, consulted with Chick often in the development of the organization and advocacy of PLA. Over the years Chick has been a major spokesperson for PLA, for example, serving on CAEL's advisory board (he was president in 1981) and publishing about learning from experience, the backbone of PLA.

While certainly not the only player in assessment writ large, one can look to the archives of CAEL publications to trace the evolution of assessment standards and practices in adult higher education. Urban Whitaker's (1986) *Assessing Learning: Standards, Principles and Procedures*, which Morris Fiddler and I updated in 2006, serves as a national standard for assessing learning. For more than a decade CAEL has offered an online certification program for faculty and administrators in Assessing Prior Learning (authored by Fiddler & Marienau). CAEL's landmark study of the academic progress over a 7-year period of 62,000 students at 48 colleges and universities yielded much-needed evidence that PLA helps adult learners gain credentials faster and at lower cost. Highlighted in Klein-Collins' 2010 report, "Fueling the Race to Postsecondary Success," are these findings: PLA students are 2.5 times more likely to persist to graduation than non-PLA students; and cost savings can be realized in the thousands of dollars. In February 2013, the Lumina Foundation and Gallup released the report "American's Call for Higher Education Redesign." Close to 100% of the 1,000 survey respondents indicated they recognized the importance of credentials beyond high school. However, only 41% without a degree or certificate reported having considered going on for further education and 61% said they were unlikely to return to school. Why not? The same situational and institutional barriers to education that Pat Cross found in 1981 persist across the decades: most notably, time and money.

PLA is moving from an institution-by-institution basis to more systemic support. CAEL has launched a new initiative designed to provide adults with easier access to PLA. "LearningCounts.org is a full-service online portal that helps students determine their most appropriate PLA method and subsequently offers them online portfolio development classes and assessment services conducted by a national network of faculty experts" (Sherman, 2013, para. 10). States such as Tennessee, Georgia, Kentucky, and others are promoting PLA through statewide policies for public institutions. I am most familiar with the Adult Learning Consortium (ALC) through the University System of Georgia. Just a few years ago, the ALC comprised four institutions; today, 13 institutions (all college levels) are members. Among the agreements to be a member of the ALC is to provide PLA to adult learners and permit transfer of PLA-earned credit across member institutions. Recognized for its leadership, the ALC now is a strategic partner in the Complete Degree Georgia initiative.

PLA and competence-based learning go hand in hand. CAEL is positioning itself to lend its leadership in PLA to advance competence-based assessment. Another piece of the Hewlett funded project—in addition to identifying competence-based programs—involved exploring competence frameworks that could be used for PLA adult learners. In collaboration with CAEL, colleagues and I conducted research involving prior learning assessors from LearningCounts.org to explore two key questions: What are some reasons to consider alternatives to course-based assessment? What are some implications for the assessment of prior learning? (Wilbur, Marienau, & Fiddler, 2012). In a nutshell, experienced assessors each evaluated prior learning portfolios—in fine arts, ethics, and nursing—using competence descriptions that the researchers provided from three different assessment tools: Lumina Foundation's Degree Qualifications Profile; AAC&U's LEAP essential learning outcomes; and School for New Learning's competence framework. In addition, each assessor used a course description match that he or she selected.

An overall finding was that "specific, flexible, and transparent assessment criteria were required for valid prior learning assessment, and these characteristics transcended course-based and competence-based approaches per se" (Wilbur, Marienau, & Fiddler, 2012, p. 2). My colleagues and I also found that competence-based assessment supports quality in important ways. For example, "competence statements with defined criteria provided specificity that enabled more accurate assessments since ambiguity and subjective interpretations were reduced" (Wilbur, Marienau, & Fiddler, 2012, p. 3). Given our experience, these findings were not surprising to us; however, we were pleased to see this theme emerge: "When clear and specific criteria guided portfolio development, the assessors said they could discern some of the students' development of ideas and reflections on their learning processes. . . . Consequently, the depth of their knowledge, application, and perspective could be analyzed more precisely, yielding a more balanced review" (Wilbur, Marienau, & Fiddler, 2012, p. 3) than might be the case with course-based assessments.

CAEL's work, along with other leaders in competence-based learning and assessment, has sparked considerable interest at the national level. Examples include foundations (e.g., Lumina, Bill and Melinda Gates), the U.S. Department of Education, the U.S. Department of Labor, and regional accrediting agencies. A scan of higher education news headlines in 2013 shows promising directions for higher education that will be of great benefit to adult learners:

- Credit hour unseated as the time-based measure of learning:
  - "The Curious Birth and Harmful Legacy of the Credit Hour" (*The Chronicle of Higher Education,* 1/21/2013)
  - "Accreditation in a Rapidly Changing World" (*Inside Higher Ed,* 1/31/13)

- "It's Official: U.S. Department of Education Approves First College to Ditch the Credit Hour" (*New America Foundations*, 4/18/2013)
- "New Directions for Higher Education: Q & A with Carnegie Foundation President Anthony Bryk About the Credit Hour" (*New England Journal of Higher Education*, 4/29/2013)

- Title IV financial aid provided for direct assessment in competence-based programs:
  - "Competency-Based Learning: A Big Deal, But Not Because of the Feds" (*Huffington Post* Blog, 4/02/2013)
  - "Competency-Based Education Heats Up With New Entrants" (*Inside Higher Ed*, 4/17/2013)

If we can crack the constraints of the credit hour and financial aid, historically two huge barriers, the paths will open for more innovations in competence-based learning and assessment for adult learners. We can look to the new pioneers—for example, Capella University, Northern Arizona University, College for America at Southern New Hampshire University—for different models of competence-based learning and assessment, including direct assessment where learning outcomes, rather than credit hours, are the recognized currency. We also can look to the Lumina Foundation and the Bill and Melinda Gates Foundation for funding of large-scale initiatives that seek to advance competence-based learning and assessment across the higher education landscape.

Higher education has indeed come a long way since Chick helped found Empire State College, edited *The Modern American College*, and oriented the Memphis State Center for Higher Education toward adult learners. Yes, many daunting challenges remain. We forge ahead as best we can because now, as then, we have so little time.

REFERENCES

Barker, R., & Gump, P. (1964). *Big school, small school*. Stanford, CA: Stanford University Press.

Bonnabeau, R. E. (1996). *The promise continues: Empire State College, the first twenty-five years*. Virginia Beach, VA: Donning.

Chickering, A. W. (1969). *Education and identity*. San Francisco, CA: Jossey-Bass.

Chickering, A. W. (1979). Adult development—implications for higher education. In V. R. McCoy, C. Ryan, & J. W. Lichtenberg (Eds.), *The adult life cycle*. Lawrence, KS: University of Kansas, Division of Continuing Education.

Chickering, A. W. (1980). Adult development: A workable vision for higher education. *Current Issues in Higher Education, 5*, 21–43.

Chickering, A. W. (Ed.). (1981). *The modern American college: Responding to the new realities of diverse students and a changing society*. San Francisco, CA: Jossey-Bass.

Chickering, A., & Claxton, C. (1981). What is competence? In R. Nickse & L. McClure (Eds.), *Competency-based education: Beyond minimum competency testing*. New York, NY: Teachers College, Columbia University.

Chickering, J. (1974). *Six years in the lives of six women* (Unpublished doctoral dissertation). Union Institute and University, Cincinnatti, Ohio.

DePaul University. (2012). *MAAPS program guidebook*. Chicago, IL: Author.

Eldred, M., & Marienau, C. (1979). *Adult baccalaureate programs* (AAHE/ERIC Higher Education Research Report No. 9). Washington, DC: American Association for Higher Education and ERIC Clearinghouse on Higher Education.

Fain, P. (2013, April 17). Big disruption, big questions. *Inside Higher Ed*. Retrieved from http://www.insidehighered.com/news/2013/04/17/competency-based-education-heats-new-entrants

Fiddler, M., Marienau, C., & Whitaker, U. (2006). *Assessing learning: Standards, principles, and Procedures* (2nd ed.). Dubuque, IO: Kendall/Hunt.

Hathaway, R. (1997). *The friendly pioneer: An informal history of the adult degree program*. Montpelier, VT: Word and Image Press.

Johnstone, S., Ewell, P., & Paulson, K. (2002). *Student learning as academic currency*. Washington, DC: American Council on Education.

Klein-Collins, R. (2010). *Fueling the race to postsecondary success: A 48-institution study of PLA and adult student outcomes*. Chicago, IL: Council for Adult and Experiential Learning.

Klein-Collins, R. (2011). Strategies for becoming adult-learning-focused institutions. *Peer Review, 13*(1), 5.

Klein-Collins, R. (2012). *Competency-based degree programs in the U.S.: Postsecondary credentials for measurable student learning and performance*. Chicago, IL: Council for Adult and Experiential Learning.

LeBlanc, P. J. (2013, April). Thinking about accreditation in a rapidly changing world. *Educause Review*. Retrieved from http://www.educause.edu/ero/article/thinking-about-accreditation-rapidly-changing-world

Lumina Foundation & Gallup. (2013). *America's call for higher education redesign*. Retrieved from http://www.luminafoundation.org/publications/Americas_Call_for_Higher_Education_Redesign.pdf

Lynch, A. Q., & Chickering, A. W. (1984). Comprehensive counseling and support programs for adult learners: Challenge to higher education. In H. B. Gelatt, N. K. Schlossberg, E. L. Herr, A. Q. Lynch, A. W. Chickering, G. R. Walz, & L. Benjamin (Eds.), *New perspectives on counseling adult learners* (pp. 45–73). Ann Arbor, MI: ERIC Counseling and Personnel Services Clearinghouse.

Lynch, A., Doyle, R., & Chickering, A. W. (1985). Model programs for adult learners in higher education. *The Phi Delta Kappan, 66*(10), 713–716.

Maehl, W. (2000). *Lifelong learning at its best: Innovative practices in adult credit programs*. San Francisco, CA: Jossey-Bass.

Marienau, C. (1999). *Principles for effectiveness for serving adult learners*. Chicago, IL: Council for Adult and Experiential Learning.

Marienau, C., & Chickering, A. W. (1982). Adult development and learning. In B. Menson (Ed.), *Building on experiences in adult development* (New directions for experiential learning, No. 16, pp. 62–84). San Francisco, CA: Jossey-Bass.

Marienau, C., & Lindquist, J. (1981). *Turning colleges toward adults*. Memphis, TN: Center for the Study of Higher Education, Memphis State University.

Schlossberg, N. K., Lynch, A. Q., & Chickering, A. W. (1989). *Improving higher education environments for adults: Responsive programs and services from entry to departure*. San Francisco, CA: Jossey-Bass.

Sherman, A. (2013). *Prior learning assessment: Making learning count*. Retrieved from http://www.evolllution.com/opinions/prior-learning-assessment-making-learning-count

Whitaker, U. (1989). *Assessing learning: Standards, principles, and procedures*. Chicago, IL: Council for Adult and Experiential Learning.

Wilbur, G., Marienau, C., & Fiddler, M. (2012). Authenticity for assurance and accountability: Reconnecting standards and qualities for PLA competence and course-based frameworks. *PLA Inside Out, 1*(2), 1–10. Retrieved from http://www.plaio.org/index.php/home/article/view/28/55

CHAPTER 9

Professional Reflections

W hen contemplating change in higher education, it helps to have a geological-time perspective. Like shifting tectonic plates, accumulated evidence and incontrovertible experiences collide, over time, with crusty traditions and unexamined assumptions. Hot magma spurts forth to maintain the status quo, protect turf, and preserve perks. Administrative habits and faculty self-interests override concerns for students and educational quality. Many of us who have wanted to rework the existing topography to create transformational and socially significant outcomes have felt the heat. But my coauthors (Part Two) and I persist. Looking back through 55 years, we see significant changes in the landscape.

We *have* succeeded in recognizing that knowledge transfer—getting right words in rote order—no matter how deep and broad, will not generate a citizenry competent enough to sustain a multicultural, globally interdependent, still emerging democracy, nor will it foster the motivation to do so. Professional and occupational preparation must meet the needs of rapidly changing work places. But we now realize that the skills, competencies, and mental models that were adequate for the factory and farm are no longer sufficient. We need to generate the complex perspectives and the cognitive, affective, and moral maturity required to respond intelligently and compassionately to international conflicts, climate changes, population explosions, and starvation. I am encouraged that, as in earlier publications, the Association of American Colleges and Universities continues to call for fundamental outcomes that are critical not only for civic engagement but also for a successful career, effective parenting, and a meaningful life. However, it is a long and rocky journey from espousing those outcomes to adapting them for particular institutional contexts, and creating the policies, practices, resource allocations, and institutional cultures required.

We have come to rely more and more on well-grounded research to anchor general policies and for continuous quality improvements within institutions. We can no longer say, as Nevitt Sanford wrote in 1962, that colleges and universities do not apply "scientific method to the understanding and evaluation of their own functioning" (p. v). Many are trying seriously to do so. But strong tensions continue among assessment, accountability, and improvement, as Peter Ewell (2009) discussed in an occasional paper published by the National Institute for Learning Outcomes Assessment. Underneath those tensions lies the difficulty in defining and assessing the interactive mix of personal characteristics and behavioral competencies called for by today's world.

In Chapter 8, Catherine Marienau ends her list of current challenges for higher education and adult learners by bringing readers up to date on competence outcomes-based learning and assessment. During the competency-based movement in the 1970s and early 1980s, Ruth Nickse at the Northwest Regional Educational Laboratory asked me to write the opening chapter for a competency-based education book she and a colleague were editing. Her suggested title was "What Is Competence?" I invited Chuck Claxton, a faculty member in the

Memphis State Center for Higher Education, to work with me. Here I quote parts of the introduction to our 40-page chapter at some length because I suspect many of the challenges we were up against at the time are still present today.

> What is competence? . . . If we can answer the question . . . the most difficult part of our deliberations will be behind, at least temporarily. . . .
>
> The authors . . . propose four basic principles that underlie the expression and development of competence . . . (1) the significance of situations and contexts that shape "competent" responses; (2) the perceptual and biological characteristics that delimit them; (3) the importance of employing diverse learning styles to achieve competence; and (4) the motivational nature of competence itself.
>
> In their second section the authors identify issues administrators and policy makers must examine as they turn their efforts to the design and implementation of programs. . . . and then there are the practical problems of the organization of instruction and its measurement. . . . It is learning *gains* that should be evaluated in a competency-based system and both our attitudes and our assessment techniques must become increasingly sophisticated to measure them.
>
> The authors then offer their own model . . . using the familiar Bermuda onion as a visual metaphor to help us think about competence levels and interactions among them. The surface layers are those aspects of competence that are most susceptible to change: called survival skills, and closely connected to basic skills, they are essential for daily living, as are those of the next layer, psychomotor skills. Underlying these in the inner

rings, which interact with those in the surface, are vocational skills; and nourishing them are intellectual and interpersonal skills. These in turn draw sustenance from even deeper layers, the generic abilities of the tendency and self-confidence to learning, which cling closely to the heart and foundation of the onion: ego development and self-determination. This metaphor will be useful to the extent that we understand the interaction of the skills and abilities, for each is dependent upon the others.

In conclusion, the authors point to some significant implications of the model for the design of competence-based programs. There is a need for altering structures of schooling to provide many diverse learning opportunities; and this will call for modification of both curricula and of instruction. Student evaluation and its reporting will be altered as well. Schools need to connect with other community agencies for a shared role in teaching and assessing competence. Finally, the authors observe that the notion that school is something that takes twelve years—no more, no less—will have to be set aside. For many, that may be the most difficult idea of all. (Chickering & Claxton, 1981, pp. 5–7)

In the mid the 1970s, research found that 90% to 95% of teaching consisted of lectures, texts, and midterm and final exams, except for associated laboratory work in the natural sciences. I don't know what the percentage would be now. I expect it is still high. But we have adapted and are improving alternatives for teaching and learning. Foremost among these has been service-learning, accompanied by other experiential alternatives that honor Dewey's (1938) basic precept that learning is the reconstruction of experience. Time for reflection has occasionally become integral for some teachers and courses. But at most institutions, these and other alternatives—learning communities, collaborative learning, student-faculty research, individually designed learning contracts—operate on the margins. They are exceptions; when, in reality, these approaches should pervade the full curriculum and be consistent with desired outcomes and available to all students depending on their preferred learning styles and educational purposes.

We also *have* begun to realize that it takes an integrated educational culture to have a significant impact on students. Culture can be integrated at the level of a department, school, college, or total university. When students, staff, faculty, student affairs professionals, and administrators pull together to sustain an integrated educational culture everyone is enriched and feels good about being identified with an organizational mission—at whatever level it occurs. But student experiences at most universities, colleges, schools, and departments remain fragmented. "Majors" may require combinations of course requirements, but seldom is the content thoughtfully integrated across courses and with other aspects of the college experience. Pedagogical strategies are rarely intentionally varied to achieve the larger desired outcomes. Rarely does collaboration among faculty members and student affairs professionals systematically integrate on-campus or off-campus out-of-class experiences with academic content and course requirements—and reflection about those interactions is marginal at best.

In the early 1970s, when increasing numbers of adult learners began to enroll, some of us hoped adult learners could be a significant force for change. There *have* been significant changes, as Catherine Marienau so aptly summarized in Chapter 8. However, many challenges remain, as her list for the CAEL *Principles for Effectiveness for Serving Adult Learners* (Marienau, 1999) indicates (see Chapter 8). She suggests that we need to merge the aims and traditions of adult higher education with a new vision for all of higher education. I certainly agree. But it's a rapidly changing landscape.

Now we have massive open online courses (MOOCs) accompanied by the rich potential of new information, communication, and interaction technologies. Perhaps this combination can drive substantial improvement. Perhaps institutions will lead with their best teaching and best teachers, acting on our best knowledge concerning ways powerful pedagogies interact with individual differences to maximize desired outcomes. Perhaps, given dramatically increased access and large numbers of globally diverse participants, sophisticated research can examine those interactions and drive continuous quality improvement. Perhaps these excellent examples, operating with sufficient scope, at sufficient scale, can influence the dominant approaches for credit-bearing, degree-generating teaching and learning.

At a different level, maybe interactions among learners with varied ethnic, religious, national, and cultural backgrounds will foster increased appreciation of and respect for those differences. Or, MOOCs might create more broad-based readiness and ability to tackle the critical challenges facing our beleaguered planet. We certainly need global learning and broad-based human development so those challenges can be productively managed rather than tearing us apart.

But that will be a long and difficult journey, even if we begin with our own colleges and universities. Consider the challenges faced by our federal, state, and local politicians, policy-makers, and diverse vested interests. We need to strengthen and sustain a multicultural, multiethnic, multireligious, internationally interdependent, pluralistic democracy. We need to identify and support policies, practices, and resource allocations that anticipate the dislocations and disruptions that will accompany global warming and the steady depletion of oil reserves. We need to contain and help ameliorate recurrent intertribal, interethnic, and interreligious conflicts. We need to address basic issues concerning public education, health care, and an aging population. We need to create a globally recognized example of participatory government where all persons are actively involved, regardless of socioeconomic status, race, national origin, or religious and spiritual orientation. To be effective, all our citizens must function at the levels of intellectual, emotional, and social complexity required to meet our global challenges.

But as I read papers and magazines, track political decision making, listen to talk shows, and experience the general culture, I see that we are far from the levels of complex functioning required to effect these changes. From my personal perspective, our political, economic, and social systems and the policies, practices, and resource-allocation decisions associated with them are functioning at the most basic levels articulated by various seminal human development theorists. I am sure not everyone agrees with me, and I invite you to make your own judgments.

Conceptual frameworks developed by human-development theorists—Loevinger; Kegan; Kohlberg; Perry; and Belenky, Clinchy, Goldberger, and Tarule—offer a sense of the kinds of persons our students need to become. I lead off with Loevinger's ego development and Keegan's evolving self because they are the most general and comprehensive. Then come Kohlberg and Perry, with their narrower focus on cognitive-moral development and intellectual-ethical development. Finally, Belenky et al. focus on "ways of knowing."

Any "grand theory" is reductionistic, given human complexity and multicultural diversity. Also, these conceptual frameworks and their associated research are almost entirely "Western" and north of the equator, with all our unrecognized and unarticulated values and assumptions. With apologies to these seminal thinkers, I try to avoid jargon and use nickel words. I will also be categorical and omit the usual qualifiers that typically accompany social science research findings. My brief renditions will sound more definitive and unequivocal than these good folks would like.

Jane Loevinger

Loevinger's research was done during the 1950s, 1960s, and early 1970s, with her major work published in 1976. It has been criticized for mainly being anchored in research on men, and we need to recognize the male-dominated culture of the time.

Loevinger (1976) posited five stages pertinent to adults: self-protective, conformist, conscientious, autonomous, and integrated. Persons at the self-protective stage externalize blame and are not characteristically self-critical. They are vulnerable and guarded, with fragile controls. The main rule is "don't get caught"; getting caught means the action was wrong. They are opportunistic, exploitative, deceitful, and competitive.

Conformists identify their own welfare with that of their particular reference group and the group is defined by its external characteristics. Belonging means security. Rules are there to be obeyed, not questioned. Right and wrong are defined by rules rather than consequences. They are given to moralistic clichés. Disapproval is a potent sanction. They are insensitive to individual differences and have stereotyped conceptions of gender roles. They value niceness, helpfulness, and cooperation.

Major elements of adult conscience are present for persons at the conscientious stage. Long-term, self-evaluated goals and ideals are important. These persons evince differentiated self-criticism and a sense of responsibility. They measure achievement by their own standards. Rules are evaluated, chosen, and internalized; they are not absolutes; contingencies and exceptions are recognized. They see things in a broader context and can see matters from another person's point of view. They feel responsible for other persons and have a sense of interpersonal mutuality. They have a sense of choice and of creating their own destiny.

Persons at the autonomous stage can acknowledge and cope with inner conflict. They express feelings vividly and convincingly. They have a high tolerance for ambiguity, can integrate ideas, transcend polarities, and see reality as complex and multifaceted. They cherish personal ties, recognize others' need for autonomy, and aspire to be realistic about themselves and others. Self-fulfillment is a frequent goal, but they also recognize the limitations of autonomy and the need for interdependence. They view life as a whole and hold to broad, abstract, social ideals.

For Loevinger, very few people reach the "integrated" stage. Thus, she has few descriptors. They have a consolidated sense of identity and transcend conflicts. While they are self-actualized, they are always open to new possibilities.

So ask yourself, which of these stages characterizes our current culture? our political rhetoric, processes, and policies? our decisions regarding domestic issues? our economic orientation and practices? our budget priorities? our approaches to varied global challenges?

Robert Keegan

Keegan's (1982) developmental perspective is anchored in the dynamic between "the yearning to be included, to be part of, close to, joined with, to be held, admitted, accompanied, and the yearning to be independent or autonomous, to experience one's distinctiveness, the self-chosenness of one's directions, one's individual integrity" (p. 107). Development occurs as we move from being embedded in one pattern toward the other polarity. How we make meaning changes as this movement occurs. We observe that former pattern with greater detachment as we become embedded in the new one.

We move from Stage 1, the "impulsive balance," by learning greater impulse control; to *have* our impulses, not to *be* them. Keegan puts the modal age for this shift from 5 to 7. Stage 2 is called the "imperial balance" because others are there to "meet my needs, fulfill my wishes, pursue my interests" (p. 91). Others, therefore, have to be controlled, manipulated, or predictable. In Stage 3, the "interpersonal balance," we no longer *are* our needs but *have* them. We now experience a shared reality with others. With this shift away from self-centeredness, we can now try to coordinate and integrate our needs with others' in relationships of mutuality, if not intimacy. In Keegan's view, mature intimacy requires an independent self. But this stage requires a significant other to feel complete, to define oneself, to make life meaningful. "There is no self to share with another: instead the other is required to bring the self into being. Fusion is not intimacy. If one can feel manipulated by the imperial balance, one can feel devoured by the interpersonal one" (pp. 96–97). In Stage 4, the "institutional balance," we realize that we are not our relationships, instead we *have* our relationships. This shift requires a relatively autonomous self that can create and give up relationships. Our emotional life is more internally managed. Personal rejection is less important than personal integrity. This ability to stand alone, without a group's approval or without fusion with another person, is a major developmental step. Stage 5 is the "interindividual balance." We now can reflect on, from some psychic distance, our own individual values, purposes, and reactions. We can try to understand the complex dynamics that govern our beliefs and behaviors. Instead of simply being that complexity, we can try to manage it, to be more intentional about the kind of person we are, to better create our own future. We can accept our impulses and our emotional and instrumental interdependence, without being owned by them.

From Keegan's perspective we must continually work to find the balance between too much independence and too much dependence. We must continually create a balance between care of the self and concern for others, from which we can speak and act authentically.

Where would you place our culture, or different segments of it? Have we moved beyond the impulsive and imperial balances? The George W. Bush administration has been called an "imperial presidency." Does that seem accurate in Keegan's terms? Where are we with regard to the interpersonal and institutional balances? Are any of our institutions or subcultures at the interindividual balance?

Lawrence Kohlberg

Kohlberg (1971) posited six stages of cognitive-moral judgment. Each stage describes characteristic expectations about how each other's actions are coordinated, how rules are knowable and sharable, schemes of social cooperation, how equilibrium of interests is achieved, and a central concept for determining moral rights and responsibilities.

Stage 1 is the morality of obedience: "Do what you are told." Stage 2 is the morality of instrumental egoism and simple exchange: "Let's make a deal." Stage 3 is the morality of personal conscience: "Be considerate, nice, and kind, and you'll get along with people." Stage 4 is the morality of law and duty to the social order: "Everyone in society is obligated and protected by the law." Stage 5 is the morality of societal consensus: "What laws the people want to make are what ought to be." Finally, Stage 5 is the morality of social cooperation. How rational and impartial people would organize cooperation is what is moral.

Which of these stages currently characterizes our culture?

William Perry

Perry's (1970) scheme of intellectual and ethical development is based on his research at Harvard University beginning in 1955, when he headed up the counseling center there. Perry's theory is probably the most well known to colleges and university administrators and student affairs professionals, and to some faculty members.

He posited a continuum of nine "positions," each of which represents a more differentiated and integrated way of thinking, seeing, knowing, and being. They are clustered within four stages, each of which builds on and incorporates the former: dualism (positions 1 and 2); multiplicity (positions 3 and 4), relativism (positions 5 and 6), and commitment in relativism (positions 7, 8, and 9).

For dualists, knowledge exists absolutely and authorities have the "right answers." Thinking about options or different points of view is confusing. When authorities have different opinions or are uncertain, they are inadequate. Alternate perspectives are not acknowledged or legitimate. In multiplicity, persons accept diversity and uncertainty as legitimate, but temporary, where authority has not yet found the answers. Questions can now have multiple answers and those who hold different beliefs are no longer simply wrong. For dualists, all opinions are equally valid outside authority's realm, within which right and wrong still prevail. Dualists are unable to adequately evaluate different points of view, and they question whether it is legitimate to do so.

In relativism, all knowledge, including authority's, is contextual and relativistic. Right-wrong thinking is only appropriate within certain contexts. These persons can differentiate between an unconsidered opinion and a considered judgment. Authorities can be valued for their expertise, but their judgments also can be evaluated. Differing perspectives are seen as pieces of a larger whole. Personal commitments are ways to orient oneself in a relativistic world. With commitment in relativism, persons have a growing realization that they need to create their own choices based on multiple truths. They begin to align choices with personal themes. Actively affirming themselves and their responsibilities in a pluralistic world helps clarify their identity; decisions concerning marriage, career, religion, and politics are made from a relativistic frame of reference.

Perry also posited two associated dynamics, "escape" and "retreat." Escape exploits the opportunities for detachment offered by positions 4 and 5 and denies responsibility through passive or opportunistic alienation. Retreat entrenches persons in the dualistic and absolutistic structures of positions 2 or 3.

Perry's scheme and his associated dynamics recall Erich Fromm's (1941) *Escape from Freedom*, and the authoritarian-personality formulations of Adorno, Frenkel-Brunswik, Levinson, and Sanford's (1950) *The Authoritarian Personality*. These social psychologists were trying to understand how Germans, one of Europe's most highly educated and culturally sophisticated people, could have been led to support Hitler, engage in Kristallnacht, and tolerate the Holocaust. After being defeated in World War 1, the Germans suffered not only humiliation but severe economic depression and uncertainty about the future. Fromm's theory is that under these conditions, the populace escaped from freedom and gave themselves to the certainties of Aryan superiority espoused by Hitler and his collaborators. The authoritarian-personality research posited a dynamic where people suck up and kick down. They needed scapegoats and the Jews, among others, were handy targets.

For me, *Escape from Freedom* and *The Authoritarian Personality* sound a lot like Perry's dualism and his escape and retreat dynamics. They also sound like Kohlberg's morality of obedience and of instrumental egoism and simple exchange.

Do we see similar responses and dynamics in the United States in response to 9/11? Does something like this lie behind some of the more extreme parts of the Homeland Security legislation accompanied by unfettered surveillance and wire tapping? Are these dynamics similar to those faced by many upright Muslims, who are longstanding citizens or residents of the United States? If so, what can be done to prepare our students to respond differently from our politicians?

Mary Belenky, Blithe Clinchy, Nancy Goldberger, and Jill Tarule

In *Women's Ways of Knowing,* Belenky, Clinchy, Goldberger, and Tarule (1986) build on Perry. They interviewed women about their experiences as learners and their changing concepts of self and relationships. These researchers analyzed 135 transcripts—90 students from six academic institutions, including a high school, and 45 persons referred by family agencies rendering information or assistance in parenting. They described five epistemological perspectives that, with some important differences, parallel Perry's scheme.

The first perspective is "silence." These women were among the youngest and most educationally, economically, and socially deprived of those in the study. They had no voice of their own. Authorities were all-powerful. These women rarely engaged in dialogue and therefore missed opportunities to speak, listen, reflect, and share. Life is a set of polarities: good-bad, win-lose. Women play stereotyped roles and are incompetent, passive, and dependent on men.

Perspective 2, "received knowledge," is similar to Perry's dualism. Learning occurs by listening carefully to authorities and getting the right answers. Structure, clarity, and predictability are important. Women in this perspective built symbiotic relationships, valued conversation, and were relieved to hear others saying "the very same things they would say" (p. 37).

With "subjective knowledge," Perspective 3, the women had moved from silence and passivity to a "protesting inner voice and infallible gut" (p. 54). No longer is knowledge absolute nor are authorities infallible. But the women are not confident about their opinions, often do not express themselves, and want others to affirm their views. They felt that truth was frequently intuited and often incommunicable.

Perspective 4 is "procedural knowledge." Absolutism and subjectivism give way to reasoned reflection. Some conclusions have more credibility than others, depending on evidence and logic. Intuitive knowing is no longer sufficient. Real knowing requires careful observation and the correct form or method. The researchers found two separate styles of procedural knowing. "Separate knowing" is when truth is established through impersonal procedures, doubt and debate, public defense, and exclusion of personal feelings or beliefs. "Connected knowing" comes from firsthand experiences, from understanding another's ideas, from conversation rather than debate, from clarifying rather than judging, from collaborating and nurturing emerging ideas rather than critiquing them.

Perspective 5, "constructed knowledge," integrates personally important knowing with knowledge learned from others. The knower becomes part of the known, weaving together reason and emotion, objective and subjective information. Different ways of knowing and different parts of the self are respected. Instead of compartmentalizing thought and feeling, conscious and unconscious, work and home, self and other, these persons look for ways to transcend boundaries. They resist oversimplification and see that answers vary depending on the context in which they are asked and the frame of reference of the questioner. Authorities are valued based on their competence, not their status. They can collaborate with other "constructivists" to seek new awareness and use intellectual competence to contribute to larger spheres and use the self as a basis for increasing understanding and expanding knowledge.

What ways of knowing underlie the approaches used on various television networks and talk shows? What do they assume about their audiences? How would you describe the differences between ABC, NBC, CBS, Fox, and PBS? What are the differences among Jim Lehrer, Rush Limbaugh, Charlie Rose, and Oprah Winfrey? How would you describe different newspapers, columnists, and editorial writers? Are there definable differences among *Time, Newsweek, U.S. News and World Report, The Nation,* and *Commentary*?

Each of you will have you own reflections on these questions. As Belenky et al. (1986) recognized, our individual responses will be shaped by our own particular mental models. From my perspective, the important thing is not so much *what* we think about the complex issues we all face, but *how* we think about them. Although, not surprisingly, I would like everyone to vote for my favorite candidates, I am more concerned with the basis on which we cast our votes and function as engaged citizens. I am mainly concerned about the intellectual, emotional, and developmental complexity on which those beliefs and behaviors rest. We are a nation blessed with richly diverse backgrounds and perspectives among our citizens. Wisdom and a healthy, happy, and productive future can be generated if we can construct global, federal, state, and local policies and practices that capitalize on that variety. The comments of my coauthors in the preceding chapters suggest that we do know how to create educationally powerful colleges and universities that can graduate engaged citizens able to help us create a well-functioning democracy.

I end these professional reflections with the developmental orientation that became the foundation for my 55-year career in higher education. That earlier research and theory continues to inform me. I recognize its limitations, but human development theory remains the best basis for my own thinking about lifelong learning, the purposes of higher education, and their potential contributions to creating a better world. I also recognize the intellectual and political challenges of acting on and assessing developmental outcomes that Jon Dalton identified in Chapter 7. Perhaps I'm just stubborn and stuck in my ways, but I continue to argue that human development, with all its richness and complexity, with all its associated educational and assessment challenges, needs to be a priority focus for all our institutions. At this historic time, our diverse 2-year and 4-year colleges and our universities, among all those around the globe, are best positioned to provide such leadership.

I cannot imagine what higher education will be like 55 years from now. When I got my first job at Monmouth College in 1958, television was not ubiquitous. There were three networks: ABC, CBS, and NBC. The state-of-the-art antenna I attached to the sugar maple behind our house brought one network station into the house on a wire. Jo and I, with our four kids, huddled in front of the television for the Smothers Brothers, the moon landing, Sid Caesar, Walter Cronkite, and a few other shows. On Saturday mornings the kids watched *Mr. Rogers*. I did the covariance analyses for my dissertation on a fancy new Marchand calculator. All the data from the Project on Student Development in Small Colleges instruments were punched into computer cards that we took to the mainframe computer at the University of Vermont for analysis. The interstate highway system was in its infancy, making its way slowly up through Vermont. Air travel was a treat. I could get to the Montpelier airport 10 minutes before a half-full Eastern Air Lines plane took me to Logan International Airport in Boston, where my connections going west, south, and occasionally east to Europe were easy. Adolescents and young adults did not encounter the vividly portrayed lifestyle alternatives with all their associated familial, occupational, and moral choices and dilemmas. Distance and blended learning were unheard of.

I cannot rehearse all the changes that have occurred since then. Nor can I predict whether faculty members will continue to be more driven by their personal disciplinary and professional interests than by what students need and want to learn; nor how much our curricula will be driven more by limited institutional priorities than by global, national, and regional educational issues. I cannot predict whether college and university presidents will be first and foremost administrators concerned with fundraising, budgets, resource allocations, and personnel decisions, or whether they will be educational leaders trying to help resistant faculty and staff respond to new realities. But there certainly will be significant challenges coming from the dynamics of accelerating technological, professional, and social changes.

In my experience, student affairs professionals have been energized by the challenges they have faced. More than any others in our institutions, they have been confronted with the new realities brought by generational changes, by increasing numbers of adult learners, and by socioeconomic, racial, ethnic, and international diversity. I hope the student-learning imperative will be taken seriously, that a comprehensive approach to student learning will be the organizing focus for all their varied professional activities. With administrators absorbed by the daunting challenges of simply keeping the institution afloat and thriving, and with faculty members absorbed by their own disciplinary and professional interests, I hope members of this significant profession will become student-learning experts. As was the case when I first started working in higher education decades ago, creating the conditions for learning remains a complex challenge. Research and theory will continue to deepen our understanding of those conditions. We will learn more and more about how the conditions for learning have to vary for the diverse subgroups of learners we need to serve and for the individual differences within them. Student affairs professionals meet these persons more fully than faculty members and administrators. Becoming knowledgeable about the implications of individual differences for educational policies and practices is critically important if students are to reach their potential and if our global imperative is to be served. I hope student affairs educators will rise to that challenge.

I wish I could be around to join other friends and colleagues to try to capitalize on this significant opportunity and to bang away at the inevitable sources of resistance. I wish I could live long enough to once again share a geological-time perspective that will undoubtedly reflect huge worldwide changes in higher education and lifelong learning. But I must, eventually, leave that challenge to younger colleagues sufficiently motivated to take it on.

REFERENCES

Adorno, T. W., Frenkel-Brunswik, E. F., Levinson, D., & Sanford, N. (1950). *The authoritarian personality: Studies in prejudice.* New York, NY: Harper and Row.

Belenky, M. F., Clinchy, B. M., Goldberger, N. R., & Tarule, J. M. (1986). *Women's ways of knowing: The development of self, mind, and voice.* New York, NY: Basic Books.

Chickering, A. W., & Claxton, C. (1981). What is competence? In R. S. Nickse & L. McClure (Eds.), *Competency-based education: Beyond minimum competency testing.* New York, NY: Teachers College Press.

Dewey, J. (1938). *Experience and education.* New York, NY: Macmillan.

Ewell, P. T. (2009, November). *Assessment, accountability, and improvement: Revisiting the tension* (NILOA Occasional Paper No.1). Urbana, IL: University of Illinois and Indiana University, National Institute for Learning Outcomes Assessment.

Fromm, E. (1941). *Escape from freedom.* New York, NY: Holt, Rhinehart, and Winston.

Keegan, R. (1982). *The evolving self: Problem and process in human development.* Cambridge, MA: Harvard University Press.

Kohlberg, L. (1971). Stages of moral development. In C. M. Beck, B. S. Crittenden, & E. V. Sullivan (Eds.), *Moral education.* Toronto, Canada: University of Toronto Press.

Loevinger, L. (1971). *Ego development: Conceptions and theories.* San Francisco, CA: Jossey-Bass.

Marienau, C. (1999). *Principles for effectiveness for serving adult learners.* Chicago, IL: Council for Adult and Experiential Learning.

Perry, W. G. (1970). *Forms of intellectual and ethical development in the college years: A scheme.* New York, NY: Holt, Rhinehart, and Winston.

Sanford, N. (1962). *The American college: A psychological and social interpretation of higher learning.* New York, NY: Wiley.

PART THREE

"Retiring" to Vermont

In January of 1995 George Johnson announced that he would retire from George Mason University at the end of the 1995–1996 academic year. I was not interested in taking chances with a new president. At the same time, my closest friend and colleague, David Potter, was thinking of leaving George Mason; he began chasing college and university presidencies. His artist wife Pam Mathews was a Hope Diamond; beautiful, brilliant, multi-faceted, she lit up every space she inhabited with a penetrating intellect, heartfelt sensitivity, and concern for her fellow human beings and social issues. She had resigned from her appointment to the National Council for the Arts when Senator Jesse Helms threatened to cut their funding because they had supported the artist who created the controversial *Piss Christ* sculpture. David, Pam, Jo, and I had become a finely woven, multicolored tapestry that warmed and enriched us all. Jo and I did not look forward to living in northern Virginia with a big hole in that fabric if Pam and David left.

Virginia was facing a budget crunch and was offering early-retirement packages to induce senior professors to leave. On April 27, 1996, I would turn 69, easily qualifying for early retirement. I met with Fred Rossini, the academic vice president, and we agreed on half pay for 2 years with continued health benefits—a very generous package—beginning in July.

Jo and I were impatient about moving back to Vermont. I had learned what George Mason University had to offer, and we had experienced enough of the northern Virginia environment. Our next, and last, move would be back to our homestead. We were more than ready to trade Virginia's around-the-clock white noise and traffic for the gurgling brook running down our little watershed, and the blare of horns for the honks of Canada geese flying north, stopping to rest and feed on our beaver ponds. We would trade Yo-Yo Ma, Wynton Marsalis, chamber music, and symphony concerts for the quacks of mallards and mergansers, the drumbeats of woodpeckers and grouse, the caws of crows and ravens. We would ramble our woods and fields instead of pounding the pavements in the District of Columbia. The following chapters share the twists and turns of our lives since we came back home.

CHAPTER 10

Home Again

When we drove up our dead-end dirt road, past the fields and ponds, to the old house and barn, it felt as though we were coming home after an around-the-world excursion filled with adventures and challenges. And in many ways we were. We had lived and worked in four strikingly different cultures: Vermont and the Northeast, Memphis and the Deep South, northern Virginia with nearby Washington, D.C., and France. We had encountered diverse persons in 57 countries on all the continents except Antarctica. We had experienced loving relationships and intimate friendships with people whose backgrounds were very different from our New England heritage, and we had successfully tackled jobs that challenged our preexisting knowledge, competence, and personal styles. All these activities and experiences kept us learning and developing in ways that made us much different now from when we were the young couple who married in 1951 and raised a boy and three girls in these buildings, on this land.

Our lives and learning certainly were not over, nor even winding down, but from now on they would be anchored here. Turning off the ignition, sitting in the silence, was like heaving a huge sigh. For the first

247

time in 45 years we could relax into a time and place, we could create this last chapter of our lives, strongly together, without wondering where we would go next. It was deeply satisfying to realize that as individuals and as a married couple, we had survived all these challenges. We 69 and 67 year olds had built a solid foundation for the new and inevitable challenges we would face with aging. There was nowhere else we would rather be in the world than right here, with children and grandchildren nearby, away from the urban and suburban life, in the midst of a natural world we could savor.

As we sat in the car together, quietly holding hands, our grandsons Lars, Gabe, and Silas burst from the house, followed by our daughter Sue and her husband, John. There was certainly plenty of energy here, welcoming us home. They carried our suitcases into the bedroom off the living room that used to be an office, where I had written *Education and Identity*. That work had triggered our departure; those perspectives and values still powered my ongoing professional activities. Dinner on the old screened-in porch, looking through the bright sun to Spruce Mountain on the horizon, recalled all those other meals with family and friends, and our weekly family councils where we sorted out our difficulties and agreed about weekly chores. An earthy odor from the freshly tilled garden down by the pond filled my nostrils. It was the same plot that I had fenced in for Jo's peas, beans, tomatoes, corn, peppers, beets, lettuce, summer squash, and prolific zucchinis, where our daughter Nancy had created the first of many strawberry patches, and now where Sue had added a ground-level, battery-charged electric-wire fence to keep out the woodchucks.

After dinner we walked down the road to our new dream house with John, who was building it with Kris, Nancy's husband. Fresh cedar siding and forest green trim blended nicely with the woods behind. They were finishing up inside and it would be completed by the end of

August. Jo and I hugged each other at the prospect of moving in. Two beavers in the pond across the road slapped their tails and dove as we walked back to the house. But dark clouds hung over the hills to the northwest. Stormy weather was on the way; if not tomorrow, later on.

When we drilled the well for our water supply, we hit 6 gallons a minute. That flow meant we needed to bleed it off to relieve the pressure on the tank and pipes in the house. Jo suggested we put in a small pool and fountain that could serve as a bird bath. My penchant for before-breakfast dips led to a kidney-shaped plunge pool. John built a dock and ladder so I could dive in and climb back out. Fifty brook trout from a nearby hatchery scattered when I dove in to wash off the sweat from working around the place.

Neither Jo nor I were enthusiastic about wide expanses of lawn. We both preferred looking out on a grassy field with its wildflowers and bird life. I seeded and fertilized a small area around the house and pond, and we let the open space down to the road simply take its course. We watched daisies, goldenrod, and brown-eyed susans bloom, and chickadees, gold and purple finches, and tree swallows feed on the seeds and bugs. The wild cherry and the old crabapple trees we had left beside the driveway attracted downy and hairy woodpeckers, along with red and white nuthatches. I put a 5-foot-by-8-inch board outside the windows looking down toward the beaver ponds, with cracked corn, sunflower seeds, and thistle seeds that attracted the birds up from the fields and down from the trees. After John finished a 10-foot cherry plank and set it up inside the windows, we watched them eat only 2 feet from our noses, while we fed ourselves on corn flakes, Raisin Bran, tuna melts, and BLTs.

I arranged to work part time with Jack Kytle, who had become dean of Vermont College as part of Norwich University when he left the Goddard presidency. After showing me a spacious office across from his on the top floor of College Hall, he described the backgrounds of faculty members from Norwich University and Vermont College who could comprise a task force I would lead to design a new doctoral program. I moved my books and files from our garage and arranged my upcoming professional travels for speaking engagements. I met with President Richard Schneider prior to a welcoming reception for me that occurred in the Wood Art Gallery on the first floor. A number of Vermont College faculty members were there. Several of them had moved from Goddard along with the low-residency program, and it was nice to see them again. This small, congenial, relaxed institution, located 6 miles from our house, mostly over dirt back roads, was a welcome change from the hard-charging culture of George Mason University and the perpetual hustle of northern Virginia. I delighted at the prospect of working with these progressive, innovative educators and helping to get a new kind of doctoral program underway.

Jo and I gloried in our woods and fields, amazed at how much they had changed during the 20 years we had been gone. We reconnected with old friends. My younger brother, Rob, who had moved to Vermont several years earlier, invited me to join a monthly poker game that had been underway since the early 1980s; Al Soule, another poker playing buddy from the 1970s, took me to two other games. Wedgewood, the indoor tennis facility Jo and I had enjoyed, had new management, but many of the former players we had known were still there. By early July we were well fixed with frequent mixed-doubles matches. I partnered with Rob and also met some new singles opponents.

A nice new chainsaw helped me drop, limb off, and cut up maples, white and yellow birch, with occasional poplar and beech, for our winter wood supply. Seven heavy loads in a 6-by-12-foot wooden trailer hitched to the Ford tractor took the fruits of my labor into the garage. The masonry heater took logs up to 12 inches in diameter and 20 inches long, so I did not often have to split larger pieces with my sledge and wedges. The tractor loads, with those heavy logs, meant I felt no guilt foregoing the upper-body machines at the fitness club. Heating with wood kept me fit and warm seven times: when I dropped the trees, cut them up, loaded the wood into the trailer, stacked it in the garage, carried it into the house, put it into the stove, and after I finally lit it.

Since we had first lived in the old farmhouse, from 1964 to 1979, and now in our new home, getting in wood has been one of the most satisfying kinds of work I've done. For me, an academic—teacher, researcher, writer, administrator—it has always been hard to know whether I've done anything really useful. Maybe my students will have learned something valuable for themselves and the world. Maybe those data, articles, books, and speeches will add some useful knowledge and contribute to better educational conditions or improved performance. Maybe those strategic plans, budgets, personnel decisions, and innovations will actually have some lasting value. But it's all very vague, abstract, and uncertain. Continued effort often depends on self-serving assumptions. Yes, I've been lucky to get some awards and recognition, and I've had some moving testimonies from students. But none of that provides the immediate and direct satisfaction of seeing 7 cords of wood—a 2-year supply—stacked in the garage. And thinning out old and deformed trees improves the stand, freeing trees to grow sound and straight for future generations

During September, after we moved in and the construction activity had ceased, deer came to browse the field and eat the dropped apples. The beavers were busy maintaining their dams, solidifying their houses, and dragging in alder and poplar branches for a winter food supply. One sunrise, as we sipped our coffee and ate muffins, two black bears ambled down our driveway and across the lower field to the upper beaver dam. Much to our surprise, the smaller of the two jumped into the water and took a swim before climbing back up and strolling into the woods. I was not the only creature to enjoy a cooling dip.

Soon we woke up to frost on the grass and leaves littering the lawn. Sweater weather was here. It had been 20 years since the flaming reds and sunshine yellows of the maples, birch, poplar, beech, and tamaracks filled our eyes and hearts. Under canopies of blue, time and again, we simply stopped in our tracks, or pulled over to the side of the road, transfixed. The setting sun's flat light brightened the colors against the ridge above the beaver ponds, where glassy waters reflected each branch, leaf, and needle. Looking out through our living-room windows were impressionist paintings that Monet, Manet, and Matisse could never produce. On afternoon walks through our woods and fields, we were small figures framed by landscapes beyond the ability of Renoir or van Gogh.

The fall foliage also heralded hunting. The bird and bear seasons were upon us; bow and rifle seasons for deer and moose filled Vermont back roads and woods with locals and down-country folks. Posting our land so we could continue rambling safely gave me a chance to walk our boundaries, nailing 8-by-12-inch signs every hundred yards or so. Some of the old red-painted blazes I had put on 41 years ago were still apparent. Though the woods and fields had changed dramatically, it was nice to realize that after being away 20 years I could still follow the lines. We were happy to have others enjoy our woods, and glad to give friends and neighbors permission to hunt, but wanted some protection from out-of-state hunters who shot neighbors' cows and occasionally each other.

Jo soon discovered the Barre and Montpelier Restorative Justice boards. These five-person boards met with convicted offenders and worked out 90-day contracts the latter could pursue instead of going to jail. Those contracts called for service activities to make amends for the individual injuries they had caused and to the particular organizations or communities that had been hurt. In addition, the contracts typically involved reading pertinent research and theory about their particular offenses and writing about how that material applied to their own personal situations and dynamics. The justice boards met weekly for an hour or two with individual offenders to track their progress. A successfully completed contract meant the person's term had been served and the offense was expunged from his or her record. Jo's wide experience and deep insights concerning human behavior, combined with her loving kindness and counseling expertise, made her an ideal board member. This volunteer work, with its attendant involvement with Vermont's criminal justice system, added a rich dimension to both our lives.

We welcomed the winter snows, eager to get out into that pristine beauty on skis and snowshoes. Signs of life not so apparent when the ground was bare enriched our walks. Deer tracks led us to their beds on the ridge above the beaver pond. Fox tracks chased rabbits. Otters slid down slopes to dine on trout and crawfish in our ponds and streams. Porcupines fed in tree tops, littering the snow with twigs. Coyotes joined forces to kill deer, leaving fur, bones, and bloody spots in cedar thickets. All around us life went on, newly apparent with each fresh snowfall.

With these and other activities, Jo and I found our way back into this environment and culture we had never stopped loving. We renewed old friendships and made new ones. During the 20 years since we had left for Memphis in 1977, we had flown separately and together, come apart and reunited. Our global travels had never taken us to any place we would rather live out our remaining years. After all the comings and goings and diverse relationships, we never met anyone else with whom we wished to create our future. We were home at last, looking forward to a golden age close to family members and friends, filled with challenging new adventures at home and abroad.

But then a new life thrust itself upon us.

CHAPTER 11

Thrust into a New Life

January 22, 1999. Jo and I were hit with a new life. Like nothing we had experienced before, it was as powerful mix of emotional, intellectual, and physical challenges. It would trigger vectors—if I can use that word—of personal development and dimensions of maturity we never knew we had.

Some people were worried about bioterrorism in the wake of anthrax hoaxes. John McCain was the presumptive Republican presidential candidate. John Grisham's *The Street Lawyer* topped the bestseller lists. A prescient *New York Times* article predicted a housing crash because many people were over their heads in debt. But for Jo and me the day started out like most others around that time.

I climbed out of bed at 5:30 a.m., jumped into my tennis clothes, and got breakfast. A scarlet and purple sunrise filled our southeast windows. Vermont Public Radio called for clear, sunny weather, temperatures in the 20s, no snow coming. I took cocoa and a muffin up to Jo, where she was composing and revising poems on her computer.

"Looks like a good afternoon for snowshoeing," I said. "I'll be home for lunch about 12."

I climbed into our faithful 1994 Nissan Pulsar and headed down the driveway onto Chickering Road, bound for my morning workout and tennis match. After 15 minutes on the cross trainer, three sets of doubles, and a shower, I went to my Vermont College office. I headed home after returning phone calls and sending off the latest draft of an article titled "The Collegiate Ideal in the Twenty-First Century" for a forthcoming issue of *New Directions in Higher Education* published by Jossey-Bass.

My ever-loving, smiling wife was there with a hug and a kiss. "How was the tennis?"

"Up and down. No concentration. Lost the first set 6-3. Then I got my feet moving, eye on the ball, and head in gear. We won the next two, 6-4 and 6-2."

"I'll make tuna melts for lunch," she said. "We can eat about 12:45."

"It's a beautiful day. We can rest a bit and snowshoe up to the bog," I said.

"The rose-breasted grosbeaks should be singing in the tops of the spruce. On our way back we can check out the fisher tracks. I've seen them going up the brook and over the beaver dam. They're fishing out the trout you put in last fall."

I took an Old Fashioned glass off the shelf, dropped in four ice cubes, filled it close to the brim with Poland Spring—the cheapest gin available in the New Hampshire liquor stores—and added a dollop of Stock vermouth. I watched about a dozen World Poker Tour hands on television until Jo announced lunch. We sipped cabernet and ate our tuna melts at the cherry plank where we looked across the fields and our dirt road to the two iced-over beaver ponds. On the outdoor shelf chickadees, woodpeckers, jays, red- and white-breasted nuthatches, and mourning doves were loading up on sunflower seeds, cracked corn, and suet.

"I'll deal with my e-mails while you take it easy for a bit," I said. "Have a good rest. I'll be down in an hour or so."

"No rush," she said, flopping on the couch.

I had worked my way through several e-mails when I heard, "Help! Chick, help!"

I jumped up. My chair back hit the floor. Bounding down the stairs two at a time, I found Jo, hands and knees on the floor between the coffee table and couch, white hair hanging down over her eyes, turtleneck sweater askew at her waist. A couch pillow rested on the floor by her shoulder. Radiation from our wood-fired heater warmed all the surfaces. Smells from our tuna-melt lunch lingered in the air.

"Help me up. I'm feeling sick. I need to get to the bathroom."

Putting a hand under each of her arms, I lifted her. She was unsteady on her feet. We hobbled around the coffee table, by the heater and cellar door, and into the john. Sliding down her slacks and panties, she dropped onto the toilet.

"I can't feel my left arm. I'm dizzy and woozy."

"Just stay put," I said.

I called our daughter Nancy, who is a medical doctor and works half time in the Central Vermont Medical Center Emergency Room. Fortunately, she was home.

"I think Jo has had a stroke. She reminds me of that woman I rented a room from in Fairfax."

"Call 911 and get her to the emergency room. I'll be there when you arrive."

I dialed 911 and Bob, who runs a nearby convenience store, answered.

"Hi, Bob. This is Art Chickering. Come quick. We need to get Jo to the emergency room."

How the hell can this be happening? I asked myself. Jo is fit as a fiddle. She was just resting on the couch. When I got back to the bathroom she was holding her head and moaning.

"I feel really strange. I don't know what's happening."

"Nancy says we should go to the emergency room. She'll be waiting for us. I called 911 and they'll be right up."

I heard a truck door slam. Two men jumped out of a black pickup. It had a flashing light over the cab and a top over the back deck. Forest, an old friend and colleague from Goddard and Empire State College, and Bob hustled in, carrying a stretcher. Forest appeared at the bathroom door. Jo cursed with embarrassment as I lifted her off the toilet and pulled up her panties and slacks. Forest and Bob helped her onto the stretcher and put her into the back of the pickup. I followed them in my car. With the light on top of Bob's pickup flashing, they sped the 10 miles to the emergency room entrance, me on their tail.

Dropping the tailgate, Forest and Bob slid Jo out and carried her in past the receiving desk and moved her onto a gurney in the trauma suite, where Nancy was waiting. I was right behind them trying to control my anxiety and hold my questions.

Nancy and Dr. Brown, the Emergency Department doctor on duty, quickly evaluated Jo. I stood by, watching, listening, and sweating. I usually keep cool in emergencies, especially when there are things I can do. But here I was helpless, with my heart racing.

Jo was able to speak, though with a slur and foul language, freely using "fuck," "shit," "goddamn it," and similar words I had never heard from her before. She could lift her arms, so her shoulders were functioning; and she could lift her legs off the gurney, so her hips worked. Both legs held her weight and she could swing and slap them on the floor when they helped her walk to the john. But her right side was functioning much better than her left. It was obvious that she had had a stroke. The most pressing task was to do a CAT scan to see if it was a brain hemorrhage that could be life threatening or just a clot creating an ischemic stroke. Lots of things happened quickly—getting her into a gown and on a heart monitor, putting an IV in the back of her left hand, drawing blood, and recording an EKG—all before she was whisked off to the CAT scan.

I dropped onto a chair, heart pounding. A nurse brought me a paper cup of icy water. After the longest 15 minutes of my life, they came back with good news. It was not a hemorrhagic stroke. It did not seem as though there was serious damage. Jo was able to talk and to walk to the bathroom, unstable as she was. They speculated that she had a mild right-frontal stroke.

Under these conditions we needed to decide whether she should stay at the hospital. The knee-jerk response usually is "yes." Most families can't handle this sort of thing at home. But Jo was clear she did not want to stay. Nancy didn't think that there was any risk not being in the hospital. All they could do was give her two chewable children's aspirin and hope that by morning the more severe symptoms would taper off. The event had happened and was not ongoing. I could play nurse and help Jo get around. So we all opted for going home. I was relieved to learn that for about 10% of strokes, within 24 hours all symptoms clear up. I leaned over the gurney and gave Jo a hug.

With me holding Jo's right arm, and Nancy her left, we walked to my car in the parking lot. Jo and I were silent as we drove home, wondering what the future might hold. My heart rate was pretty much back to normal and the sweat was drying. I backed into the garage so her door was next to the entryway. She opened the door and started to get out but her left leg did not seem to function. I supported her as we tottered into the house and she settled into the living room rocker.

By now it was dinner time. Jo was not hungry, so I just warmed up some leftover curried pumpkin and squash soup she'd made the day before, and we were fine with a couple of slices of Nancy's homemade bread. I poured a glass of the cabernet and gave Jo a mug of Red Zinger tea from the pot on the stove. Her left arm and hand had no feeling and did not work, so she ate and drank with only her right hand. Her speech was a bit slurred as she cursed "this goddamn stroke." We watched the *Jim Lehrer News Hour* until 8:00 and then headed upstairs for bed. Her left side was heavy on me as she managed the stairs, stepping up with her right foot and dragging her left up behind her. I pulled down the sheet and blankets on her side of the bed and helped her sit. She undressed with her right hand, pulled her nightgown out from under her pillow and let it drop over her head to her waist. Leaning back, she slid her legs under the covers. I pulled the blankets up under her chin, gave her a long kiss, and rested my head on her chest.

Despite the doctor's reassuring diagnosis, I was scared and weepy. We had no idea what the future might be. We held each other for a few minutes. I roused myself and turned on a Jean-Pierre Rampal flute concerto already set to go on the CD player downstairs. After brushing my teeth, I slid into bed beside her. We were both drained from the stress of the last 5 hours. Jo almost immediately fell sound asleep, perhaps soothed by Rampal's beautiful music. I was not soothed. My mind was like a clothes dryer, full of tumbling questions.

I remembered Bernice, my landlady the first 2 years I was at George Mason University. We both usually got up about 7:00 a.m. Almost every morning we chatted over breakfast at her kitchen table. One day in April she did not appear. I ate my breakfast, washed the dishes, got my attaché case, and started out the door to my car. But I felt uneasy. I turned, went to her bedroom door, and knocked. I heard a low moan. When I opened the door, Bernice was on the floor beside her bed. Her right temple was bleeding from a small cut, apparently from hitting her head on the side table when she fell getting out of bed. Her bewildered, frightened eyes fixed on mine. She could not speak or get off the floor. I lifted her onto the bed, ran to the kitchen phone, and dialed 911. Then

I called her boyfriend, Ed. Both he and an ambulance pulled up about the same time. With him there to make decisions, I left for work.

Bernice's stroke was serious. Though her motor skills came back in 4 or 5 months, her speech took 3 or 4 years to partially recover. She was at a rehab center the rest of that spring and continued weekly therapy for 3 years. I moved out but we kept in touch and eventually she was able to communicate and work again.

What were Jo's prospects? What kind of handicaps might she have? What about my work at Vermont College and Norwich University designing a new doctoral program, my speaking and writing commitments, and the workshops on spirituality in higher education? As I tossed and turned, tears ran. I choked down sobs so as not to wake Jo. Finally I dropped off to sleep.

I heard a scream and jumped out of bed. The clock said 1:18 a.m. Jo was on the floor beside the bed, trying to get up.

"I have to pee," she said.

I lifted her under the arms and helped her to the toilet.

"Thanks," she said.

I pulled the bathroom door shut and got back into bed. Then came a thump and another scream. I lunged for the bathroom. Jo had fallen again. Her left side had bounced off the bathtub, but she had not hit her head on it or on the nearby sink. Her left leg clearly was not functioning. We hobbled back to the bed. If she needed to get up again, she would wake me. Fortunately that was not necessary. My clothes-dryer mind slowed down and we both slept until 5:30 a.m., our usual waking time.

At 9:00 a.m. we met with Dr. Mark Yorra, our primary care physician, at the hospital. We discussed whether home health care with a physiotherapist would be sufficient or whether we should go to the Mt. Ascutney Hospital and Health Center, which specialized in rehabilitation services for brain injuries. With its day-long regimen and overnight care it might lead to a quicker and more complete recovery. In Windsor, Vermont, about an hour and a half southeast, it was a manageable drive—no matter how bad the winter weather might get. Mark called Ascutney and arranged for Jo to be admitted the next day. I was relieved that we had a plan. I could reschedule my professional responsibilities, go to the rehab center each afternoon, and stay through dinner. Nancy could ride with us tomorrow and help clarify any questions.

I packed clothes and toiletries per Jo's instructions, along with three books she was reading, and picked Nancy up the next day. The sunshine and fresh snow did not lighten my feelings of gloom and foreboding. Despite our acceptance at the rehab center, the future was still uncertain, promising only disciplined work on Jo's part and helplessness for me. None of us spoke much. Vermont's classical music station treated us to Vivaldi's *Four Seasons* and Prokofiev's *Lieutenant Kijé*, two of our favorites. They made the silence more bearable, but it did little for our spirits. Just before 2:30 p.m., we drove up to the small hospital on a hilltop with a nice view of Mt. Ascutney, whose name it took.

I checked Jo in while an attendant wheeled her to a room with two empty beds, and Nancy brought her small suitcase. After finishing the paperwork I found Jo stretched out on the bed nearest the window, with Dr. Naomi Banbury sitting beside her. About 5 feet 9 inches tall, with graying hair and a pleasant smile, she welcomed me and got right down to business.

Jo has suffered an ischemic stroke. She will participate in the acute rehabilitation program, which provides intensive help for patients with significant impairment. Her rehabilitation team will include a physiatrist, an internist, a case manager, a nurse, a speech and language pathologist, an occupational therapist, a physical therapist, a therapeutic recreation specialist, and a registered dietitian. Each day Jo will be up and dressed in street clothes. She will spend up to 5 hours a day with a variety of therapies. The entire team meets daily to evaluate and modify plans as needed, and meets weekly with us to discuss Jo's progress and develop new goals. A home evaluation will recommend useful adaptations or special equipment needed. In cases like this, we can expect Jo to be here 4 to 6 weeks.

Family and friends are welcome to visit and attend therapy sessions to better understand Jo's capabilities and how to help her achieve increasing independence. But it's important to recognize that she will need plenty of rest during the day. There are no overnight accommodations. Even though there is a spare bed in Jo's room, no one is permitted to stay there.

At the end of the briefing, Dr. Banbury asked if we had any questions.

"That's a lot of information to absorb," I said. "I don't have any questions right now. How about you, Jo?"

"I'm pretty overwhelmed. I guess we'll just have to take it one day at a time."

"Well," Dr. Banbury said as she left, "If anything comes up, don't hesitate to ask me or any other staff members."

This clearly is no minor stroke, I thought. My stomach churned. My mouth was dry.

"That's some team you'll be working with. This whole program certainly sounds a lot better than having home health-care people come to our house. It's great that I and others can come and visit any time."

"It does sound good, but don't feel you need to be running down here every day," Jo replied.

"This place has an excellent reputation, and I can see why," Nancy said. "Do you feel like a cup of tea?"

"I'd like a cup of tea but then I need to take a nap before supper. It's been a busy day."

What a spirit, I thought. Just another "busy day." If anyone can work her way through these challenges, Jo can.

Walking down the hall we went by five other double rooms and found the cafeteria on the right. Nancy made Red Zinger for her and Jo and I found half-and-half in a small refrigerator under the counter to go with my sweetened coffee. We rejoined Jo in her room.

"Now that you have a sense of what you'll be doing, is there other stuff you need?" I asked.

She took a sip of tea. "It's plenty warm here, so I could use my sandals. They're easy to put on with one hand. My blue sweat suit would be nice. And I really want my copies of Thich Nhat Hanh's *Peace Is Every Step* and *Call Me by My True Names*. If ever I needed his perspectives, with all he went through, it's now. I wonder whether I can be 'mindful' with my head and gut feeling the way they do."

She sipped more tea and wiped her eyes with the back of her right hand. I reached out and took it in mine.

"If anything else occurs to you, just have them call," I said. "I'll be back tomorrow morning with the things you want. I love you and will miss you tonight."

Nancy pressed her hand and wished her well. We walked out to the car in silence. Before I got in to drive, Nancy took me in her arms and held me tight. Sobbing, I felt as though an atom bomb had dropped onto our beautiful landscape, blowing away all the flowers and trees, leaving an overhanging mushroom cloud with dangerous fallout. Would I have the strength and wisdom to cope?

I asked Nancy, "So what do you think Jo's prospects are?"

"I don't have a very good idea. I deal with stroke victims in the emergency room, but once they're stabilized I don't see them anymore. It's more severe than we thought when she first came in. They say that most of the progress occurs during the first few weeks and not much after the first 6 months. We'll just have to see how it goes."

"I want to be here as much as I can. I'm going to cancel my trips during the next few weeks and put off whatever work I can."

"I'll know my ER schedule for March this coming week. Once that's set I should have lots of time to come down."

It was around 6 p.m. when I got home after dropping Nancy off. I headed for the refrigerator, filled a glass with ice, and pulled Old Crow bourbon, Stock sweet vermouth, and Angostura bitters out of the liquor cabinet for a hefty Manhattan. It was just past the time when Jo and I usually sat down to watch the news. I had enough on my mind without adding political comings and goings, as well as the starvation and violence that seemed to be daily staples. I took my drink to the plank by our northeast-facing windows, looked out over the beautiful snowy fields, iced-over beaver pond, pine and spruce trees, and tried to digest this whole experience.

This seems more serious than we first thought. What lies in store for this energetic, adventurous love of my life? What kinds of lives will we be able to create? Will she recover her independent thinking and participate in the activities that so enrich her life and mine? Will we be able to snowshoe and ski together through the beautiful woods we love and know so well? Will she get back on her 3.5 tennis team this summer? What about the Intergenerational Elderhostels we had been discussing for next summer with Lars, Gabe, and Courtney, three of our grandchildren? How much would my professional trips for keynote speeches, workshops, and consultations need to be curtailed? I would need to call the Fetzer Institute in the morning to let them know I would not be coming to their weekend workshop on spirituality and higher education.

These practicalities brought me back to the present. As usual, Jo had the refrigerator well stocked. I figured out which food would spoil fastest and looked at my calendar to see what lunches and dinners I would be eating at home instead of at the rehab center. My frugality and flexibility saved me from rampant ruminations about an unknown and unknowable future. For better or worse, I can compartmentalize thoughts and feelings pretty well. I have a high tolerance for ambiguity, and I'm able to take things as they come. I went to the fridge, took out some hamburger meat, cut up two onions, slopped some garlic oil into our large cast-iron frying pan, and dropped it all in. With teary eyes, mostly from the onions, I guess, I made myself another copious Manhattan and poured a glass of cabernet. After I cleaned up the supper dishes, the booze and wine helped me crash in bed.

The next morning I packed a bag with the clothes and books Jo wanted. I also grabbed my copy of *Learning That Lasts*, a 576-page volume by Alverno College friends and colleagues, which had just come out from Jossey-Bass. They had asked me to review their original manuscript, and I recommended turning it into two separate books, but they decided to go ahead with publishing it in one volume. I was interested to see how it came across in this final version, and it would keep me occupied for several visits while Jo was resting.

I got to Ascutney around 9:15 a.m. When I walked in, a young woman at the front desk said that Dr. Banbury would like to see me. Jo was not in her room, and I tossed her clothes and books on the bed. Dr. Banbury's door was open. She was sitting behind a large brown wooden desk. Three shelves of medical books and pamphlets were on the wall behind her. A mug of coffee was steaming in front of her.

"Good morning. If you'd like some coffee, help yourself and I'll get out Jo's folder."

When I came back she handed me a single sheet of paper.

"Here is our initial team conference report. It gives you our assessment of how Jo is as we start rehabilitation."

I read through the report, overwhelmed by how much work was in store for Jo. The goals noted were for Jo to learn to speak clearly, think logically/sequentially, walk independently, and gain increased sensitivity/motion in her left leg. The discharge goal was for Jo to return home with me as the primary caregiver, with help from the Central Vermont Home Health Agency.

The report continued with a list of Jo's impairments and capacities:

- Short-term and immediate memory are impaired; long-term memory and problem-solving skills are mildly impaired. Abstract reasoning is moderately to severely impaired. Left neglect present. Patient is not completely oriented to place or time.
- Patient's speech is dysarthric. She is able to state her wants/ needs. Language is inappropriate at times; information can be tangential and/or irrelevant; thoughts are disorganized.
- Self-care/grooming supervision required with minimal assistance at sink side, and with a roll-in shower chair; moderate to maximum assistance with dressing and toileting.
- Primary issues for rehab are patient's left neglect and poor safety awareness.

Jesus Christ, I thought. This is going to be hell for Jo. Lots of grueling work and agonizing time for her here and for both of us when she gets out.

In shock and sadness I asked Banbury, "How the hell can something like this happen to my wife? She doesn't drink or smoke. We eat good food and keep our weight under control. She's active and in good shape. Then out of the blue she gets hit."

"You're right. She does not have any of the preconditions that often lead to a stroke. Sometimes, for reasons we don't understand, a piece of plaque will come loose, float through the blood stream, and lodge in the brain."

"Well, it sure would be nice to know what happened."

"I wish I could be more definite, but we just don't know."

"If you get any further ideas I'd like to hear them. What is 'left neglect?'"

"With this kind of stroke to the right side of the brain, you lose awareness of what is going on to your left. For example, if Jo were given a circle and asked to draw in the numbers for a clock, she would put in those from 12 to 6 but leave out 7 through 11. When she moves around the rehab center in her wheelchair she will tend to bump into door jams, chairs, tables, and so forth that are on her left. It can be a safety issue until she becomes more aware of it."

"And what is dysarthric speech?" I asked.

"Disjointed. Words don't flow smoothly."

"You comment on inappropriate language. I have never heard such cursing and foul language from Jo before. What's going on?"

"It's what we call emotional disinhibition. She has diminished capacity for the self-censoring that we use all the time. And she is also subject to dramatic mood changes, from being ecstatically happy to very sad. This can be one of the most difficult things to live with. It will diminish as she recovers, but it will take time."

"This has been helpful. Daunting, but helpful. Anything else I need to know now?"

"You'll get one of these reports each week after our interim team meetings. They will give you a good sense of how things are going."

She stood up, came around from behind her desk, and held out her hand. I squeezed it with both of mine, not surprised by her strong return grip. Holding back tears of pain, anger, and frustration, I thanked her and picked up my untouched mug of coffee.

I went to Jo's room. Stretched out on the bed, she turned to look me squarely in the eyes. I recognized that look and knew something important was coming.

"I feel like half a person. I can't talk or think straight. I don't want to live like this."

I sat, silent. No, no, no, don't leave me, I thought.

"This is a huge shock for both of us, coming out of nowhere," I said. "I can hardly stop myself from lashing out at someone, someplace. You've been healthy, active, no smoking or drinking, keeping your weight under control. No wonder you feel depressed and don't want to live like you are now. It's hard for me to imagine how you feel, but I believe we can work our way through this. Our life may be different, but it will still be us. However, if it's all too painful, too much of a struggle, too limited, I'll help however I can."

I reached out and took her right hand in mine. We sat there, holding hands, in silence. Voices passed in the hall. A car pulled up outside, a door slammed, and then it drove away.

"This seems to be an excellent facility," I said. "We don't really know what kind of recovery you may make. Let's give it a chance. We've talked about death and dying before. If you still feel like you do now when they kick us out of here, you know Nancy and I will help you check out in any way you want. She and Luke will be here tomorrow and you can see how you feel then."

"Well, I don't know. Maybe I'll feel better after I sleep awhile."

She turned her head away and closed her eyes. I let go of her hand and got my copy of *Learning That Lasts*.

When she woke up, I suggested we go to the rec room to see if we could find something enjoyable to do until supper. In the hall, just before the rec room door, was a large tank, maybe 5 feet long, 3 feet high, and 2 feet wide. The bubbling water was perfectly clear, full of multicolored tropical fish. We stopped, entranced by the beauty of that microenvironment, full of diverse organisms, apparently living in happy harmony with each other. Clearly someone knew enough about this little part of Ascutney to give it the kind of competent, loving care each inhabitant required. We just watched quietly. We had snorkeled with fish like these when we were diving off a rented, bareboat sailing in the British Virgin Islands and at Pennekamp Coral Reef State Park next to Key Largo in Florida. We were with these fish and more when we spent 4 days on the Great Barrier Reef during a consulting visit to Australia. Would sailing, diving, swimming, and further travels be part of our future?

Instead of continuing into the rec room, we turned back to the empty cafeteria. I got Jo a mug of tea and myself coffee. I told her a bit about *Learning That Lasts* and my thoughts about reorganizing my work schedule and travel plans.

"Don't turn your life inside out just to come down here and spend time with me."

"I want to be here to see how things are going and how I can be helpful. We can just see how it works out and plan accordingly. The writing will still be there when I get to it, and passing up a conference or consultation or two will not make a big difference in the scheme of things."

My professional work can wait indefinitely, I thought. Nothing will be worth doing anyway if we cannot work our way through this.

Back in her room after a leisurely dinner, I stretched out beside her. We held each other quietly, deep in our own thoughts and feelings. After a final kiss goodbye, I handed her *Peace Is Every Step* from the table beside her bed. Nancy and grandson Luke would be down tomorrow, and I would be back Monday midmorning, In the meantime, if she thought of anything she wanted from home she could call me.

Driving home I could not help ruminating about Jo's sadness and despair. How deep were those feelings? How much will she have to give up, and will she want to do so? Like summer thunderheads, will this bring lightning shocks and a deluge, or will it blow over, leaving a clear horizon?

I decided not to call Nancy about Jo's despair but just to wait and see what developed. I was confident about the perspective Nancy would bring if Jo expressed similar suicidal feelings to her. I drove up to the old farmhouse where our daughter Sue, her husband, John, and our three grandsons were, and brought them up to date on Jo's condition and our plans. Their sympathy and support gave me strength. At home, I called Alan, who lived in Olympia, Washington, and our daughter Peri, who lived in New Hampshire with her husband, Andrew, to share what Banbury had told me about Jo's condition. Peri would come over for a visit early in the coming week.

After a restless night, I was up for an early breakfast and off to my Vermont College office. After plowing through about 25 e-mails, I worked on writing "Creating Community Within Individual Courses." I had an April deadline for this piece to be published in the Spring 2000 issue of the *New Directions for Higher Education* series.

I went home about 3:30 p.m. in sparkling weather, no wind, with the temperature in the mid-20s—perfect for a nice snowshoe walk in our woods. The snow was about three-and-a-half feet deep and there were few deer tracks. A flock of crows flew up from a cedar thicket about a quarter of a mile down our watershed. I found blood on the snow, with hair and bones scattered about. The deer had yarded up and the coyotes had taken one. It must have been pretty easy. Fox tracks showed where they had cleaned up the leftovers, and the crows were gleaning the last morsels.

When the snow gets deep and the going gets tough, deer act the same way many humans do. They huddle together in a sheltered spot, often in a clump of cedars where they can browse on the low branches. But, even though during the rest of the year they range all over their territory, when they have nipped off all the branches they can reach, up to a height of 7 or 8 feet, they will not venture out of the thicket.

Gradually, they get weak and starve, easy pickings for any coyotes that find them. I had often used this analogy consulting about the dynamics of institutional change. Musing about this behavior, I continued through our familiar woods and wondered whether Jo and I would end up hunkering down, just giving up on creating the best life we could with whatever possibilities there were.

After going up to the bog and back, I got home as dusk was falling. I stoked up the masonry heater. It would be nice to have some hot buttered rum, with a handful of cloves and sweetened with our own maple syrup. Each February and March, Sue, John, Nancy, and Kris tap about 130 trees on the hillside above our house. Grandsons Lars, Gabe, Silas, and Luke help collect the sap. Our Christmas presents always include a gallon from the 20 to 25 gallons of syrup they make. I was just settling down to watch *Meet the Press* when Nancy called about their visit. After giving Jo a hug, 4-year-old Luke had gone exploring. While he was away, Jo told Nancy how sad and frustrated she was feeling, ready to call it quits, after what had been a rich and wonderful life. Nancy's response was similar to mine. She said she was willing to help her die after she completed the Ascutney rehabilitation program but urged Jo to wait and see how things go. Then Luke burst into the room, oblivious to Jo's tears and wet pillow.

"Mormor, wait 'til you see what I found. There's a bunch of awesome fish in a huge tank. Come on. Get in your wheelchair. I'll push you."

He rolled Jo down the hall. His delight and excitement was a bright beacon for Jo. By the time they finished watching and talking about all the creatures in the aquarium, she was beaming and ready to share some tea and cookies. There was no more talk of suicide after that. I was relieved. When she puts her mind, talents, and strong will to something, she can usually do it. She would work hard at the rehabilitation process and make whatever improvements were possible.

No matter how difficult the circumstances, life seems to evolve into routines that fit those circumstances. Mornings I followed my past schedule—up at 5:30, workout and tennis at the fitness center, at the office by 9:00, and work until 11:30 or 12:00. I went home for lunch but sometimes stayed in town to eat and do business. After lunch I drove to Ascutney, went to Jo's therapy sessions, had afternoon tea, and came home after dinner. Occasionally, I would stay home when friends or family went to visit Jo, which gave me a chance to catch up on housework, bill paying, and other life-management requirements.

Our weekly reviews of the detailed team reports showed steady progress. As recommended, bars were installed at the end and along the side of the downstairs bathtub, and a railing for going upstairs. I got a wheelchair and a transfer bench so that Jo could sit down beside the tub, swing her legs into it, and slide her body over to wash. She would continue to sleep on a Castro convertible bed until a therapist cleared her for going upstairs. She would be ready to come home on Saturday, March 6. Jo was delighted to be getting out. From the first day it had been an emotionally and physically challenging ordeal.

Nancy joined me for the drive to bring Jo home. When we arrived at the rehab center midmorning, Jo was packed and sitting up in bed reading *Peace Is Every Step*. We wheeled Jo to Dr. Banbury's office, where we reviewed the discharge summary, which read, in part:

> Mrs. Chickering initially demonstrated profound weakness involving her left side which appeared to have progressed from her initial insult three days previously. Nonetheless, throughout the course of her hospitalization she did demonstrate gradual improvement with good isolation in her lower extremity. She was ambulating with standby assistance with the use of a quad cane without the use of assistive device

or bracing. Left upper extremity did demonstrate gradual improvement although she still had reduced isolation at her wrist and fingers. She was able to use her hand in a gross patterning activity.

Mrs. Chickering initially had significant emotional lability, reduced insight, and judgment. This gradually improved . . . although she still demonstrated left sided neglect. Neuropsychological testing demonstrated persistent reduced insight, however it was determined that she would be safe at home alone once she was declared independent with her general overall mobility. At the time of discharge, she was still standby for wheelchair transfers in the bathroom and in order to manage her clothing. She was also standby for gait because of occasional tendency to leave behind her lower left extremity with ambulation. . . .

At the time of discharge Mrs. Chickering was ambulating with standby assistance. She was using her wheelchair for long distances. She is going to have physical and occupational therapy as well as speech therapy at home and strict instructions were given to the family concerning her specific physical therapy intervention and the need to not change her status including going up stairs and maintaining supervision until cleared by physical therapy. She is not to return to driving. She may need follow-up neuropsychological testing. She will be seen back by me in one month. She will have follow up occupational therapy for left upper extremity function and speech for her cognitive changes.

Dr. Banbury emphasized the importance of the follow-up physical and occupational therapy and that we should strictly abide by the limitations she outlined. It was clear that there was plenty of work to be done for an indefinite time. But Jo was happy and animated during the drive home. We told her about the bathtub bars and the new railing for getting upstairs. The Castro had clean, warm, linen sheets. I recorded a number of our favorite television programs and stocked up on food so she could teach me how to cook. The Central Vermont Medical Center had been notified and their physical rehabilitation unit was ready to receive us.

When we got home, I stoked up the masonry heater while Nancy made tuna melts, Jo's favorite lunch. Tears came to Jo's eyes and mine as we sat at the plank looking at the birds feeding outside the window. Fifty yards downhill, deer tracks dented the snowy fields with the frozen beaver ponds and wooded hillside behind them. We didn't talk much; all three of us were lost in thought. Unanswerable questions flooded my skull. Would Jo ever get out there on skis or snowshoes again? Would she be able to explore our fields, woods, and bog to check out the wild flowers, birds, and animal life? Would she drive again and resume volunteer work on the Barre and Montpelier Restorative Justice Boards? Would she be active again in our Quaker meeting? Would I be able to learn to cook well enough so we could continue to have the leisurely drinks, hors d'oeuvres, and dinners we enjoyed so much with friends? What changes would I need to make in my professional life to help Jo with her therapy, manage the household, and care for our gardens and woods?

The stove crackled and rumbled along, warming us with its radiant heat. Unarticulated love flowed among us. There were no pronouncements or predictions. There was no happy babble. I cleaned up the dishes. Nancy hugged Jo and said a weepy goodbye. I helped Jo onto the Castro for a nap. Taking a lined pad from the file cabinet by my upstairs desk, I came back to the plank to list all the things to be done to begin creating our new life.

I had a lot to learn. There were mundane tasks—cooking, cleaning, friendly correspondence, and such—that Jo had always handled. More important, there was how to be a caregiver. Balancing doing things for Jo and letting her do as much as she could on her own was complicated. It included everything—helping her sit down and get up out of a chair, walk around the house and manage stairs, take things out of the refrigerator and put them back in, use the stove, microwave, and toaster oven. She wanted to regain as much independence and ability to care for herself as possible. Dealing with the risk/benefit tradeoffs was intellectually, interpersonally, and emotionally demanding. Jo's stroke offered us both a significant opportunity for personal growth and for deepening our relationship if we could manage these myriad challenges and not get burned out or diminished by them.

Gradually, we settled into a new lifestyle and new routines that recognized Jo's limited mobility and single-handedness. No more tennis or walks in the woods, but on hands and knees she could still be outside and weed the flower gardens. I mowed the lawns, tended and harvested our vegetable garden, and worked with chainsaw, tractor, and trailer getting in our winter wood supply. With coaching from Jo, my cooking repertoire slowly expanded, though it was still pretty basic: cereal, eggs, or muffins with coffee and cocoa for breakfast, tuna melts with dill pickles or peanut butter and raisin sandwiches for lunch. For dinner, I cooked meat, potatoes, vegetables, salads, pastas with pesto and other sauces, or cheese omelets with cut-up apples and basil. Due to her medications, Jo could no longer drink wine, but I continued having wine with lunch and dinner, and a couple of drinks as well.

My part-time professional work took me to Vermont College most mornings and afternoons for meetings, correspondence, and conference calls. At home, an office in the upstairs bedroom worked well for writing and e-mail communications. With advance food preparation and help from Sue and Nancy, Jo was able to manage when I joined a five-person task force in Denver to help create the National Survey of Student Engagement. That summer I also contributed to the Kellogg Forum on Higher Education Transformation in Battle Creek, Michigan.

Jo started most days at the computer in her bedroom office, writing poems. Often these were inspired by nighttime ruminations or dreams jotted down on a lined pad under the bedside light. I brought her juice, cocoa, and a muffin or cereal before I went for my early-morning tennis. During the day, she spent more time reading and listening to books on tape than in the past. Evenings usually found us in front of the tube, starting with the news and finishing off with something recorded earlier: a classic movie, a show on PBS (maybe a British comedy), figure skating, or tennis matches.

Life went on, slowed from a busy hustle to a more deliberate pace. Patience and forbearance became critical. It was challenging for Jo as she continually tried to improve her balance and stability walking, and exercised her left hand, pushing her fingers out flat and helping them to move separately. Going through her morning exercise routine on the bed and getting dressed with one hand took discipline and time. For this energetic, independent, athletic woman, needing help with various activities and routines was like Sisyphus struggling to push an immense boulder uphill only to have it roll back down, if not to the bottom, at least part way. For me, learning to go with this much slower flow, trying to balance stepping in to give help with standing back and letting her struggle, was an ongoing, emotionally challenging part of our daily lives. Jo's remarkable spirit, fighting off frustration and despair, finding joy in small successes and interesting experiences, sustained us both.

Erik Erikson (1950) described eight stages of life, each character-ized by tensions between opposing developmental challenges. The last two are "generativity versus self-absorption or stagnation" and "integrity versus despair." Generativity occurs when we are caring for others and doing meaningful and creative things that benefit society. Significant relationships are in the workplace, community, and family. If that is not going on, we can become self-absorbed and stagnant. Integrity occurs when we look back on our lives feeling happy, content, fulfilled, that life has meaning and we have made a contribution, accepting death as completing a life well lived. It's fair to say that we were on the generativity and integrity sides of Erikson's dichotomies.

Our years from 2001 until the winter of 2008, when another life-changing experience brought home new realities, were generative and integrated for both of us. An authorized instructor had cleared Jo to drive with her right hand using an automatic transmission and a "necker nob" on the steering wheel. She drove wherever she needed to go and was active in our Quaker meeting, serving as co-clerk for a year and as a consistent member of Ministry and Counsel, which takes responsibility for spiritual leadership and helping individual members. She organized potluck discussion groups addressing various Quaker-related concerns. We served on "clearness committees" for individuals and couples facing personal problems or relationship difficulties. As a member of the Barre and Montpelier Restorative Justice Boards, she helped individual offenders design and carry out "contracts" that made amends to individuals and communities hurt by their behavior. In face-to-face meetings, she helped these people mend their own flawed perspectives and self-perceptions. Most days she worked on poems, sharing her insights and commenting on current events and daily experiences. She filled spiral notebooks that became presents for me and our kids. And as always, her wisdom and support bolstered my responses to various professional challenges.

When the Norwich University faculty, despite President Schneider's support, turned down the doctoral program proposal I had helped design, I felt like a fifth wheel at Vermont College. Goddard had discontinued its resident undergraduate program, concentrating exclusively on its successful low-residency programs. The board of trustees had recruited Mark Schulman for the vacant presidency. Impressed by his inaugural address, I asked about a part-time position and we settled on special assistant to the president, with a $5,000 annual stipend and $2,000 for professional travel. It was satisfying to come full circle back to the institution where I launched my career 55 years earlier and from which I had learned so much. It felt good to carry that affiliation with me as I spoke and consulted around the country, and wrote for various higher education publications.

Professional and community activities did not stop Jo and me from spending lots of time together in other parts of the world. Winter snow and ice are difficult for Jo to navigate with her cane and uncertain footing, so we often found relief with friends in Florida and Hawaii. I had become a regular contributor and resource person for the annual Institute on College Student Values, organized by my friend and colleague Jon Dalton at Florida State University, held in Tallahassee in early February. Our longtime friends Rich and Mimi Rice, in St. Petersburg, Florida, generously welcomed us for a week or two before and after that event. We also visited Corinne and Nat Schulman, former New England compatriots, at their home on the shore of Kaneohe Bay on Oahu. In February, Jo and I joined Peri and Andrew in Mexico for a University of Vermont-sponsored program exploring Oaxaca's interesting complex of cultures and diverse healing alternatives. These vacations helped us make it through the Vermont winters since Jo could not go out to ski and snowshoe.

In September of 2001 and 2002 we took the long drive to Stratford on Avon, west of Toronto, for 4 days of Shakespeare plays, and then to Niagara-on-the-Lake for 4 days at the Shaw Festival. For the next 4 years we attended the Shaw Festival, joined by Rich and Mimi. We also visited them in the fall at Mimi's family homestead on Lake Ozonia in the Adirondacks. During July 2003 and 2004 we went to conferences on spirituality and higher education in Sedona, Arizona, organized by Paul Elsner, chancellor of the Maricopa County Community College System. Our individual and joint lives were rolling along nicely, adapted to the now-familiar limitations in Jo's mobility and use of her left arm and hand.

In February 2008, as she was on a back road headed into Montpelier for her workout, Jo drove into a snowdrift. It had snowed the night before and although the road had been plowed there was limited contrast between the road surface and the drifts alongside. She was taking this back dirt road because it seemed safer than coping with the traffic on Route 2. Our car had all-wheel drive, so she backed out without difficulty, but was shaken by this experience as she continued into town. A couple of weeks earlier she had barely missed a woman and small girl, not seeing them until they were just off the right front fender.

Her vision was becoming increasingly restricted. She could no longer see in dim light and going out in the dark evenings was a serious challenge. Her limited vision also made walking more difficult because she could not clearly see where she was going or rough spots on the surfaces. Though we were not really housebound, our life increasingly revolved around activities at home or that we could do together else-where. Jo, in her usual courageous and inventive fashion, invested more time and energy writing poetry. Now that our shared outdoor activities, community contributions, and travels had become limited, I searched for something new that we could do together. Goddard had a Master of Fine Arts in Creative Writing (MFAW) program with residencies just 4 miles away. I had always enjoyed writing my professional books and articles. We could work together on a memoir about our 57-year marriage. We could revisit the ups and downs of our years together, share thoughts and drafts, and at least create something our children might like to read.

President Mark Schulman and his leadership team approved a

tuition waiver for me beginning with the January 2009 term and said Jo could participate in the residencies. I hoped they would let Jo work along with me informally even though she would not be registered. I was assigned Nicola Morris, a veteran Goddard faculty member, as an advisor. In our second meeting, she suggested that Jo continue her poetry writing instead of trying to work on prose drafts with me. Nicky would read and give her feedback on poems she could submit as part of the writing packets sent to my advisor. All this would be informal and off the record, not part of the degree program. We were delighted with that generous offer. Jo was thrilled to pursue poetry writing, which she had been doing throughout our marriage. We went through the residency eating our meals and taking workshops together, enjoying encounters with fellow participants. I included three or four of Jo's poems in my packets along with my own narratives, annotations, and a letter about my writing process. With excellent feedback from Nicky, we were setting off on a challenging and absorbing journey. For me, it was especially interesting to be back at Goddard, experiencing firsthand, as a student, the educational process I used as the basis for creating Empire State College and had been advocating in various forms during the 50 years since I joined the faculty in 1959. I appreciated the general program design, the active learning in the residency workshops, and the rigorous expectations for the five packets during the term, with the supportive and tough-minded feedback from my advisor. With master's and PhD degrees already behind us, the credential was irrelevant. As Shakespeare's (n.d.) Hamlet said, "The play's the thing" (p. 74). It was the process, the shared activities, that enriched our lives.

When the first term of the residency concluded, Nicky told Jo she could not continue to work with her. Besides, it would probably be more helpful if Jo found a local poet with whom she could meet on a regular basis. She recommended Sherry Olson, who had been on the tennis team with Jo. Sherry had been an MFAW advisor and worked locally with individuals and groups. She and Jo met weekly at our house for an hour or so, going over original drafts and revising earlier work during the summer and fall. Those meetings were instructive for Jo and enjoyable for both of them.

By the winter of 2010, Jo had generated enough work to think about putting together a book. Andy Christiansen, one of Alan's classmates and a good friend, heard of Jo's work and suggested we see if Earline Marsh might help. She was active in the Poetry Society of Vermont and coordinated monthly evening readings at the Red Hen, a bakery and eatery nearby in Middlesex. She had published poetry books and knew the territory. Earline agreed to help as a managing editor for Jo, for a small stipend. They scanned Jo's abundant creations and settled on "Saying Yes to Life" as the thematic organizer and title for a finished collection that was published in March 2011. That project was a wonderful addition to our lives.

After graduating from the MFAW in June 2012, I decided to tackle this memoir to share my growing up, current life, and key aspects of my professional career. With help from five wonderful coauthors, I hoped we might provide some useful historical perspectives.

REFERENCES

Chickering, A. W. (2000). Creating community within individual courses. In B. Jacoby (Ed.), *Involving commuter students in learning* (New directions for higher education, No. 109, pp. 23–32). San Francisco, CA: Jossey-Bass.

Chickering, J. (2011). *Saying yes to life.* East Montpelier, VT: Author.

Erikson, E. (1950). *Childhood and society.* New York, NY: W. W. Norton & Co.

Shakespeare, W. (n.d.). *Hamlet, prince of Denmark.* Retrieved from http://www.gutenberg.org/dirs/etext98/2ws2610.pdf

CHAPTER 12

Now at 86

My internal alarm wakes me up at 5:23 a.m. Jo stirs. I pull the chain on the small lamp beside the clock and give Jo a good-morning kiss. Slipping into my flannel shirt, dungarees, wool socks, and beat-up sneakers, I'm ready for the day.

"How'd you sleep?" I ask Jo.

"Quite well. Those back spasms seem to be gone, so I got to the bathroom easier and didn't thrash around so much. How about you?"

"Very well. I only had to get up once, around 4:00. What do you feel like for breakfast? Cocoa, oatmeal, eggs, Raisin Bran and blueberries, or just muffins?"

"Oatmeal and cocoa this morning. It's cold. I'll be working out and need something hot and substantial."

Downstairs, I open the drafts and the firebox door on our wood-burning stove, stir the embers from last night's fire, and arrange five pieces of old shingles in a way that 60 years of starting wood fires have taught me will effectively catch the embers. Two cups of water and a teaspoon of salt in a saucepan go onto the stove. Flames flash inside the partly open firebox door, ready for several pieces of seasoned maple.

After putting half a can of wet food in Sheba's cat dish, I adjust the drafts to channel the heat to the stove's four-plate cooking surface where the saucepan sits.

Jo turns on the Peter, Paul, and Mary CD she likes for her exercise routine. The house fills with their familiar songs that were so much part of our lives during the 1960s. I sing along, while I gather coffee, milk, orange juice, and maple syrup from the fridge. Water and 2 tablespoons of grounds go into the small coffeemaker, and milk goes into the "I Love You Mom" mug our daughter Peri gave Jo a few years ago. I put the maple syrup pitcher and warm water from the teakettle in another saucepan on the stove. Boiling water vibrates the lid of the oatmeal pan and I add a cup of oatmeal and two handfuls of raisins. The coffeemaker bubbles. Jo's cocoa mug goes into the microwave. The stove warms two of our favorite old crockery bowls.

"About 10 minutes to breakfast!" I shout.

"I'll be down soon. Just finishing my leg lifts."

I fill two glasses nearly full of orange juice and put a tablespoon full of soy protein powder in each. Stirring them and drinking mine, I dance over to put place mats on our dining room table.

Jo comes down the stairs, one at a time, leading with her left leg. Taking her cane from the railing at the bottom stair, she walks carefully, keeping the wall, kitchen counters, and peninsula close to her right side, then lowers herself at the table. I carry over a tray with her orange juice, cocoa, and oatmeal with raisins, a splash of milk, and syrup, and my coffee and cereal bowl.

Our weeks have a steady routine. Monday mornings we drive 10 miles to First in Fitness, where Jo works out until around 9:00 a.m. while I also work out or go food shopping. Tuesday, Wednesday, and Thursday I go to the gym to work out and play tennis from 7:30 to 9:30 a.m. Then it's home to check my e-mails and write while Jo works on poems. Lunch is tuna melts or other open-faced sandwiches, milk for Jo, a martini or two and wine for me. During lunch we watch a Charlie Rose interview, part of a classic movie, or *Masterpiece Theatre*. Jo stretches out on the couch for a nap, and I go upstairs to deal with any new e-mails and respond online to a chess move from my friend Peter in Norway. Then I turn to journal articles, consultations, or professional presentations. I am honored to have been invited to speak at the Institute on College Student Values that Jon Dalton started more than 20 years ago. It will be nice to share that experience again with all those good folks. And then a major highlight will be the formal launch of this book at the 2014 NASPA Annual Conference.

By 3:30 or 4:00 p.m., Jo wakes up and reads on her Kindle until I am ready to come down for our late-afternoon Scrabble game. Between plays I fix drinks. For her, ginger ale with ice, hot tea, or warm apple juice. For me, whatever booze seems to suit the day. I put more wood in the stove, work on making dinner, and by the end of the game we are usually ready to eat. We listen to the recorded *PBS NewsHour* while we eat, keeping up to date on political comings and goings and economic news, but fast-forwarding through the hard-to-watch scenes of violence, starvation, and natural catastrophes. We finish the shows we started at lunch, or go to new ones we recorded—*Nature, NOVA, Poirot*, or *The Daily Show*. At 9:00 p.m. we head up for bed. A good-night kiss and we drop off to sleep.

Then a major storm hit. Early Saturday morning, February 23, 2013, Jo woke up with diarrhea and vomiting. A highly infectious intestinal flu was going around that usually lasted 24 hours. It continued all day Saturday and Sunday. She became too weak to walk so I was wheeling her back and forth from our upstairs bed to the toilet. Sunday evening the bug hit me as well. Between getting to the toilet eight times myself and helping her, I didn't get much sleep. On Monday morning I started to feel better, but Jo's illness continued, and by that afternoon she was getting so weak I feared she would no longer have the strength to get on and off the wheelchair and toilet.

I called our daughter Nancy, who was with another daughter, Susan, at the Kirkwood Mountain Ski area in California to watch our grandsons Lars and Silas compete in the Freeskiing World Tour event (which Lars won!). Nancy suggested taking Jo to the Central Vermont Medical Center. Mark Yorra, our primary care physician, agreed and made the referral. Jo was able to bump down the stairs on her rear and we made it to the car and the emergency room. By 8:00 p.m. it was clear that Jo would need to stay overnight, so I drove home and crashed into bed.

At about 10:30 p.m., I was awakened. "Art, you need to get to the hospital! Jo is in critical condition!" My brother Rob, who had been called by the hospital, had driven from his nearby house and was yelling from downstairs. When I got to the hospital, I learned that her kidneys and liver had stopped functioning and that her body was shutting down. They thought she had an infected gall bladder and were taking her by ambulance to the Surgical Intensive Care Unit at the Fletcher Allen Health Center in Burlington, Vermont. The doctor at the hospital let me know I should go with Jo because she might not make it through the night. My son-in-law, John, always a rock of support when needed, drove me. I spent a restless night on a recliner in the waiting room.

The next morning Jo was still with us and they let me into her room. Her eyes were closed. I kissed her forehead and held her hand. My eyes locked on the monitor above her bed that showed heart rate, blood pressure, respiration rate, and blood oxygen level. I watched her blood pressure drop as low as 54/17 and heart rate to 34. John returned to join my vigil. Jo's intravenous fluids included a broad-spectrum antibiotic to fight the infection, a saline solution to remedy the dehydration, and dopamine to keep her heart functioning at an appropriate level. At about1:00 p.m. a doctor took me to the waiting room and told me an echocardiogram that morning had revealed that the valve to Jo's aorta had shrunk previously, limiting blood flow to fight the infection that I and others fought off easily. A heart attack had been brought on by the stress of the infection. She could not get enough blood to her kidneys and liver. Unless she turned this around in the next 2 hours she might not make it. Stunned, I made my way back to her bedside.

Nancy stayed informed about the situation by phone and notified Peri, Susan, and our son Alan about the serious state of affairs. Peri, who had just started a week of consulting with the chief of the U.S. Forest Service and his staff, flew up from Washington, D.C. John brought her from the airport. Jo had enough energy to greet her warmly.

The afternoon wore on and Jo still lived. Her blood oxygen level was in the low 80s when it should be in the high 90s, and a nurse said Jo was "confused." At one point, flat on her back, Jo said, "I need to lie down." Later, she said, "Okay, I'm ready to go home now."

At 8:00 p.m., with John and Peri there to stay with Jo, I went to a room John had reserved at the nearby Sheraton. Peri joined me about 11:00 p.m. I slept fitfully, partly because of my anxiety and partly because of my painful hip and knee. (A hip replacement was in my future.) When we went to the hospital to join Jo for breakfast, we learned that her heart rate and blood pressure had dropped sharply during the night but that they had been able to revive her.

Patrick Delaney, a tall red-headed attending doctor, took me aside. "She is on a knife edge. Is your 'Do Not Resuscitate' decision still firm?"

"We do not want her to be intubated or on a ventilator, but please keep her heart going with dopamine to maximize her chance of kidney and liver recovery," I replied.

During the day, we watched her vital signs vary as they lowered and increased the dopamine dosage and as she struggled to recover.

Our grandson Gabe and his fiancée, Sera, arrived from Arlington, Massachusetts, to help out, and Jo was glad to see them. Gabe volunteered to stay overnight with her. When I went to the hospital that evening, her kidneys were improving and her liver was showing signs of recovery, but there was still a long way to go. She made it through the night, and with the help of intravenous fluids and expert attention from the doctors and nurses, Jo was still hanging on and making progress the next morning.

Peri, John, and Gabe were with me when two nurses came in to adjust her upper body and roll her over, which they did every 2 to 3 hours to minimize bedsores. As they rolled her to her left side, the monitor showed her heart rate and respiration plunging to 0. My eyes were glued to the monitor as I kissed Jo on the forehead and said, "Don't go, don't go!" John held her right hand, Peri her left, and Gabe stood at the foot of the bed. We all cheered her on. "Come on, Jo, you can do it. Stay with us!" I experienced eternity for 10 to 15 seconds. Then a "1" appeared on the heartrate monitor. Then a 2, 4, 8, 15. Dr. Delaney rushed in and took her still face in his hands. "Joanne, Joanne, Joanne." No answer. He injected a shot of atropine to stimulate her heart. We watched the rate gradually climb back into the 70s and 80s and her respiration resume. She opened her eyes and said, "Hello." I turned away, burying my face in my hands, weeping and shuddering with relief.

That event marked the turning point of her recovery. It was as though she had decided to beat this thing. The energy in Jo's voice came back. During the next few days the recovery rates for her kidneys and liver accelerated. She gradually tapered off the dopamine and was able to stop the saline solution and antibiotics. By Friday, March 9, she was well enough to be transferred to the rehabilitation center in Berlin, 20 minutes from our house. She came home a week later.

Jo's survival—and my health—were powerfully boosted by the

loving presence of John, Peri, and Gabe, and amplified when Nancy and Sue returned. Nancy calls it a "miracle," a gift to witness in her own family. I also recognize the importance of other sources of support. Jo's sangha sisters were "mindful" of her condition. This group of eight women has been an important part of Jo's life since she had her stroke in 1999. Our Quaker meeting held her in the light. Peri's husband, Andrew, and his other attunement practitioners sent energy her way. Many others from their own spiritual and cosmic perspectives were there for her—testimony to her total inclusiveness.

I had my own problems. In January 2013, X-rays showed I needed my right hip replaced. A surgeon at the nearby Central Vermont Medical Center did a great job on May 6. Two weeks later, I was getting around with a cane, free from pain for the first time in 8 months. By June 6 I was walking without a cane and cleared to drive. Jo and I had weathered our respective hospitalizations and resumed our former "normal" life, with its various limitations.

We live with the loss of stamina, with memory lapses, and with arthritic aches and pains that plague many others like us in their 80s. Jo's handicaps—difficulty walking, tunnel vision—determine how we live. But small and gradual adjustments are manageable as they come. A walker has replaced her cane around the house. A stair lift helps her get up to our bedroom and her study. Thus, our lives continue to evolve, not really getting worse, just different.

Death, over the horizon, sails toward us, still far enough away that the tops of the masts are not apparent. But we do not dread that prospect. Jo and I have agreed that if circumstances arise so that one of us wants to go, the best way would be dropping off to sleep outside on one of those below-zero nights when the moon is so bright you can read a newspaper. We enjoyed snowshoeing and skiing under many of those moons when she was able. Helped by our long-loved partner keeping warm nearby, why not just go to rest with the firmament full of those memories? Selfishly, we each hope to go first so as not to suffer the inevitable pain and adjustments of life without the other. That moonlight fantasy will probably give way to some self-administered alternative with help from our daughter Nancy. Vermont is forward-looking, as usual, and recently legalized physician-assisted suicide.

Our financial affairs are in order. Our bodies will go to the Dartmouth-Hitchcock Medical School for use as cadavers; our ashes, returned when they have finished, to be sprinkled on our gardens. If I go first, Jo can stay in this place she loves so much, with help from our children and from friends and neighbors who already lend a hand. We have money enough to support a live-in companion if that becomes necessary.

I am full of questions if she should die first. How would I live? Would I be immobilized by grief? Drink all day? How long would I wander the woods and fields crying? In contrast to the first 50 or so years of my life, when strong feelings were well sealed off, my emotions are close to the surface. Tears flow readily. There will be plenty of those as I make my way through the aching emptiness of life without Jo. What kind of life would I create? Would I continue professional writing, speaking, consulting? I still enjoy doing occasional workshops and consulting. Would I continue creative writing, working more on my autobiography or other creative nonfiction? Jo and I jumped into writing in 2009 to enrich our life together, and it has been a great source of learning, sharing, reminiscing—challenging and satisfying. But without her along, much of the joy and flavor would be gone. Maybe I could pick up my trombone and find some orchestra or group to join. There are many opportunities for volunteer work nearby.

What about another woman? Jo hopes I'd quickly partner up with some damsel on my knee with whom I'd laugh, dance, and plan each day for play and work. Turning to another woman would be fine with her. But as I scan through those I know and have known, personally and professionally, I realize that though some are attractive and interesting, none are candidates for a long-term partnership. I have no inclination to go scouting. I can cook, clean, and handle all the household chores well enough for me. If I need a hit of sex there are women available without living in, though nowadays it hardly seems worth the time and energy.

Companionship to fight off loneliness may be what I'll need, perhaps sharing the place with another man. It would have to be an easy, relaxed fit. If our old friend Seward Weber, whom Jo and I have known and spent time with since 1952, were still alive and alone that might have worked. Though his standards for order and cleanliness were higher than mine, I wouldn't mind trying to live up to them. Andy Doe, a tennis-playing buddy and good friend off the courts, has very similar social values and political interests, and similar tastes in reading, music, and theatre. But he is a very private person, emotionally connected to his family homestead, so that would not be a possibility. The basic problem, of course, is that any other man in his 70s or 80s will be pretty well set in his ways and his places, just as I am. I would not leave this home for any other person, location, or amount of money. Whatever life I create, for whatever years might remain, will be based here, close to children and grandchildren, in the middle of these woods, fields, and ponds I love and know so well.

For now, fortunately, those are all hypotheticals. On November 22, 2013, Jo and I celebrated our 62nd wedding anniversary. Here we are, in our mid-80s. Individually and jointly we have said yes to life. We have turned toward challenges, not away from them. Loving, working, and becoming are still built into the fabric of our weekly routines. We write—poems for Jo, professional books, articles, and an autobiography for me. We nurture our children and grandchildren and are nurtured by them. Our love for each other deepens even as the challenges of aging increase. We sustain local, national, and global friendships. We care for our own precious land and water and for the larger environment. We continue becoming, along trajectories projected by our rich personal and shared histories. Over the years we have been on top of the Rockies, down in Death Valley, and to most of the elevations and climates in between. Now, in this temperate zone, we look forward to future years together, whatever challenges and new learning they may bring.

Arthur Chickering
Curriculum Vitae

Personal Data

Birthdate and place: April 27, 1927, Framingham, Massachusetts

Marital Status: Married to Joanne Nelson, November 1951

Children: Alan, Susan, Peri, and Nancy Chickering

Education

1948	Summer study. University of Dijon, France
1950	AB, Modern Comparative Literature. Wesleyan University
1951	AMT, Teaching of English. Harvard Graduate School of Education, Cambridge, Massachusetts
1958	PhD, School Psychology. Teachers College, Columbia University, New York, New York
2012	MFA in Creative Writing. Goddard College, Plainfield, Vermont

Professional Experience

1945–1946	Private, U.S. Army
1946–1950	Varied part-time employment during college
1951–1955	Secondary school teacher (English, Spanish, French) and coach (football, baseball, tennis). Wardlaw School, Edison, New Jersey
1955–1958	School psychologist. Woodmere Hewlett School System, Woodmere, New York
1958–1959	Chairman, Department of Teacher Education. Monmouth College, Long Branch, New Jersey
1959–1965	Psychology teacher and coordinator of evaluation. Ford Foundation Experiment in College Curriculum Organization, Goddard College

1965–1970	Program director. Project on Student Development in Selected Small Colleges, Plainfield, Vermont
1970–1971	Visiting scholar. Office of Research, American Council on Education, Washington, D.C.
1971–1977	Vice president and professor. Empire State College, Saratoga Springs, New York
1971–1975	Program director. Project on Strategies for Change and Knowledge Utilization, Saratoga Springs, New York
1977–1987	Distinguished professor of higher education and director of the Center for the Study of Higher Education. Memphis State University, Memphis, Tennessee
1987–1996	University Professor. Leadership and Human Development George Mason University, Fairfax, Virginia
1991–1992	Interim dean. Graduate School of Education, George Mason University, Fairfax, Virginia
1993–1994	Visiting professor. University of Grenoble, Grenoble, France
1995–2004	Board member. Wordbridge Playwright Institute, Eckerd College, St. Petersburg, Florida
1996–2001	Visiting distinguished professor. Vermont College at Norwich University, Northfield, Vermont
1996–present	Senior associate. New England Resource Center for Higher Education, Plainfield, Vermont
1997–2001	Team member. Kellogg Forum for Higher Education Transformation, Plainfield, Vermont
1998–2001	Project director. W. K. Kellogg Foundation Civic Engagement Cluster, Plainfield, Vermont
1997–2000	Team member. Fetzer Institute Project on Authenticity, Wholeness and Integrity in Higher Education, Plainfield, Vermont
2001–2004	Distinguished professor. Vermont College at Norwich University, Northfield, Vermont
2002–2005	Co-coordinator. Educo International Alliance, Plainfield, Vermont

| 2004–2010 | Special assistant to President Mark Schulman. Goddard College |
| 2010–2012 | Special assistant to President Barbara Vacarr. Goddard College |

Honors

1954–1955	Eleanor Colford Morris Fellowship, Teachers College, Columbia University
1955	U.S. Public Health Stipend, Teachers College, Columbia University
1969	American Council on Education Book Award for *Education and Identity* (Jossey-Bass, 1969)
1972	Outstanding Service Award, National Association of Student Personnel Administrators
1975	Distinguished Service Citation, Sex Information and Education Council of the United States
1980	Contribution to Knowledge Award, American College Personnel Association
1984	Senior Scholar, American College Personnel Association
1984–1985	Distinguished Research Award, Memphis State University
1985	E.F. Lindquist Award, American Educational Research Association
1985	Newman Award, Lourdes College, Sylvania, Ohio
1985	Honorary Doctorate of Humane Letters, University of New Hampshire, Durham, New Hampshire
1989	Distinguished Service Award for Innovation in Higher Education, International Council for Innovation in Higher Education
1990	Diplomate Senior Scholar Award, American College Personnel Association
1990	Morris T. Keeton Award, Council of Adult and Experiential Learning: For contributions to research, theory, and program development
1991	Honorary Doctorate of Humane Letters, Empire State College
1995	Distinguished Service Award, Council for Independent Colleges

1999	Arthur W. Chickering Scholarship Award, established by the Adult Higher Education Alliance
2000	Howard R. Bowen Distinguished Career Award, Association for the Study of Higher Education: For "extraordinary scholarship, leadership, and service"
2000	American College Personnel Association Diamond Honoree for Outstanding Contributions to the Field of Student Affairs
2003	National Defense University, Department of Defense, Certificate of Appreciation for Educational Excellence through Teaching, Technology and Transformation
2006	Spirit of Educo Award: For outstanding service and special contributions
2013	Goddard College Excellence Award

Grants

1963–1964	National Institute of Mental Health, study of relationships between personality characteristics and interpersonal attraction, $10,000
1965–1970	National Institute of Mental Health, Project on Student Development in Small Colleges, a 4-year study of student characteristics, college characteristics, attrition, student change, and the relationships among these in 13 small colleges across the country, $450,000
1971–1975	National Institute of Mental Health, Strategies for Change, a 4-year project to assist planned changes in curriculum, teaching, and evaluation in eight participating colleges and universities, to study the processes of institutional change and resistance to change, and to identify effective strategies for varied administrative and faculty styles and characteristics, $395,000
1972–1973	Lilly Foundation, Postgraduate Teaching Interns, $50,000
1972–1975	Fund for the Improvement of Postsecondary Education, Developing Cost-effectiveness Models for Postsecondary Education, $500,000
1973–1976	Danforth Foundation, Center for Individualized Education, $333,000

1978–1981	Fund for the Improvement of Postsecondary Education, Higher Learning for Diverse Adults, $369,000
1980–1981	Exxon Foundation, Evaluation of FIPSE Special Focus Projects on Adult Learning, $14,000
1981–1984	National Institute of Mental Health, Higher Education for Adult Mental Health, $458,055
1983–1986	Kellogg Foundation, Project LEARN, $198,050
1988–1989	Lilly Endowment, create an Institutional Self-assessment Guide for Improving Undergraduate Education, $24,800
1989–1990	Lilly Endowment, support distribution of Faculty and Institutional Inventories to diagnose faculty behaviors and institutional environments consistent with "Principles for Good Practice in Undergraduate Education," $35,000
1990–1991	Lilly Endowment, survey institutional users of the "Principles for Good Practice in Undergraduate Education" and the Faculty and Institutional Inventories for *New Directions for Teaching and Learning*, $5,000
1997–2001	W. K. Kellogg Foundation, create a cluster of 10 institutions that would undertake major transformations to strengthen civic learning and social responsibility among college students, $832,000

Board Memberships

1971–1985	Member, Board of Scholars, Higher Education Research Institute, Los Angeles, California
1976–1987	Chairman and member, Board of Trustees, Council for Adult and Experiential Learning, Chicago, Illinois
1978–1984	Panel of Advisors, Institute for Higher Education, University of New England, Armidale, New South Wales, Australia
1979–1983	Editorial Board, *Journal of Higher Education*
1981–1985	Chairman and member, Board of Directors, American Association for Higher Education
1983–1986	Editorial Board, *Continuum: Journal of the National University Continuing Education Association*

1984–1992	Board of Trustees, Goddard College
1985–1989	Commission on Continuing Higher Education Management, National University Continuing Education Association
1987–1990	Advisory Board, W.K. Kellogg Foundation National Fellowship Program
1984–1990	Editorial Board, *Journal of Higher Education Management*
1989–1994	Editorial Review Board, *Human Resource Development Quarterly*
1990–1996	Member, National Review Panel, Higher Education Reports, ERIC Clearinghouse on Higher Education, Association for the Study of Higher Education
1993–2001	Board member, Educo School for Leadership Development, Environmental Awareness, and Multicultural Understanding
1994–1996	Board of Trustees member, National Society for Experiential Education
1996–2000	Board of Contributors member, *About Campus*
2003–2006	Board member, Pyralisk Center for the Arts, Montpelier, Vermont
2005–2007	Chair, Steering Committee, Osher Central Vermont Lifelong Learning Institute, Burlington, Vermont
2010–2012	Board member, Vermont Philharmonic Orchestra, Montpelier, Vermont
2013–2015	Board member, Plainfield Cooperative, Plainfield, Vermont

Professional Associations

American Association for Higher Education (Board chair)

American College Personnel Association (Distinguished scholar)

American Psychological Association (Member)

Council for Adult and Experiential Learning (Board chair)

Association for the Study of Higher Education (Board member)

National Society for Experiential Education (Board member)

Professional Ski Instructors of America (Member)

International Experiences and Professional Contributions

1945–1946	Rio de Janeiro, Brazil: U.S. Army service
1947–1948	France: Summer study and volunteer work
1950–1959	Europe: Occasional travel
1965–1972	Europe: Occasional consultation and educational conferences
1973	Guatemala: One month of study, travel, and writing
1974	Scandinavia and England: Summer study, consultation, and travel
1976	India: Six weeks of consultation and travel
	Venezuela: Two weeks of consultation concerning new forms of postsecondary education
1977	England: Professional presentations, "Improving University Teaching"
1978	Australia: Two weeks of workshops and professional presentations regarding adult development and learning
	People's Republic of China: Three weeks of visiting universities
1980	Lausanne, Switzerland: International conference "Improving University Teaching" professional presentation
	Gottingen, Germany: Consultation at the University of Gottingen concerning curriculum concepts and faculty development
1981	London, England: Consultation concerning assessment of experiential learning
1982	Paris, France: Consultation regarding adult learners, Organization on Economic Cooperation and Development
	West Berlin, Germany: Professional presentation, "Improving University Teaching"
	Edinburgh, Scotland: Presentation at meeting of International Association of Applied Psychology
	Bournemouth, England: Consultation concerning institutional size and educational consequences
1983	Dublin, Ireland: Presentations, "Improving University Teaching"
1984	Australia: Consultation concerning adult learners

	Papua, New Guinea: Consultation concerning teacher education and higher education in developing countries
1987	Yugoslavia and Russia, Soviet Union: Travel and university visits
	London, England: Keynote speaker, International Conference on Experiential Learning
	Norway: Climbing in Jotunheimen Mountains
	Spain: Visit to Mondragon Cooperative Systems as advisor to W.K. Kellogg Foundation Leadership Program fellows
1988	Austria and Switzerland: Travel
1989	Moscow, Leningrad, and Tbilisi, Soviet Union; and Helsinki, Finland: Advisor to W.K. Kellogg Foundation Leadership Program fellows
	San Jose, Costa Rica: Keynote speaker, International Conference on Innovation in Higher Education
1990	Ecuador: Travel
1991	Budapest and Tokaj, Hungary: Leadership Development Program for Hungarian School Principals
	Prague, Czech Republic: Keynote speaker, annual meeting of the Czechoslovakian Association of Adult Educators
1993	Grenoble, France: Visiting professor, University of Grenoble
	Paris, France: Task force member, Implications of Communication and Information Technologies for Higher Education, Organization for Economic Cooperation and Development
1996	South Africa and Republic of Botswana: Travel and consultation concerning leadership development for Educo Africa, and concerning professional development strategies for the Botswana Department of Wildlife and National Parks
1998	Dublin, Ireland: Consultation with National College of Industrial Relations, and presentation ("Student Development: From Rhetoric to Reality") for series on Higher Education for the 21st Century
1999	Limerick, Ireland: Consultation on strategic planning for the University of Limerick

2001	Costa Rica and Ecuador: Travel
2002	Bahia, Brazil: Organizational meeting with Educo International Alliance
2003	Japan: Meetings with Shinji Shumeikai representatives
	Bhutan: Travel with members of the International Crane Foundation
2004	Bavaria, Germany: Co-coordinator, Educo International Alliance Annual Meeting
2005	Bulgaria: Co-coordinator, Educo International Alliance Annual Meeting
2006	Oaxaca, Mexico: Program participant, "Syncretism: Spirituality, Religion and Healing"
2007	Iceland: Resource Person, Intergenerational Elderhostel
2009	Mexico and Belize: Intergenerational Elderhostel

Books

1969	*Education and identity*. San Francisco, CA: Jossey-Bass.
1974	*Commuting versus resident students*. San Francisco, CA: Jossey-Bass.
1977	*Experience and learning*. New York, NY: Educational Change.
	Developing the college curriculum: A handbook for faculty and administrators. With D. Halliburton, W. Bergquist, & J. Lindquist. Washington, DC: Council for the Advancement of Small Colleges.
1981	*The modern American college: Responding to the new realities of diverse students and a changing society*. (Ed.). San Francisco, CA: Jossey-Bass.
1989	*Improving higher education environments for adults: Responsive programs and services from entry to departure*. With N. Schlossberg & A. Q. Lynch. San Francisco, CA: Jossey-Bass.
1993	*Education and identity* (2nd ed.). With L. Reisser. San Francisco, CA: Jossey-Bass.
	Getting the most out of college. With N. Schlossberg. Boston, MA: Allyn & Bacon.

1996	*Getting the most out of college* (2nd ed.). With N. Schlossberg. Upper Saddle River, NJ: Prentice Hall.
2006	*Encouraging authenticity and spirituality in higher education.* With J. Dalton & L. Stamm. San Francisco, CA: Jossey-Bass.
2008	*How to talk about hot topics across campus: From polarization to moral conversation.* With R. Nash & D. L. Bradley. San Francisco, CA: Jossey-Bass.

Articles, Chapters, and Reports

1964	Dimensions of independence. *Journal of Higher Education, 35*(1), 38–41.
1965	Improving psychological services. *Journal of School Psychology, 3*(4), 43–48.
	Does our performance match our claims? *Improving College and University Teaching, 13*(1), 35–37.
	Faculty perceptions and changing institutional press. In C. Bagley (Ed.), *Design and methodology in institutional research* (pp. 75–84). Proceedings of the National Institutional Research Annual Forum, Stony Brook, NY, May 3–4, 1965. Athens, GA: Association for Institutional Research.
1966	*An experiment in college curriculum organization.* With G. Beecher, W. G. Hamlin, & R. S. Pitkin. Plainfield, VT: Goddard College.
	How big should a college be? *Liberal Education, 52*(3), 281–292.
	Institutional differences and student characteristics. *Journal of the American College Health Association, 14,* 168–181.
1967	The young adult: A new course for the college personnel curriculum. *Journal of the National Association for Women, Deans and Counselors, 30*(3), 98–11.
	Talking with college students. *Improving College and University Teaching, 15*(1), 30–32.
	College residences and student development. *Educational Record, 48*(2), 170–186.
	Curriculum, teaching, and evaluation—Implications for student development, mental health, and counseling. *Journal*

of the Association of Deans and Administrators of Student Affairs, 5(2), 1–18.

Institutional objectives and student development in college. *Journal of Applied Behavioral Science,* 3(3), 287–304.

Development of autonomy. *American Journal of Orthopsychiatry,* 37(2), 203–204.

1968   Curriculum, teaching, and evaluation—Implications for student development. *Liberal Education,* 59(2), 1–18.

Research and action: Third annual progress report. With D. Campagna, W. Hannah, & J. McDowell. Plainfield, VT: Project on Student Development in Small Colleges.

1969   Institutional differences and student development. With J. McDowell and D. Campagna. *Journal of Educational Psychology,* 60(4), 315–326.

The process of withdrawal. With W. Hannah. *Liberal Education,* 55, 551–558.

Student-faculty relationships—Bedrock for college governance. Retrieved from http://files.eric.ed.gov/fulltext/ED038910.pdf

1970   Civil liberties and the experience of college. *Journal of Higher Education,* 41(8), 599–606.

1971   The best colleges have the least effect. *Saturday Review,* 48–50, 54.

Comments on 'participative education and the inevitable revolution' by Albert R. Wright. *Journal of Creative Behavior,* 5(1), 44–54.

Cultural sophistication and the college experience. *Educational Record,* 52(2), 125–128.

Educational outcomes for commuters and residents. With E. Kuper. *Educational Record,* 52(3), 255–261.

Research for action. In P. Dressel (Ed.), *The new colleges: Toward an appraisal* (pp. 1–24). Iowa City, IA: American College Testing Service.

1972   Undergraduate academic experience. *Journal of Educational Psychology,* 63(2), 134–143.

Institutional objectives and student development in college. In K. A. Feldman (Ed.), *College and student* (pp. 89–102). New York, NY: Pergamon Press.

Social change, human development, and higher education. In E. J. McGrath (Ed.), *Prospect for renewal*. San Francisco, CA: Jossey-Bass, 14–29.

A new model for higher education. *Liberal Education, 58*(4), 509–519.

How many make too many? In C. G. Benello & D. Rossopolos (Eds.), *The case for participatory democracy* (pp. 213–227). New York, NY: Viking Press.

1973   The best colleges have the least effect. In G. Stricker & M. Merbaum (Eds.), *Growth of personal awareness: A reader in psychology* (pp. 157–163). New York, NY: Holt, Rinehart and Winston.

Personality development and the college experience. With J. McCormick. *Research in Higher Education, 1*(1), 43–70.

College advising for the 1970s. In J. Katz (Ed.), *Services for students* (New directions for higher education, No. 3, pp. 69–80). San Francisco, CA: Jossey-Bass.

1974   Education and identity: Implications for residence hall living. In D. A. DeCoster, & P. Mable (Eds.), *Student development and education in college residence halls* (pp. 76–86). Washington, DC: American College Personnel Association.

1975   Assessing students and programs—A new ball game. In S. Baskin (Ed.), *Organizing nontraditional study* (pp. 53–74). San Francisco, CA: Jossey-Bass.

Nontraditional responses to the needs of new learners. In *Conference report on quality revolution*. Belmont, NC: Sacred Heart College.

Adult development: Implications for higher education. In C. E. Cavert (Ed.), *Designing diversity 1975: Proceedings of the Second National Conference on Open Learning and Non-Traditional Study* (pp. 203–219). Lincoln, NE: University of Mid-America.

Developing intellectual competence at Empire State. In N. R. Berte (Ed.), *Individualizing education through contact learning* (New directions for higher education, No. 10, pp. 31–40). Tuscaloosa, AL: University of Alabama Press.

1976   Developmental change as a major outcome. In M. Keeton (Ed.), *Experiential Learning: Rationale, characteristics, assessment* (pp. 62–107). San Francisco, CA: Jossey-Bass.

The double bind of field-independence versus field-dependence in program alternatives for educational development. In S. Messick (Ed.), *Individuality in learning: Implications of cognitive styles and creativity in human development* (pp. 79–89). San Francisco, CA: Jossey-Bass.

Problems in the postsecondary education of adults. With J. Chickering and P. Durcholz. Paper presented at the Latin American Conference on Innovative Forms of Postsecondary Education, Caracas, Venezuela.

1977   Part I. Curricular rationale. In G. H. Quehl & M. Gee (Eds.), *Developing the college curriculum* (pp. 1–34). Washington, DC: Council for the Advancement of Small Colleges.

Vocations and the liberal arts. In D. W. Vermilye (Ed.), *Relating work and Education* (pp. 125–140). San Francisco, CA: Jossey-Bass.

Love and work. *A.G.B. Reports, 19*(5), 14–19.

Evaluation in the context of contract learning. *Journal of Personalized Instruction, 2*(2), 96–100.

1978   Four critical years: A book review. *Higher Education Review, 1*(2), 1–5.

Lifelong learning by handicapped persons. With J. N. Chickering. In M. C. Reynolds (Ed.), *Futures of education for exceptional students: Emerging structures.* Minneapolis, MN: National Support Systems Project, 1–65.

1979   [Review of the book *Investment in learning: The individual and social value of American higher education,* by H. R. Bowen]. *Journal of Higher Education, 50*(3), 349–353. The Ohio State University Press.

Adult development: Implications for higher education. In
V. R. McCoy, C. Ryan, & J. W. Lichtenberg (Eds.), *The adult
life cycle* (pp. 191–207). Lawrence, KS: University of Kansas,
Division of Continuing Education.

What is competence? With C. S. Claxton. In R. Nickse &
L. McClure (Eds.), *Competency-based education* (pp. 5–41).
New York, NY: Teachers College Press.

Adult development: Implications for teaching and learning.
Community Services Catalyst, 9(2), 4–11.

1980   Adult development: A workable vision for higher education.
Current Issues in Higher Education, 5, 1–12.

How do students define quality? With J. N. Chickering.
In L. Kramer (Ed.), *Issues in Higher Education* (Vol. 4,
pp. 17–30). Proceedings of the Third National Conference
on Off-Campus Credit Programs: The Quality Issue, New
Orleans, LA, October 26–29, 1980. Manhattan, KS: Kansas
State University, Division of Continuing Education.

1981   Integrating liberal education, work, and human development.
American Association for Higher Education, 33(7), 1–16.

Potential contributions of college unions to student development.
In W. M. Klepper (Ed.), *College unions at work: The impact of
college unions and their programs on today's students* (pp. 23–27).
Stanford, CA: Association of College Unions–International.

Curriculum. In D. K. Halstead (Ed.), *Higher education: A biblio-
graphic handbook* (Vol. 2, pp. 127–152). Washington, DC:
National Institute of Education, U.S. Government Printing Office.

1982   Liberal education and work. *National Forum, 62*(2), 22–23.

Critical role of value development in student development. With
R. E. Thomas & P. Murrell. *NASPA Journal, 20*(1), 3–13.

Adult development and learning. With C. Marienau. In B. Menson
(Ed.), *Building on experiences in adult development* (New direc-
tions for experiential learning, No. 16, pp. 62–84).
San Francisco, CA: Jossey-Bass.

Crediting service learning. With R. J. Doyle. In S. Goodlad (Ed.),
Study service (pp. 187–201). Berkshire, England: NFER-Nelson.

Institutional size, higher education and student development. With R. Thomas. In S. Goodland (Ed.), *Economics of scale in higher education* (Research into higher education monographs, No. 57, pp. 41–56). New York, NY: McGraw-Hill Education.

Theoretical bases and feasibility issues for mentoring and developmental transcripts. With R. Thomas & P. R. Murrell. In R. D. Brown & D. A. Decoster (Eds.), *Mentoring-transcript systems for promoting student growth* (New directions for student services, No. 19, pp. 49–65). San Francisco, CA: Jossey-Bass.

1983   Education, work and human development. *The Journal of Continuing Higher Education, 31*(2), 2–6.

Education, work and human development. In T. C. Little (Ed.), *Making sponsored experiential learning standard practice* (New directions for experiential learning, No. 20, pp. 1–6). San Francisco, CA: Jossey-Bass.

Quality from the students' point of view. *AASCU Studies.* Washington, DC: American Association of State Colleges and Universities.

1984   Faculty evaluation: Problems and solutions. In P. Seldin (Ed.), *Changing practices in faculty evaluation* (pp. 91–96). San Francisco, CA: Jossey-Bass.

Education and identity revisited. With R. E. Thomas. *Journal of College Student Personnel, 25*(5), 392–399.

Comprehensive counseling and support programs for adult learners: Challenge to higher education. With A. Q. Lynch. In G. W. Walz and L. Benjamin (Eds.), *New perspectives on counseling adult learners* (pp. 45–74). Ann Arbor, MI: ERIC Counseling and Personnel Services Clearinghouse, University of Michigan.

Foundations for academic advising. With R. E. Thomas. In R. R. Winston, Jr., T. Miller, S. Ender, & T. Grites (Eds.), *Developmental academic advising* (pp. 89–117). San Francisco, CA: Jossey-Bass.

1985   Foreword. In T. M. Rocco & L. W. Murphy (Eds.), *Instructional and staff for structures for nontraditional programs* (pp. v–ix). Scarecrow Press for the Alliance.

Model programs for adult learners in higher education. With A. Q. Lynch & R. J. Doyle. *Phi Delta Kappan, 66*(10), 713–716.

1987   Seven principles for good practices in undergraduate education. *American Association for Higher Education Bulletin, 39*(7), 3–7.

College residences and student development. *Educational Record, 48*(2), 179– 186.

The life cycle. In E. Steltenpohl & J. Shipton (Eds.), *Orientation to college for adults* (pp. 44–55). Lexington, MA: Ginn Press.

1988   Linking educators and researchers in setting a research agenda for undergraduate learning. With M. Mentkowski. *The Review of Higher Education, 11*(2), 137–160.

Individual enhancement as the personal purpose of education. With A. Q. Lynch. In C. V. Willie & I. Miller (Eds.), *Social goals and educational reform* (pp. 105–136). Westport, CT: Greenwood Press.

1989   Encouraging student development through student employment. With I. Frank & V. Robinson. *Journal of Student Employment, 1*(2), 5–15.

Faculty inventory: 7 principles for good practice in undergraduate education. With L. Barsi & Z. Gamson. Racine, WI: Johnson Foundation.

Institutional inventory: 7 principles for good practice in undergraduate Education. With L. Barsi & Z. Gamson. Racine, WI: Johnson Foundation.

Framework for a workshop on good practice in undergraduate education. In C. H. Pazandak (Ed.), *Improving undergraduate education in large universities* (New directions in higher education, No. 66, pp. 85–88). San Francisco, CA: Jossey-Bass.

Profiles in adult learning [VHS]. United States: California State University Center for Innovative Programs.

An interview with Arthur W. Chickering, J. G. Krivoski, J. G., & R. M. Nicholson. *The Journal of College and University Student Housing, 19*(2), 6–11.

1990   Grades: One more tilt at the windmill. In S. H. Barnes (Ed.), *Points of view on American higher education* (pp. 170–175). Lewiston, NY: Edwin Mellen Press.

Linking campus and state initiatives. With D. Potter. In
P. Seldin (Ed.), *How administrators can improve teaching*
(pp. 143–161). San Francisco, CA: Jossey-Bass.

1991   Classroom teaching, personal development and professional
competence. In L. Lamdin (Ed.), *Roads to the learning society*
(87–98). Chicago, IL: Council for Adult and Experiential
Learning.

Contributing to (and learning from) a video conference on dating
violence. In R. Edgerton, P. Hutchings, & K. Quinlawn, (Eds.),
The teaching portfolio. Washington, DC: American Association
for Higher Education.

*Applying the seven principles for good practice in undergraduate
education* (New directions for teaching and learning, No. 47).
With Z. F. Gamson. San Francisco, CA: Jossey-Bass.

Reshaping the university for the metropolitan area. With D. Potter.
Metropolitan Universities: An International Forum, 12(2), 7–20.

The 21st century university: The role of government. With
D. Potter. In R. R. Sims & S. J. Sims (Eds.), *Managing
institutions of higher education into the 21st century: Issues and
implications* (pp. 10–30). New York, NY: Greenwood Press.

1992   Maintaining momentum and quality in a time of decline: A case
study. With D. Potter & M. Scherrens. *Journal for Higher
Education Management, 7*(2), 53–65.

A pedagogiai innovacio menedzsdelese (Leadership for improved
education). Report published by the Hungarian Center
for School Improvement, with support from the German
Marshall Fund, Budapest, Hungary.

1993   TQM and quality education: Fast food or fitness center. With
D. Potter. *Educational Record, 74*(2), 35–36.

1994   Helping students take charge: Empowering lifelong self-development. *AAHE Bulletin, 47*(4), 3–5.

Empowering lifelong self-development. *NACADA Journal,
14*(2), 50–53.

1995   Considering the public interest. With D. Stewart. *Liberal
Education, 81*(2), 12– 19.

Communicating high expectations. Introduction to article by R. Scott & D. E. Tobe, *Liberal Education, 81*(2), 38.

A conversation with Arthur W. Chickering. *CAEL Forum, 18*(1), 1–3.

Liberal education, work, and human development. In E. Steltenpohl, J. Shipton, & S. Villines (Eds.), *Orientation to college* (pp. 224–229). Belmont, CA: Wadsworth.

Your preferred learning style. With N. K. Schlossberg. In E. Steltenpohl, J. Shipton, & S. Villines (Eds.), *Orientation to college* (pp. 80–86). Belmont, CA: Wadsworth.

Reflections on excellence in learning and teaching in adult higher education: An interview. *Alliance Newsletter*, Winter, 8–11.

1996   The values and feelings of today's students. Book review. *Planning for Higher Education, 24*(3), 42–43.

Implementing the seven principles: Technology as lever. With S. C. Ehrman. *AAHE Bulletin, 49*(2), 3–6.

The university learning center: A driving force for collaboration. With J. O'Connor. *About Campus, 1*(4), 16–21.

Key influences on student development. With L. Reisser. In F. K. Stage, G. L. Anaya, J. P. Bean, D. Hossler, & G. D. Kuh (Eds.), *College students: The evolving nature of research* (pp. 196–204). Needham Heights, MA: Simon & Schuster.

Moving on: Seniors as people in transition. In J. N. Gardner & G. Van der Veer (Eds.), *The senior year experience: Facilitating integration, reflection, and transition* (pp. 37–50). San Francisco, CA: Jossey-Bass.

1997   Academic and student affairs: Collaboration to strengthen liberal education. In C. E. Coombs (Ed.), *Proceedings, fourth annual general education symposium* (pp. 3–12). Boston, MA: Berklee College of Music.

Why we should encourage student activism. *About Campus, 2*(6), 2–3.

Moving on. With N. Schlossberg. In J. N. Gardner & G. Van der Veer (Eds.), *The senior year experience* (pp. 37–50). San Francisco, CA: Jossey-Bass.

1999   The collegiate ideal in the twenty-first century. In J. D. Toma & A. J. Kezar (Eds.), *Reconceptualizing the collegiate ideal* (New directions for higher education, No. 105, pp. 109–120). San Francisco, CA: Jossey-Bass.

          Strategies for change. *The Academic Workplace, 10*(2), 3–7.

2000   Creating community within individual courses. In B. Jacoby (Ed.), *Involving commuter students in learning* (New directions for higher education, No. 109, pp. 23–32). San Francisco, CA: Jossey-Bass.

          [Review of the book *Best practices in adult learning*, edited by T. Flint]. *CAEL Forum and News, 23,* 34–35, 39.

          Teaching and technologies for human development. With C. Payne & G. Poitras. *Educational Technology, 41*(5), 46–51.

2002   Bottom line—Making our purposes clear. With L. Stamm. *About Campus, 7*(2), 30–32.

2003   Reclaiming our soul: Democracy and higher education. *Change, 35*(1), 38–44.

          Strengthening civic learning. *All About Mentoring, 25,* 3–8.

2004   Higher education: Current challenges and needed changes. *LAANE Newsletter, 16*(2), 1–11.

2006   Authenticity and spirituality in higher education: My orientation. *Journal of College and Character, 7*(1), 1–5.

          Every student can learn–If. *About Campus, 11*(2), 9–15.

          Strengthening spirituality and civic engagement in higher education. *Journal of College and Character, 8*(1), 1–5.

2007   Foreword. In M. R. Diamond (Ed.), *Encountering faith in the classroom: Turning difficult conversations into constructive engagement* (pp. xi–xiii). Sterling, VA: Stylus.

          Strengthening democracy and personal development through civic engagement. In S. R. Reed & C. Marienau (Eds.), *Linking adults with community: Promoting civic engagement through community-based learning* (New directions for adult and continuing education, No. 118, pp. 87–95). San Francisco, CA: Jossey-Bass.

Turning toward challenge. *The LLI Review, 3,* 352–361.

2009   Goddard legacies. *All About Mentoring, 36,* 3–7.

Developing global perspective for personal and social responsibility. With L. A. Braskamp. *Peer Review, 11*(4), 27–30.

2010   Civil discourse in the age of social media. With R. Junco. *About Campus, 15*(4), 12–18.

Our purposes: Personal reflections on character development and social responsibility in higher education. *Liberal Education, 96*(3), 54–59.

Dear Alan. *All About Mentoring, 38,* 4–5.

Coauthor Biographical Notes

Jon Dalton is professor emeritus of the Educational Leadership and Policy Studies Department and former vice president for student affairs at Florida State University. He is a past president of the National Association of Student Personnel Administrators (NASPA) and a senior scholar of the American College Personnel Association (ACPA).

George D. Kuh is adjunct professor of education policy at the University of Illinois and chancellor's professor emeritus of higher education at Indiana University, Bloomington. He currently directs the National Institute of Learning Outcomes Assessment, co-located at Indiana University and the University of Illinois. Founding director of the widely used National Survey of Student Engagement (NSSE), he has written extensively about student engagement, assessment, institutional improvement, and college and university cultures, and consulted with more than 350 colleges and universities in the United States and abroad. His recent publications include *Student Success in College: Creating Conditions That Matter* (Jossey-Bass, 2010); *Piecing Together the Student Success Puzzle: Research, Propositions, and Recommendations* (ASHE Higher Education Report, Vol. 32, No. 5; Jossey-Bass, 2007); *High-Impact Educational Practices: What They Are, Who Has Access to Them, and Why They Matter* (Association of American Colleges and Universities [AAC&U], 2008); and, with coauthor Ken O'Donnell, *Ensuring Quality and Taking High-Impact Practices to Scale* (AAC&U, 2013). He's been awarded seven honorary degrees, and in 2001 he received Indiana University's prestigious Tracy Sonneborn Award for a distinguished career of teaching and research. NASPA named its Award for Outstanding Contribution to Literature and Research after him in 2011. He earned a BA at Luther College, an MS at St. Cloud State University, and a PhD at the University of Iowa.

Catherine Marienau has more than 40 years of experience in mentoring, assessing, teaching, and program development in individualized, competence-based programs for adults at bachelor's, master's, and doctoral levels. Since 1983, she has served as professor and faculty mentor in the School for New Learning (SNL) at DePaul University. At SNL, Catherine works with adult learners in the following programs: Bachelor of Arts with an Individualized Focused Area; Master of Arts for Applied Professional Studies (founding director); and Master of Arts in Educating Adults (program coordinator). In addition to several publications noted in Chapter 8, she is coauthor with Kathleen Taylor and Morris Fiddler of *Developing Adult Learners: Strategies for Teachers and Trainers* (Jossey-Bass, 2000).

R. Eugene Rice is senior scholar at the Association of American Colleges and Universities. He received his PhD in religion and society from Harvard University and is a graduate of Harvard Divinity School. For 10 years he served as director of the Forum on Faculty Roles and Rewards and the New Pathways projects at the American Association for Higher Education (AAHE). Before moving to AAHE, he was vice president and dean of the faculty at Antioch College, where he held an appointment of professor of sociology and religion. Earlier, he was program executive and senior fellow at the Carnegie Foundation for the Advancement of Teaching, where he was engaged in the national study of the scholarly priorities of the American professoriate and collaborated with the late Ernest Boyer on *Scholarship Reconsidered: Priorities of the Professoriate* (Jossey-Bass, 1990). His work on that topic is available in the *New Pathways* working paper series in an essay titled "Making a Place for the New American Scholar" (Stylus, 1996), and appears in *Faculty Priorities Reconsidered: Rewarding Multiple Forms of Scholarship,* edited by KerryAnn O'Meara (Jossey-Bass, 2005).

Recently, Rice has been working on faculty initiatives that have potential for improving conditions in developing countries torn by violent civil conflict. He has been in the West Bank working with Palestinian universities and in Liberia assisting with the initiation of national professional development programs. During the major part of his career, Rice was professor of sociology and religion at the University of the Pacific, where he helped initiate the first of the experimental "cluster colleges"—Raymond College—and served as chairperson of the Department of Sociology. His teaching and research focus on the sociology and ethics of the professions and the workplace. In *Change* magazine's survey of leadership in American higher education, Rice is recognized as one of a small group of "idea leaders" whose work has made a difference nationally.

John Saltmarsh is codirector of the New England Resource Center for Higher Education at the University of Massachusetts Boston, as well as a faculty member in the Higher Education Administration doctoral program in the Department of Leadership in Education in the College of Education and Human Development. He is the author, most recently, of a coedited volume with Mathew Hartley, *To Serve a Larger Purpose: Engagement for Democracy and the Transformation of Higher Education* (Temple University Press, 2011) and a book with Edward Zlotkowski, *Higher Education and Democracy: Essays on Service Learning and Civic Engagement* (Temple University Press, 2011).